# CHRIS WALSH

# Leadership In The River

## *Obeying God In Our Leadership*

GREAT
BOOKS

*First published by Great Books 2021*

*Copyright © 2021 by Chris Walsh*

*All rights reserved. No part of this publication may be reproduced, stored or transmitted in any form or by any means, electronic, mechanical, photocopying, recording, scanning, or otherwise without written permission from the publisher. It is illegal to copy this book, post it to a website, or distribute it by any other means without permission.*

*Chris Walsh asserts the moral right to be identified as the author of this work.*

*Scripture quotations taken from the Amplified® Bible (AMP), Copyright © 2015 by The Lockman Foundation. Used by permission. www.lockman.org*

*Scripture quotations are taken from the Holy Bible, New Living Translation, copyright ©1996, 2004, 2015 by Tyndale House Foundation. Used by permission of Tyndale House Publishers, Carol Stream, Illinois 60188. All rights reserved.*

*Scripture taken from the New King James Version®. Copyright © 1982 by Thomas Nelson. Used by permission. All rights reserved.*

*Scriptures taken from the Holy Bible, New International Version®, NIV®. Copyright © 1973, 1978, 1984, 2011 by Biblica, Inc.™ Used by permission of Zondervan. All rights reserved worldwide. www.zondervan.com The "NIV" and "New International Version" are trademarks registered in the United States Patent and Trademark Office   by Biblica,   Inc.™*

*Scripture quotations from The Authorized (King James) Version. Rights in the Authorized Version in the United Kingdom are vested in the Crown. Reproduced by permission of the Crown's patentee, Cambridge University Press*

*Scripture quotations marked MSG are taken from THE MESSAGE, copyright © 1993, 2002, 2018 by Eugene H. Peterson. Used by permission of NavPress, represented by Tyndale House Publishers. All rights reserved.*

*First edition*

*Cover art by Roy Kamau*

# Contents

# Introduction

Over the past ten years, we have met weekly with leaders in both business and ministry and read the Proverb chapter of the day. And we deliberately sought God for wisdom. He has answered and given us a portion of His excellence. We have learned that Holy Spirit-led leaders, thoroughly grounded in the Word of God, are the greatest need of this generation.

As I have read these two contradictory commandments from Proverbs, I hope you see this.

> *"Answer not a fool according to his folly, lest thou also be like unto him. Answer a fool according to his folly, lest he be wise in his own conceit" (Prov 26:4-5 KJV).*

To the business owner with a foolish employee, how are they to respond?

Verse 4 says to not respond to their foolishness, yet verse 5 says to answer and correct them. Is this situational ethics?

No, this is wisdom in working human relationships in the business world which requires a walk with God that causes the leader to know what to do in each complicated situation.

Over the years, we have received many precious pearls of insight into the Scripture. So, I have compiled this rich storehouse of truth into a series of motivational leadership talks that I'm sure will be of great use to many in the kingdom.

# 1

# Workers In The Vineyard - Be Led

*Matt 20:13 But he answered one of them, Friend, I am doing you no injustice. Did you not agree with me for a denarius?*

Take what belongs to you and go. I choose to give to this man hired last the same as I give to you.

Am I not permitted to do what I choose with what is mine? [Or do you begrudge my being generous?] Is your eye evil because I am good? 16 So those who [now] are last will be first [then], and those who [now] are first will be last [then]. [d]For many are called, but few chosen.

Four things I see in this that are helpful to me:

1. **Every man cuts his own deal.** Job and financial opportunities come to us all the time; we decide what we are worth. Certain positions pay only specific amounts. Some money is always better than no money; however, we should be looking to be in the right field, working for the right Master that values us and rewards us well for our efforts. If we are self-employed, Jesus is directly our Master. We need to be diligently seeking Him for His direction, promotion, provision, favor, and means of maximizing our effort for maximum result.

2. The opportunity offered **was open to many**, but only a few even showed

up at the place of service.

3. The pay was not based upon longevity, faithfulness, or service but **only upon the generosity of the Master.** Our income can radically increase when we obey Jesus. Availability trumps ability; obedience trumps sacrifice and hard work.

4. **Only a few may make the grade.** Luke 19:13 And he called his ten servants, and delivered them ten pounds, and said unto them, Occupy till I come.

Read this parable carefully. The Lord called ten servants. Only three showed up to report on their stewardship. The one who buried his talent lost it, which means that only two out of ten servants were ever heard from in Scripture again. Eight disqualified themselves! It is imperative that we not only listen to the voice of Jesus but that we obey quickly and give it everything we've got! What is He saying to You today? How can we maximize our effectiveness for the King today?

> *"By whom we have received grace and apostleship, for **obedience** to the faith among all nations, for his name."* **Romans 1:5**

> *"And Samuel said, Hath the Lord as great delight in burnt offerings and sacrifices as in obeying the voice of the Lord? Behold, to obey is better than sacrifice, and to hearken than the fat of rams."* **1 Samuel 15:22**

'Father, life is busy with many opportunities to work, grow, learn, and move forward. Help us to fully obey You, that we might maximize our eternal impact today and every day. We ask, knowing we are heard and answered, for we ask in Your name, Lord Jesus. Amen.'

# 2

# Leadership vs. Management

Have you ever noticed that there is a difference between leadership and management?

While leaders must manage, they also create and produce revenue out of nothing. Strict management manages well-fixed budgets and resources but is not responsible for creating the revenue they manage. Leaders, by faith in God and His promises, literally create something out of nothing.

> **Luke 18:27** *"And he said, The things which are impossible with men are possible with God."*

> **Mark 9:23** *"Jesus said unto him, If thou canst believe, all things are possible to him that believeth."*

Yes, faith comes by hearing and hearing by the Word of God. Love is the currency of the kingdom by which everything works as Galatians 5:6 says, 'but faith which worketh by love.'

Therefore, you must receive the love of God to recognize your worth. John 1:12 But as many as received him, to them gave he power to become the sons of God, even to them that believe on his name

You are a child of the King, powerful in Him, and only because you have received Him. There is no way you can love your neighbor as yourself, unless you receive the love of God for yourself. If you don't know God loves you deeply and intimately so that your self-worth is established in Him, then your neighbor is in trouble.

We are talking about impossibilities, though, and Jesus said that all things are possible to them that believe. Believe what, you may ask?

Believe that you are precious! Royalty! A child of the King! The Lord has adopted you into the most potent family this earth has ever seen, the family of the Most High God!

You may be in the crosshairs of hell, but heaven's arsenal responds with howitzers in the hands of angels. He has charged His angels to watch over you. The 91st Psalm declares that Heaven has not lost track of you or me. Jesus will never leave you nor forsake you, and the host of heaven walks with you. You have guardian angels, and because you serve the Lord of glory, King of heaven.

> *Psalms 34:7 The angel of the LORD encamps round about them that fear Him and delivers them.*

Though you may feel alone and helpless, however, Jesus will never leave you nor forsake you, and the specific angels assigned to you are delivering you from your current circumstance and trial. Even though you might not be able to see, touch, hear or feel them right now, they are with you, and they fight for you!

## LET YOUR SPIRIT FREE

In the book, *The E-Myth Revisited,* the author recounts a fictitious account with a business owner named Sarah and the importance of developing systems to produce excellence in her world without her having to do it all herself. In the dialogue, he accidentally stumbles upon a spiritual law, the law of creating your world with your faith-filled words!

> *Hebrews 11:3 "Through faith we understand that the **world**s were **framed** by the word of God, so that things which are seen were not*

*made of things which do appear."*

*Romans 10:6 "But the righteousness which is of **faith speaketh**."*

*2 Corinthians 4:13 "We having the same **spirit of faith**, according as it is written, I believed,and therefore have I spoken; we also believe, and therefore speak."*

In dreaming of what her business could be, Sarah decided to unlock her spirit and create a slogan for her business. As she thought on it, I quote:

*"There will be no stuffing of the spirit here, my business will say. Maybe I should put it up above the door to remind everyone who comes in what our purpose is."* She grinned. *"Or maybe better yet, 'Let thy spirit run free!' Yes, that's better. It even feels better!"* She laughed out loud at the joy of it.

As she continued, it became so clear to me, what a miraculous gift speaking can be.

I saw that Sarah wasn't so much talking to me, but to herself. She discovered that miracles lived within her, within her experience, within her relationship with her aunt, within her extraordinary imagination. She found truths she didn't know before. She tapped into the wealth that was waiting there inside of her to be unearthed, to be explored, to be treasured as the words came tumbling forth.

As though the words, once freed by speaking them, combined with the air to become something else again: A vision, Understanding, Expansion.

Do you see the principle? God placed a dream within her that she had not yet articulated. She believed in the goal in her heart but had never yet spoken it into existence. When she began to speak, miracles began to happen! God, the Creator, and author of all creativity breathed up on her dream, just as He breathed upon His own dream way back in the days of creation. When He would speak, and His Breath, the Person of the Holy Spirit, would create and bring into existence what He spoke. And it was good!

What is your dream? We all have one, for we are created in the image and likeness of God. It needs to be articulated and written down and quantified into some action plan. Don't die taking to the grave your dream unspoken, unrealized, unfulfilled.  Speak it!  If only to a close friend or into your microphone on your computer, speak it.

*Let Your Spirit Free! Create!* **Let thy spirit run free!**

Like Sarah, the princess of God, miracles will unlock from deep inside of you. Because when you received Jesus into your heart, your heart became the fertile soil of His beauty, His dreams, His creativity. Your lips became His voice in this generation, and your world and your work now become an expression of His creativity and love in the earth.

Speak the dream!

Let's Pray:

> *'Father, I come before You, and I see that some of these deep, beautiful things on the inside of me are Your things that, like Mary, I have pondered in my heart for years.  Flow through me Holy Spirit with Your words erupting from the depths of my heart. Write your eternal dreams on the canvas of time. Make my life the beautiful expression of Jesus in my generation. Amen.'*

# 3

# When You Fast

Each year, as I seek the Lord, there comes a time when I deliberately fast and pray – a time to let go of agendas, offenses, even daily disciplines that are not bearing any fruit in my life. Time to reflect and receive fresh vision and direction, to replenish, and then launch out again in His plan and destiny of my life.

Hear the words of Jesus:

> *Matthew 6:16–18 "Moreover, when ye fast, be not, as the hypocrites, of a sad countenance: for they disfigure their faces, that they may appear unto men to fast. Verily I say unto you; They have their reward. But thou, **when thou fastest,** anoint thine head and wash thy face; That thou appear not unto men to fast, but unto thy Father which is in secret: and thy Father, which seeth in secret, shall reward thee openly."*

As a Rhema Graduate, I have heard Kenneth E Hagin teach on many subjects, but his book, *A Common Sense Guide to Fasting,* has been a great help to me over the years.

As I prepare to do my particular yearly fast of 'no pleasant food,' I am encouraged by this quote from brother Hagin's book:

*"Remember how Daniel fasted 21 days? He ate no "pleasant bread." We need to realize there is more than one way to fast. Daniel didn't eat anything he wanted, but he did eat a little something. This is harder to do sometimes.*

*You see, it's a matter of keeping the flesh under; keeping the body under and not letting it dominate you. You dominate it instead.*

*If you wanted to go a step further, you could fast things other than food. You might say, "Now, Lord, I'm going to leave off watching television and spend that time praying." (Daniel said he gave up eating pleasant bread. So why wouldn't it be all right to leave off other things that might be pleasant to us?)*

*A well-known evangelist, when he was pastoring, decided to give God 10 percent of his time in prayer. He began to pray at night after his family was in bed. He prayed for two hours and 40 minutes each night. To do that, he had to sacrifice his television time. God has given him an internationally known ministry."*

Over the years, I have been drawn repeatedly back to these verses of Scripture as I fast:

*Isaiah 58:6 "Is not this the fast that I have chosen? To loose the bands of wickedness, to undo the heavy burdens, and to let the oppressed go free, and that ye break every yoke?"*

As I fast and pray, I recognize that we have spiritual enemies that, if not directly preventing our success, always try to contain us in some measure to their control. I am believing for God Almighty to break their bands of wickedness, to remove their heavy burdens, to let me go free from all demonic oppression, and oppression by ungodly people. A yoke is something by which you harness an animal. Forces that are driving and prodding me into pathways other than the glorious liberty of the Spirit of God must go by the power of Jesus!

*Isaiah 58:7 Is it not to deal thy bread to the hungry, and that thou bring the poor that are cast out to thy house? When thou seest the naked, that thou cover him; and that thou hide not thyself from thine own flesh?*

These verses are a 'heart check' for me. I should already, always, continually be feeding the hungry, clothing the naked, caring for those less fortunate. Yet, here I check myself as to how well I am doing this as a man of God. Do I have clothes I can give away? Can I provide shelter for someone who can never repay me? Am I living and walking in the love of God? *'and that thou hide not thyself from thine own flesh?'* In the Amplified Bible, it says: *"and that you hide not yourself from [the needs of] your own flesh and blood?"*

Here is where the rubber meets the road. How well am I exemplifying the love of Jesus to my own family members?

Fasting is hard on our pride and selfish natures – it seems it is easier to love strangers than family members who are not living the way WE think they should. God loves them, and, if we are to represent Him, we must, too, no matter what they have done or are doing. Maybe a simple telephone call, card, or birthday gift will break the ice on relational walls of bitterness, grudges held generationally – rationalized because: 'that's just the way we are.' Nope, there is a cross for our sin, and our lack of love towards family is one that must die. We are called to love.

Back in college, I took a couple of courses in computer programming. We would write modules in Pascal (I know, for all you 'C++' programmers it is a dinosaur) where we would tell the computer IF (this condition is met), THEN (this must happen). In the previous verses, God was telling us to DO certain things in both prayers, in attitude, and in action.

IF we do these things, then we qualify for THEN He will do these things:

*Isaiah 58:8 Then shall thy light break forth as the morning, and thine health shall spring forth speedily and thy righteousness shall go before thee; the glory of the Lord shall be thy reward.*
*Then shalt thou call, and the Lord shall answer; thou shalt cry, and*

*he shall say, Here I am.*

The real purpose of fasting is to seek God, who is life, love, purity, power, strength, purpose, direction, power, holiness, healing, and prosperity. God is love!

Light speaks of revelation to me:

*Psalm 119:130 "The **entrance of thy words** giveth light; it giveth understanding unto the simple."*

Here we see revelation and healing from the throne of God, justification before our enemies, and the glory of God deposited in our lives. We see intimacy, the thing we desperately need, and the deepest needs of our heart met by the Lord Himself – we call, and He answers! Sometimes the greatest miracle in life is to be granted a supernatural understanding of a situation.

The Scripture has another 'if.' If thou take away from the midst of thee the yoke, the putting forth of the finger, and speaking vanity.

Here's my translation: Stop gossiping, wasting your precious conversations with words empty of substance and power, judging, pointing fingers at others – your life has never been about them anyway. It's about you and Jesus! Change your words, change your life – SPEAK THE WORD OF GOD, the Words of power!

And if thou draw out thy soul to the hungry, and satisfy the afflicted soul;

In my life, 'drawing out my soul to the hungry' is to pour my love out in teaching, preaching, encouraging, instructing people with the bread of life, the Word of God. People are hungry for love, the greatest need of all. The only thing that will meet the true hunger of every heart is Jesus! He will heal the afflicted soul! Yes, we work and supply natural food, but what about loving and injecting life into our particular world? Money will not do this unless used in love to alleviate human suffering and meet legitimate needs. If we do these things then shall thy light rise in obscurity, and thy darkness be as the noonday:

*Isaiah 58:11 And the Lord shall guide thee continually, and satisfy thy soul in drought, and make fat thy bones: and thou shalt be like a watered garden, and like a spring of water, whose waters fail not.*

*And they that shall be of thee shall build the old waste places: thou shalt raise up the foundations of many generations; and thou shalt be called, The repairer of the breach, The restorer of paths to dwell in.*

Much can be said here, but this speaks of the result of our work and effort. Jesus walks with us and does signs, wonders, and miracles, and others' lives are changed. They catch the vision and move in His love and power, and the result of their work is the foundations of many generations being raised up. We become repairers of the breach, restorers of the way, the one right path, the pathways of purpose, the straight and narrow path, the walk of faith with Jesus! Notice here that it is those whose lives we touch that build up the waste places, raising up the foundations of many generations and make fat thy bones: These simple words have great depth and meaning. Medically, we know that the marrow of our bones actually produces our blood cells.

*Leviticus 17:11 For **the life** of **the** flesh **is in the blood**: It seems that as we fast, God does a deep, deep work in our bodies, strengthening our bone marrow, infusing us with His life.*

Faith only comes by hearing and hearing by the Word of God. God is love, and He is not looking for a hunger strike from you and me. He wants us to draw near to Him, meet with Him, and let Him direct our lives for good.

Are you struggling to make something happen?

Consider fasting and praying – it works!

# 4

# When God Does Business

The following is an old message I preached at one of our leadership breakfasts. I believe its message is rather timely for America. One by one, we need to choose to do right for God's sake alone, and our country will change.

*"Hey, I didn't do anything illegal"* is a statement I have heard out of the mouths of some business leaders.

Remember, we have been adopted into a royal family; we have now become children of the Most High God through Jesus. We are kings and priests unto Him!

We are no longer merely governed by the laws of the land in which we live but also by the courts of heaven, where truth, mercy, and holiness reside.

In many cases, I would have to agree that these people operated in the confines of the laws of the land. Yet, what about the laws of God? In trying to survive in today's 'jungle warfare,' we are forced to compete as business leaders. We find ourselves lying, cheating, stealing, or violating sacred trusts to make a buck.

*"Our Constitution was made only for a moral and religious people. It is wholly inadequate to the government of any other."* John Adams

I think about Ananias and Sapphira (Acts 5), who were struck dead for lying to the Holy Spirit in the presence of a man of God, anointed by God to raise up His church.

Yet, let's break this down into a modern-day contract negotiation.

It would be fair in construction to take bids or estimates from vendors, suppliers, and contractors on a project We would then compile the bids, add an acceptable profit and overhead, and submit the completed proposal to the client.

Contracts are then issued and performed. When the contractors completed their work, the vendors or suppliers would then invoice according to their initial approved estimates, and we would pay them based upon the percentage of work completed. If there were additions or subtractions to the contract, these are documented and paid accordingly.

This, however competitive it might become, is honest business.

Yet, here are a couple of scenarios that are not only common in the business world but, in many cases, have become the law of the jungle.

Let's say, for instance, that I want to make more on the electrical portion of the job, so I tell my electrician the amount of the other two bids, telling him to match the lowest bid, or he does not get the job. This is unfair in that it is now a corrupt bidding process. I have immediately disqualified the other two bidders by secretly disclosing their numbers to my buddy.

Or, I have been awarded the contract, and I have so much money allocated for each trade or portion of the work. I then shop the bid by lying to contractors saying, 'I only have $5000.00 into this project for electrical. Can you do it for this? And we will make it up on the next one."

When perhaps, acceptable profit and overhead are 20-25%, and I have $10,000.00 allocated for the work. The honest way to do this is to ask contractors, "How much are you willing to do this job for?" and let them bid it fairly.

In a free-market economy, competition will keep the bids on track.

This scenario is precisely what Ananias and Sapphira did.

Now, let's say that the job goes well, and my suppliers invoice me, but I tell them that 'we ran into some additional expenses on this job. We are all having to settle on 90 cents on the dollar.' In other words, I get paid the full amount of the contract but pay my suppliers 90 cents on the dollar and pocket the remainder. This is lying, cheating, and stealing.

Let's look at Ananias and Sapphira for a second:

> *Acts 5:1–11 But a certain man named Ananias, with Sapphira, his wife, sold a possession,*
>
> *And kept back part of the price, his wife also being privy to it, and brought a certain part, and laid it at the apostles' feet.*
>
> *But Peter said, Ananias, why hath Satan filled thine heart to lie to the Holy Ghost and to keep back part of the price of the land?*
>
> *Whiles it remained, was it not thine own? And after it was sold, was it not in thine own power? why hast thou conceived this thing in thine heart? Thou hast not lied unto men, but unto God.*
>
> *And Ananias hearing these words fell down and gave up the ghost: and great fear came on all them that heard these things.*
>
> *And the young men arose, wound him up, and carried him out, and buried him.*
>
> *And it was about the space of three hours after, when his wife, not knowing what was done, came in.*
>
> *And Peter answered unto her, Tell me whether ye sold the land for so much? And she said, Yea, for so much.*
>
> *Then Peter said unto her, How is it that ye have agreed together to tempt the Spirit of the Lord? Behold, the feet of them which have buried thy husband are at the door and shall carry thee out.*
>
> *Then fell she down straightway at his feet and yielded up the ghost: and the young men came in and found her dead and, carrying her forth, buried her by her husband.*
>
> *And great fear came upon all the church, and upon as many as heard these things.*

I have a picture come to mind of one of the Levitical high priests, perhaps an Old Testament prophet, who saw that God was about to make a new covenant with all humanity through Jesus. They saw how the Law, with all its holy ordinances and principles, would be fully satisfied in Jesus. All the punishment sin-sick humanity deserved would be poured out upon this

One, the Lamb of God, and how God our Father, would receive His sacrificial death as an atonement for our sins. After He had raised Jesus from the dead, how God could now pour out love, and mercy, and blessing upon anyone who believed. Perhaps this man had spent his entire life consecrating Himself to God's laws and service in the temple, well aware of God's holiness. Perhaps He cried out the throne, knowing in the future that an undeserving people were now going to enter into the covenant He had given his life to uphold, and from the depths of His heart, He cried: 'God, forsake not Your Holiness!"

And God heard and performed a precedent-setting example in the courts of Heaven – sin would still be judged, and unfortunately for Ananias and Saphira that day, their lies cost them their lives.

These two did what is the everyday business in the United States today. They sold a piece of land and then had a private meeting to discuss what they were going to do with the money. They decided that because of the big revival going on at the church. They ought to make an offering at the temple because it was the politically correct thing to do:

> *Ac 4:34 Neither was there any among them that lacked: for as many as were possessors of lands or houses sold them and brought the prices of the things that were sold, others, touched by the Spirit of God, were doing it, so they decided to join the noble, God-fearing community and give into the Gospel.*

Yet, they decided to try and make themselves look good at church while padding their pockets with a nice little profit.

The funny thing about sin is that it costs more than a person is willing to pay and generally takes a person further than one was willing to go.

Notice, in Acts 5:2, how: **they did not have to give the entire purchase price** of the land in the offering.

Ananias and Saphira could have declared how much they were going to give and placed that amount in the offering. They then could have left the meeting, blessed of God and favored of man.

Yet, like many business people I have met, they told one story but lived another.

It cost them their lives.

> *Prov 1:7 The fear of the LORD is the beginning of knowledge: but fools despise wisdom and instruction.*

How many lies do we have to tell before we become liars? Just one.

How much do we have to steal before we become a thief? Just once.

How often can we accept a bribe or shop bids, before we become a cheat? Just once.

Whatever happened to sin?

It seems that the discussion of sin in the church is no longer politically correct, yet the Gospel is this:

> *1 Tim 1:15 This is a faithful saying, and worthy of all acceptation, that Christ Jesus came into the world to save sinners, of whom I am chief.*

If the apostle Paul could call himself the chief of all sinners, how much more I, and you, before a holy God.

The gospel, or good news, is that Jesus Christ died upon the cross to pay for our sins. He will forgive, but only if we humbly ask Him with the intent of going our way and sinning no more.

> *1 John 1:9 If we confess our sins, he is faithful and just to forgive us our sins and to cleanse us from all unrighteousness.*

10 If we say that we have not sinned, we make him a liar, and his word is not in us.

I love this verse that I describe this way: If you sin, immediately tell Jesus and ask for His forgiveness. When you do, He will hear, and He will forgive you and give you strength and grace to not do it again and wisdom to know what to do next. He, in His amazing love, will cleanse you from your filth and will even make the impossible possible, in mending the unmendable, fixing the unfixable, cleaning up the mess we made.

This is repentance. This is the cross. This is grace. This is the love of God.

Perhaps you are in this place today:

You have been a mover and shaker, trying to get things done in this brutal world we call the business world. Yet, your words have become lies, and the truth is no longer the bedrock upon which you build your life.

> *1 Cor 10:13 There hath no temptation taken you but such as is common to man:  but God is faithful, who will not suffer you to be tempted above that ye are able; but will with the temptation also make a way to escape, that ye may be able to bear it.*

> *1 Corinthians 10:13 Amplified Bible (AMP) For no temptation (no trial regarded as enticing to sin), [no matter how it comes or where it leads] has overtaken you and laid hold on you that is not common to man [that is, no temptation or trial has come to you that is beyond human resistance, and that is not [a]adjusted and [b]adapted and belonging to human experience, and such as man can bear]. But God is faithful [to His Word and His compassionate nature], and He [can be trusted] not to let you be tempted and tried and assayed beyond your ability and strength of resistance and power to endure, but with the temptation, He will [always] also provide the way out (the means of escape to [c]a landing place), that you may be capable and strong and powerful to bear up under it patiently.*

Now, this verse is written to those who are enduring temptation or trial.

The people I am speaking today have already blown it and have sinned, yet unlike Ananias and Sapphira, you are still alive.

God is love. He is merciful, and though there may be brutal consequences to your sin, you are alive. He will walk with you as you bear them, and more importantly, He is not done with you, for there is a fate far worse than death.

There is a certain, eternal place called hell, and Jesus and I are working very hard to see that you don't have to go there.

> *Rev 21:8 But the fearful and unbelieving, and the abominable, and murderers, and whoremongers, and sorcerers, and idolaters, and all liars, shall have their part in the lake which burneth with fire and brimstone: which is the second death.*

In a book entitled *A divine revelation of Hell*, a lady claims to have been taken by Jesus into hell and shown around. Everyone knows Him there, for He sent them there:

> *Rev 1:18 I am he that liveth, and was dead; and, behold, I am alive forevermore, Amen, and have the keys of hell and death.*

His heart is always to seek and save the lost, but if His offer of forgiveness and restoration is rejected, He only has two other options: (1) You can die, your life cut short because of your sin, but your soul saved that you might make Heaven, instead of hell. (2) You may eternally reject His blood and refuse to change your ways, and in that case, you will go to hell.

In one account in hell, the woman witnessed a man in a prison cell, tormented in flames, screaming in pain. He saw Jesus and cried: *"Jesus, give me one more chance. You know I will do better this time!"* Jesus looked at him with eyes of steel, and said: *"You are still a liar, even here!"*

There is a day of judgment where we will appear before Jesus alone. No excuses, every word and action of our life on complete display. No one to blame but ourselves. What we do this day can prepare us for that day. Run for your life!

Leave people, places, and things that corrupt you. Choose truth, holiness, and honesty before God, at all costs, no matter how much money is involved, or what people might think.

**How much is eternal life worth?**

No one can keep your individual appointment with God on that day but you yourself.

Decide to watch your words and actions today.  All we have is today. Yesterday is gone; tomorrow is only a dream.  Work for your God-given vision, but live in truth today. His name is 'I AM,' and now faith is! He is an ever-present help in times of need, and we all need Him.

Before we pray, I give you the following story:

* * *

Who was United States Senator Edmund G. Ross of Kansas? I suppose you could call him a "Mark. Nobody." No law bears his name. Not a single list of Senate "greats" mentions his service. Yet when Ross entered the Senate in 1866, he was considered the man to watch.  He seemed to surpass his colleagues, but he tossed it all away by one courageous act of conscience. Let's set the stage.

Conflict was dividing our government in the wake of the Civil War. President Andrew Johnson was determined to follow Lincoln's policy of reconciliation toward the defeated South. Congress, however, wanted to rule the downtrodden Confederate states with an iron hand.

Congress decided to strike first. Shortly after Senator Ross was seated, the Senate introduced impeachment proceedings against the hated President. The radicals calculated that they needed thirty-six votes and smiled as they concluded that the thirty-sixth was none other than Ross'. The new senator listened to the vigilante talk. But to the surprise of many, he declared that the president "deserved as fair a trial as any accused man has ever had on earth." The word immediately went out that his vote was "shaky." Ross received an avalanche of anti-Johnson telegrams from every section of the country. Radical senators badgered him to "come to his senses."

The fateful day of the vote arrived. The courtroom galleries were packed. Tickets for admission were at an enormous premium.

As a deathlike stillness fell over the Senate chamber, the vote began. By the time they reached Ross, twenty-four "guilties" had been announced. Eleven more were certain. Only Ross' vote was needed to impeach the President. Unable to conceal his emotion, the Chief Justice asked in a trembling voice, "Mark. Senator Ross, how vote you? Is the respondent Andrew Johnson guilty as charged?" Ross later explained, at that moment, "I looked into my open grave. Friendships, position, fortune, and everything that makes life desirable to an ambitious man were about to be swept away by the breath of my mouth, perhaps forever." Then, the answer came — unhesitating, unmistakable: "Not guilty!" With that, the trial was over. And the response was as predicted.

A high public official from Kansas wired Ross to say: "Kansas repudiates you as she does all perjurers and skunks." The "open grave" vision had become a reality. Ross's political career was in ruins. Extreme ostracism and even physical attack awaited his family upon their return home.

One gloomy day Ross turned to his faithful wife and said, "Millions cursing me today will bless me tomorrow...though not but God can know the struggle it has cost me." It was a prophetic declaration. Twenty years later, Congress and the Supreme Court verified the wisdom of his position by changing the laws related to impeachment.

Ross was appointed Territorial Governor of New Mexico. Then, just prior to his death, he was awarded a special pension by Congress. The press and country took this opportunity to honor his courage, which, they finally concluded, had saved our country from crisis and division.

* * *

You can make courageous daily decisions, to tell the truth, no matter what others are doing.

# 5

# The Golden Ladder of Giving

The following account was written by a friend of mine, Pastor Dan Stratton, from New York City. I love its thoughts. So, I shot him a message and asked his permission to post it here on the blog.

* * *

A while back, I had dinner with an elderly gentleman who was doing work around the world. He spoke of building shopping centers in Ghana. His name was Daniel, and his son's name is Joseph. Joseph and I were classmates at Yale. However, I was introduced to Daniel through Obie who has been my friend now these past eight years or so.

A group of politicians and business leaders had come from Africa to discuss potential work that we might do together. We met at the Havana Club at the top of the 6's, where Obie has been a member for some years. We were there as Obie's guests.

Obie is an established African American businessman – a Harvard graduate and a solid Christian. Daniel is a Jewish businessman who has done amazingly well in the real estate market and a devout Jew.

Our discussion began. Obie challenged the motives for this potential partnership as he spoke to the contingency from Africa. Amongst this group were men who had been to prison with Nelson Mandela and had been part of the formation of the new government in South Africa. We looked for common ground.

Daniel and I found common ground in an old document written by Moses Maimanodes. I was introduced to this as the Golden Ladder of Charity. Daniel challenged me and said that the thought would best be understood and communicated as the Golden Ladder of Justice. He said that the difference was this, *"Charity is something we can choose to do or not do. Justice is a duty. Justice must be done."*

In this Golden Ladder, Maimanodes bemoans the fact that so many with such good intentions create division through their giving. He says that it is not enough to give. He describes a wisdom and a process that must be considered to ensure that the giver doesn't subjugate the recipient. If the recipient is minimized in any way, he says, eventually, there will be a significant backlash that will leave both parties diminished.

The steps of giving have eight rungs.

1. To give with reluctance or regret is the gift of the hand but not the heart.
2. To give cheerfully, but not proportionately, and not until solicited. Otherwise, the sufferer could have distress.
3. To give cheerfully and proportionately, but not until solicited.
4. To give cheerfully, proportionately, and unsolicited, but the giver gives directly into the hand of the receiver, exciting in him the painful emotion of shame.
5. To give cheerfully, proportionately, proactively, but the giver does not know the recipient. The recipient still knows the giver.
6. To give cheerfully, proportionately, and proactively; whereas, the giver knows the recipient, but the recipient does not know the giver.
7. The chamber of Silence — total anonymity. Giving cheerfully, proportionately, and proactively, whereas neither the giver nor the recipient knows each other.
8. Anticipating needs and preventing poverty, preventing suffering through education, infrastructure, and access, giving to someone so

that they never experience a day where they have to raise their hands to ask for help.

I have written extensively on the emotion and the pain experienced as we walk through these eight steps of revelation. Growing to give without the need to be recognized is a process that few are unaware of.

In every exchange, every conversation would bid us all well to keep in mind that even Wisdom is a gift that can subjugate the hearer if we are not careful.  This subjugation will create a backlash.  Taking heed to give as anonymously as possible is a journey toward selflessness."

Carefully consider that which you have received. Has it created in us anger or worse, a hatred for the giver? Reconcile that, or you will receive that same anger paid back to you when you give.

And carefully consider when you give. Your motive maybe some form of recognition that will cost you and the recipient far more than the resources exchanged.

I say this into the realm of need that exists on our precious planet earth. None of these thoughts are mine. I have just discovered them on my "school of hard knocks" journey."

This is the end of Pastor Dan's account. But I have been meditating on several Scriptures, that lead my thoughts towards the worship component of our giving.

* * *

How about this one:

> *Hebrews 7:8 AKJV And here men that die receive tithes; but there he* receiveth them, *of whom it is witnessed that he liveth.*

Here, we see that when we give, we first present our offering to God as an offering, then to whoever He directs us to give in this life. Charity then, true charity – must be worship to God.

In this passage, that I often teach on concerning tithing, I see the spirit of giving, and on this, I will expound. When I give to the poor, if possible, I do what I can to remain anonymous. For Jesus Himself said:

> *Matthew 6:3 AMP But when you give to the poor* and *do acts of kindness, do not let your* **left hand** *know what your right* **hand** *is doing [give in complete secrecy].*

We understand' that 'the poor we will always have with us,' and we seek to honestly empower, support, and bless them to the best of our ability through the love of God that works through us. It is good to meet needs without expecting anything from them as part of our worship and obedience to God Himself. Though I may not expect anything from the poor, I do expect things for them – as I honestly seek to better their condition, be it through education, job creation, or economic development initiatives.

In Matthew 25, we see how God will judge us, individually and in the work of our organizations, by how well we feed the hungry, clothe the naked, get water to the thirsty, visit the sick and the prisoner. Again, in these passages, I see the spirit of worship injected between the lines of the text – God loves all people – and one of the ways we worship is to serve and meet the needs of people that He created in His image.

We must do it in faith to please Him, for it is written:

> *He who is gracious* and **lends** *a hand to the* **poor lends** *to the Lord, And the Lord will repay him for his good deed (Proverbs 19:17).*

No matter how wealthy our work and gifts make us, we humbly recognize that it is only by the hand of an Almighty Creator, the Author of all life, that we have been able to prosper. No matter how wealthy we become, we are limited in our abilities to alleviate human suffering. He is limitless and prepared to repay us any amount He might require us to give.

Sometimes that giving is only seen privately, between Him and us in prayer like when Nehemiah was rebuilding the wall of Jerusalem and was legitimately owed his wages and expenses while he was there. Yet, he saw the oppression and needs of the people, and we read:

### Nehemiah's Example

*Nehemiah 5:14-19 Moreover, from the day that I was appointed to be their governor in the land of Judah, from the twentieth year to the thirty-second year of King Artaxerxes, for twelve years, my relatives nor I have eaten the governor's food* allowance. *But the former governors who were [in office] before me put heavy burdens on the people and took food and wine from them in addition to forty shekels of silver [as an excessive monthly salary]; even their servants assumed authority over the people. But I did not do so because of the [reverent] fear of God. I also applied myself to the work on this wall; we did not buy any land, and all my servants were gathered together there for the work. Moreover, there were at my table a hundred and fifty Jews and officials, besides those who came to us from the nations that were around us. Now the following were prepared for each day: one ox and six choice sheep; also, fowls (poultry) were prepared for me, and in intervals of ten days, all sorts of wine* were provided in abundance. *Yet, for all this, I did not demand the governor's food* allowance, *because the servitude was heavy on these people.* **Remember me, O my God, for good, according to all I have done for these people.**

Read the whole chapter – he used his position and authority to make financial wrongs right and to set the people of God free from unjust interest.

I find myself often surrounded by glaring financial needs, children that need food each day to live, orphans that need school tuition and supplies, and ministries that need buildings. I long to help them all, yet I am ONLY responsible for assisting those that God places upon my heart.

Yes, we are to give, but with selflessness and purity of heart, that we might see God in every area of our lives.

May we give generously, often, in faith, to glorify Jesus in all we do. Let's Pray:

*'Father, flow through me in generosity and love as I worship You in my giving. Help me to become more selfless than selfish, equipping and empowering people to the best of my ability. Release to me more resources and wealth to further make this world a better place. Help me to alleviate human suffering wherever it may be found, to use my position, authority and influence to break policies that oppress people rather than empower them in the pursuit of the dreams You have placed in every human heart. I ask this, knowing that You hear me, for I ask in Your name, Lord Jesus, Amen.'*

# 6

# Governing in the Fear of the Lord

*James 3:1-2 My brethren, be not many masters, knowing that we shall receive the greater condemnation. For in many things, we offend all. If any man offend not in word, the same is a perfect man and also able to bridle the whole body.*

## Controlling the Tongue

*NLT James: 3 Dear brothers and sisters,[a] not many of you should become teachers in the church, for we who teach will be judged more strictly.2 Indeed, we all make many mistakes. For if we could control our tongues, we would be perfect and could also control ourselves in every other way.*

Do you want to be perfect?

I do like this verse in James because the Word of God shows us how to do it.

We know that as we grow in the things of God and are given resource and responsibility, we are expected to remember that we are continually stewards of God over the things He has given us. We are wise to seek Him diligently, humbly, often for His help to continuously do right.

Here we see a faithful, productive leader described:

*Matt 24:45 Who then is a reliable and wise servant whom his lord hath made ruler over his household to give them meat in due season? (meat today equals food, jobs, opportunity, justice and truth for starters)*

*Matt 24:46 Blessed is that servant, whom his lord when he cometh shall find so doing. Notice here that Jesus Himself watches over our work. We are His children and ambassadors in the earth, but there is an Almighty throne in heaven that speaks and judges the affairs of men.*

*Psalm 82:1 God presides over heaven's court; he pronounces judgment on the heavenly beings:*

That would be us, saints.

Then there is the selfish, self-centered leader:

*Luke 12:48 But he that knew not, and did commit things worthy of stripes, shall be beaten with few stripes. For unto whomsoever much is given, of him shall be much required: and to whom men have committed much, of him they will ask the more.*

We will give an account of our leadership and will be judged for it.

Sure, God is love and is raising us up to be set in position, and when in our area of service, God is still growing, promoting, and expanding us for the sake of the harvest!

Yet, I see here one of the ways we can measure our own development: our words.

We cannot bridle our own tongues, the Scripture states, but the Holy Spirit can!

He can help us shut our mouths and will purify our hearts and motives, if we let Him.

> *Luke 6:45 A good man out of the good treasure of his heart bringeth forth that which is good, and an evil man out of the evil treasure of his heart bringeth forth that which is evil: for of the abundance of the heart, his mouth speaketh.*

We see that the words that we speak, reflect what is in our hearts, and if we want to do what Jesus said:

> *Matt 5:48 Be ye therefore perfect, even as your Father which is in heaven is perfect. How can any person be perfect? It's impossible! No! It is not!*

> *Matt 12:36 But I say unto you, That every idle word that men shall speak, they shall give account thereof in the day of judgment.*

The word idle here means non-working or non-productive.

We should be living lives with purpose and using our words on purpose to work both in the Spirit and in the natural. All of our words should be working words, productive words, words of faith, that God can use to get things done here in the earth.

Other ministers have taught extensively on the importance of governing our words. I would highly recommend the materials by Charles Capps- *The Dynamics of Faith and Confession*

> *Matt 6:34 Take therefore no thought for the morrow: for the morrow shall take thought for the things of itself. Sufficient unto the day is the evil thereof.*

I find myself in a season of looking at what words I am speaking each day, and how well I am bringing them to pass.

Don't waste your words. Use them on purpose to declare the promises of

God and tighten the reign on what you promise people that you are going to do.

Application:

If you have made promises that you cannot fulfill, confess your sin before God and trust Him to clean up the mess you've made. Ask Him for favor with the people you have let down.

Contact the people, wherever possible, and tell them. Ask for their forgiveness and offer to do what you can to fix the mistake you made. If you cannot correct it, do not commit! Leave your case before God.

Separate yourself from people or situations that continually cause you to break your word. Negative people, places, and things need to go in your life. You do not have to respond to every telephone call or email but can quietly obey God and be led by the Holy Spirit as to what to do about creditors, painful relationships, or abusive situations. The servant of the Lord does not strive.

If someone is offended, determined to pick a fight, and unreasonable, quietly eliminate them from your life, gently, with no rancor, bitterness, nor wrath. Our primary responsibility is to walk right before God, not them.

Eventually, God will do one of two things with them.

> *Prov 16:7 When a man's ways please the LORD, he maketh even his enemies to be at peace with him.*

Along the way, He may need to get their attention, and Psalm 110:1:

> *The LORD said unto my Lord, Sit thou at my right hand until I make thine enemies thy footstool.*

We are called to love our enemies. When He delivers them into our hands, we must be humble and seek to restore them. For our motive is never self-vindication but, rather, the expansion of His kingdom!

Deliberately keep an account of our words each day! When in morning devotion, take a pen and paper and write down your personal directives from the Lord and the things you SAID you were going to do the day before. If you finished all that you said you were going to do, Glory! If not, repeat steps one through three as required, and then do what you need to do that day!

When you are not sure what to say or are radically tempted to say something you know you cannot pray in other tongues. Emotions are powerful things, but they must come under the Lordship of Jesus! Bridling our tongue is a work of the Holy Spirit. He gave this gift not as a badge of spirituality but as an enduement of power to get things done on the earth. Remember, when we pray in the Spirit, our heart of hearts, our human spirit, is speaking directly to God the exact and perfect will of God for our lives personally. Some of the things that need to be said, you do not have enough knowledge or understanding to pray yet. So, Holy Spirit comes along and does for us what we cannot do for ourselves. He prays through us perfect, holy prayer. Holy Spirit prayer must be a part of our daily walk with Jesus, for He alone knows the times, seasons, relationships, and reasons for the circumstances we face daily.

Perfection means perfect words each day!

One day at a time!

Let's Pray:

*'Father, I fully surrender to You again today! Set a clamp on my mouth to NOT say things that are wrong to You. Help me to know what I must say, and what I must only pray. In Your name, I pray, Lord Jesus. Amen'*

# 7

# Morality Produces Prosperity

Some time ago, I read a famous book entitled: *As a Man Thinketh* by James Allen.

> *I quote: "It is popularly supposed that a greater prosperity for individuals and nations can only come through political and social reconstruction. This cannot be true apart from the practice of the moral virtues in the individuals that comprise a nation. Better laws and social conditions will always follow a higher realization of morality among the individuals of a community, but no legal enactment can give prosperity to, nay, it cannot prevent the ruin of, a man or a nation that has become lax and decadent in the pursuit and practice of virtue."*

The moral virtues are the foundation and support of prosperity, as they are the soul of greatness. They endure forever, and all the works of man which endure are built upon them. Without them, there is neither strength, stability, nor substantial reality, but only ephemeral dreams. To find moral principles is to have found prosperity, greatness, truth, and is, therefore, to be strong, fearless, joyful, and free. James Allen 'Excerpt from *As a Man Thinketh*' Bryngolen, Ilfracombe, England.

As I read this quote, I am reminded of the verse we all quote at election time:

*Pro 14:34 Righteousness exalteth a nation: but sin is a reproach to any people.*

Regarding the moral man:

*Psa 37:6 And he shall bring forth thy righteousness as the light, and thy judgment as the noonday.*

I wonder how many of us fight to do right daily in the little battles, as we love our families, teach our children, and walk forward in truth without compromise.

Let's Pray:

*'Father, help me to do right before You today for the right reasons, setting an example of honesty, integrity, holiness, and true righteousness before my family today. I want to be one of the pillars of truth that You rebuild this nation on. In Your name I pray, Lord Jesus, Amen!'*

# 8

# The Law of the Bad Apple

John Maxwell – The Law of the Bad Apple:

As I read John's Book, on the *17 Indisputable Laws of Team Work*, he talks about how one bad attitude poisons the whole team. He gives a little checklist of attitudes that we might hold that are stemmed from selfishness and pride that need to die. As I read them, I saw some of them in myself. So, I am going to share them with you, so that you can join me at the cross, and we can repent and think and act like Jesus.

1. *Thinking the team wouldn't be able to get along without you.*
2. *Secretly (or not so secretly) believing that recent team successes are attributable to your personal efforts, not the work of the whole team.*
3. *Keeping score when praises or perks are handed out to other team members.*
4. *Are you having a hard time admitting when you made a mistake? If you don't believe you are making mistakes, you need to check this.*
5. *Are you bringing up past wrongs from your teammates?*
6. *Do you believe that you are grossly undervalued or underpaid?*

These are John's list, but I got to thinking about how deceptive these attitudes are, and how they can sneakily enter our thinking.

*"Everything can be taken from a man but one thing: To choose one's*

***attitude in any given set of circumstances, to choose one's way."***
*Viktor Frankl, a concentration-camp survivor.*

*Philippians 2:15 Do all things without murmurings and disputings: That ye may be blameless and harmless, the sons of God, without rebuke, in the midst of a crooked and perverse nation, among whom ye shine as lights in the world.*

Perhaps you are more humble than I am and a better team player than I. But I need to grow in this area. I have always been a bit of a 'lone ranger,' isolating myself in academia. In sports, I became self-focused in anything I competed in (swimming and triathlon). My competition was generally me against the clock. I would go off into my own particular rhythm or zone and competed with myself to be the best I could be. Although I had other teammates where we encouraged each other for the sake of the team, we generally all thought this way, seeking personal excellence. Because when it was time to race, we were totally alone with the clock. Even if there were other competitors fiercely pushing us on either side, attitudes could be like worms eating into the sweet fruit our lives should be bearing.

I read this illustration and thought it appropriate here: *"Both the humming-bird and the vulture fly over our nation's deserts. All vultures see is rotting meat because that is what they look for. They thrive on that diet. But hummingbirds ignore the smelly flesh of dead animals. Instead, they look for the colorful blossoms of desert plants. The vultures live on what was. They live in the past. They fill themselves with what is dead and gone. But hummingbirds live on what is. They seek a new life. They fill themselves with freshness and vitality. Each bird finds what it is looking for. We all do."* Steve Goodier, Quote Magazine, in *Reader's Digest,* May 1990

Would anyone else want to join me on my journey from independence, individualism, and introversion to become a team player?

Let's pray:

*'Father God, I see how I often am in the press toward the mark of the*

*high calling in Christ Jesus for my sake instead of perhaps the best interests of Your Body, Your Church, Your dream team. Forgive me for my selfishness, stinking thinking, and an elitist, proud attitude. Help me to be the best I can be in flowing with other leaders and team members. In Your name, I pray, Lord Jesus. Amen.'*

# 9

# Mining for Gold

I have an uncle in the Yukon, Canada, that is a heavy equipment mechanic and a gold miner in the summer. From what I understand, over the past couple of hundred years, prospectors have panned most of the creeks to retrieve nuggets and easily recovered gold deposits; however, there is still much gold in the north. To retrieve it, though, one must move tons of earth and run it through huge sluice boxes that separate the dirt from the gold. Since the price of gold is so high currently, it is worth the time to fly bulldozers and earth-moving equipment deep into the bush to carve into the gold-rich soils. Fortunes have been made in doing this.

Well, I am mining a different type of gold, the more precious gold of spiritual revelation and truth, eternal in its worth and consequence.

> *Isaiah 45:3 and I will give thee the treasures of darkness and **hidden riches** of secret places, that thou mayest know that I, the Lord, which call thee by thy name, am the God of Israel.*

Recently, I saw a bibliography in the back of one of the 'Go get 'em' motivational business books I had just read, and I decided to photocopy it and to deliberately read these books at a rate of two per week. Compared to the study of the Word of God, I find them light reading, and I have been able to blaze through many of these books quickly.

What I am looking for is a revelation, truth, principles of motivation, leadership, and success that apply to raising up the healthy end-time Christian ministries I am called to develop.

As I was reading a classic entitled: *As a Man Thinketh*, by James Allen, I came across the following excerpt that jumped out at me, and I hope it blesses you:

*"All that a man achieves or all that he fails to achieve is a result of his own thoughts. In a justly ordered universe, where loss of equipoise would mean destruction, individual responsibility must be absolute. A man's weakness and strength, purity, and impurity, are his own and not another man's: they are brought about by himself, never by another. His condition is also his own and not another man's. His suffering and his happiness are evolved from within. As he thinks, so he is; as he continues to think, so he remains.*

*A strong man cannot help a weaker unless the weaker is willing to be helped, and even then, the weak man must become strong of himself; he must, by his own efforts, develop the strength which he admires in another. None but himself can alter his condition. (Allen, 45, 46).*

As I thought about this, I had several Scriptures flash across my mind for your consideration and meditation:

*Prov 23:7 For as he thinketh in his heart, so is he:*

*1 Corinthians 13:5 doth not behave itself unseemly, seeketh not her own, is not easily provoked, **thinketh** no evil;*

*Deut 31:6 Be strong and of a good courage, fear not, nor be afraid of them: for the LORD thy God, he it is that doth go with thee; he will not fail thee, nor forsake thee.*

*Isa 35:4 Say to them that are of a fearful heart, Be strong, fear not: behold, your God will come with vengeance, even God with a recompense; he will come and save you.*

*Joe 3:10 Beat your plowshares into swords, and your pruninghooks into spears: let the weak say, I am strong.*

*Rom 15:1 We then that are strong ought to bear the infirmities of the weak, and not to please ourselves.*

*1 Cor 9:22 To the weak became I as weak, that I might gain the weak: I am made all things to all men, that I might by all means save some.*

*2 Cor 13:9 For we are glad, when we are weak, and ye are strong: and this also we wish, even your perfection.*

The practical outcome of this for Christians everywhere was twofold: on the one hand, they were freed from the tyranny, superstition, and oppression of Rome; but, on the other hand, with freedom came individual responsibility before God. No longer could the single Christian rely simply on his membership in the physical organization of a church for the salvation of his soul; in no small degree, it now devolved upon him. Salvation was not something one was physically born into because one's parents were Christian or because one had received "infant baptism" and made a member of the church before he could even understand what he was doing, but salvation was something spiritual which one had to enter into as the result of a conscious decision he alone had made.

No longer could anyone else decide this matter for the individual – not one's mother or father; not one's priest or bishop; not one's pastor or elder – it was an individual decision for which the individual alone was responsible. From this point on, no human intermediary could stand between God and man: man now stood naked and alone before his Maker. The frightening words of the Apostle Paul loomed heavily over his head.

*"Wherefore, my beloved ...work out your own salvation with fear and trembling!" (Phil. 2:12)*

Heaven or Hell? – it was his choice! Remaining an "infant in the Lord" or growing up into full Christian maturity? – it was his choice. Being obedient or disobedient? – it was his choice!

> *"The church could assist by providing the Christian with a nurturing and Biblically-based environment which was conducive to growth in the Spirit; other Christians could help in their fellowship and friendships – but even here, the individual had to make a conscious decision to avail himself of these "helps." There was no way other Christians and the church could force themselves on the individual and decide for him. In the end, he alone was responsible, and he alone would have to answer for his decisions."* November 21, 1998, Written By S.R. Shearer

This thought is why Paul had us 'press towards the mark of the high calling of God in Christ Jesus.'

> *James 4:8 Draw nigh to God, and he will draw nigh to you. Cleanse your hands, ye sinners; and purify your hearts, ye double-minded.*

> *2 Tim 2:19-20 Nevertheless the foundation of God standeth sure, having this seal, The Lord knoweth them that are his. And, Let everyone that nameth the name of Christ depart from iniquity. But in a great house, there are not only vessels of gold and silver, but also of wood and of earth; and some to honor, and some to dishonor. 21 If a man, therefore, purge himself from these, he shall be a vessel unto honor, sanctified, and meet for the master's use and prepared unto every good work.*

Each of us will stand before God, alone to give an account of our lives, personally. Not only for what we did, but, I am also convinced, for what we should have done, had we fully obeyed Jesus in our generation.

As I read through these 'Go get em' motivational books, I find a blend of

Biblical principles (which always bring true success) and humanism where it seems as if the works of men will add to the power of God.

While it is true that works of faith, performed in obedience to the Holy Spirit, will produce tremendous results in both this world and the next, works of man, done according to Biblical principles, may allow a person to amass great wealth in this life, but without eternal reward. God honored His Word in the person's life, yet the man may or may not have done with the fruits of his labor what God intended, hoarding up for himself the blessings of God, without concern for the gospel, and the needs of humanity. The benefits remain temporal rather than eternal and are no indication of that man's actual state before a holy God. So, I advise you:

> *Matt 6:33 But seek ye first the kingdom of God, and his righteousness, and all these things shall be added unto you.*

I believe that in this hour, the regular schedule and business of life not suffice.

> *Heb 11:6 But without faith, it is impossible to please him: for he that cometh to God must believe that he is, and that he is a rewarder of them that diligently seek him.*

'God is calling a people to Himself and is wanting to be sought out for His plans, purposes, and pursuits in this generation,' quote from Kenneth E. Hagin: I urge you to deliberately carve time out of your busy schedule, even if it means skipping a couple of hours of sleep each morning, to spend time in the Word, in prayer, in praying in other tongues, in worship, seeking His face, until He speaks to you specifically and clearly about your particular giftings and callings. Your appointment in this life.

> *1 Thes 5:9 For God hath not appointed us to wrath, but to obtain salvation by our Lord Jesus Christ.*

Let's pray:

> *'Father, help me to discipline myself to deliberately seek You in prayer, praise, and Your Word daily. Speak to me today, and correct me, and redirect me, where I have gone astray. Meet with me, Papa God, and meet the deepest pangs of hunger in my heart with Your love and truth that makes me free, as I honor and serve You, Lord Jesus. Free indeed! Amen!'*

# 10

# The Responsibility of Abraham

God promised Abraham to multiply his seed as the sand of the seashore and stars of the heavens. His life is an example of what it looks like when God makes one healthy, wealthy, and wise.

For those of us growing as leaders, determined to do things God's way, I got to thinking about how much responsibility and courage it would take to manage and lead 400 employees and their families.

> *Gen 14:14 And when Abram heard that his brother was taken captive, he armed his trained servants, born in his own house, three hundred and eighteen*

> *Gen 17:23 And Abraham took Ishmael his son, and all that were born in his house, and all that were bought with his money, every male among the men of Abraham's house; and circumcised the flesh of their foreskin in the selfsame day, as God had said unto him.*

(Not sure how many exactly, from the 318 and decades later, so I guessed 400)

This promise is for us today, too. Yet, I have been meditating on the life of Abraham and thinking about the responsibility he walked in before God and man, so here are my thoughts...

**The responsibility of Abraham:** We are blessed with the blessing of Abraham.

> *Gal 3:29 And if ye be Christ's, then are ye Abraham's seed, and heirs according to the promise.*

But something I hear so little about is **the responsibility of Abraham**.

Sure, he was called of God, and God blessed and multiplied him, but then what? How did he handle the blessing? Well, let me make a few points:

He had the responsibility to establish God's covenant in the earth.

He tithed.

He had to develop raw land into agricultural use.

He raised up an army to secure his land.

He was given authority from heaven on earth.

He had to look after at least 400 families in his employment.

He had a responsibility to believe what God said.

Let's look at these:

1. *He had the responsibility to establish God's covenant in the earth.*

> *Gen 12:1 Now the LORD had said unto Abram, Get thee out of thy country, and from thy kindred, and from thy father's house, unto a land that I will shew thee: And I will make of thee a great nation, and I will bless thee, and make thy name great; and thou shalt be a blessing: And I will bless them that bless thee, and curse him that curseth thee: and in thee shall all families of the earth be blessed. So Abram departed, as the LORD had spoken unto him, and Lot went with him: and Abram was seventy and five years old when he departed out of Haran.*

He had to know he heard the voice of God because it initially cost him everything. He had to leave his religion, his family, his relatives, his nation, and his culture to obey God. God told him that He would make him into a great nation and would give him fame and honor. His power manifest through him would make the earth a better place. Yet, initially, it cost him everything. Probably all his relatives and his wife thought he was nuts. No one had ever done this before. Of course, he had Noah to think about. No one had ever built an ark before, either...bottom line. If we want to be like Abraham, we must be willing to leave our father, mother, relatives, nation, and culture to obey God in this generation fully.

Hear the words of Jesus:

*Matt 10:33-39 But whosoever shall deny me before men, him will I also deny before my Father which is in heaven.*

*Think not that I am come to send peace on earth: I came not to send peace but a sword.*

*For I am come to set a man at variance against his father, and the daughter against her mother, and the daughter in law against her mother-in-law.*

*And a man's foes shall be they of his own household.*

*He that loveth father or mother more than me is not worthy of me: and he that loveth son or daughter more than me is not worthy of me. And he that taketh not his cross, and followeth after me, is not worthy of me.*

*He that findeth his life shall lose it: and he that loseth his life for my sake shall find it.*

He may ask us to stay in our community to exhibit His love there. But in my case, He told me to leave my family, my country, my culture, my career, and my fiancé, to fully obey Him. As I see prayers answered and His fingerprints upon the earth through my life, I am keenly aware of the spiritual responsibility I carry. Though no one else on the earth understands me, He does. And it is to Him that I must give an account of my obedience. One day, we will all die. On that day, we each have an individual appointment with the King to give an account of our lives. To whom much is given, much is required...**Whatever He says, DO IT!**

*2. Abraham tithed:*

> *Heb 7:1 For this Melchisedec, king of Salem, priest of the most high God, who met Abraham returning from the slaughter of the kings, and blessed him; To whom also Abraham gave a tenth part of all; first being by interpretation King of righteousness, and after that also King of Salem, which is, King of peace; Without father, without mother, without descent, having neither beginning of days, nor end of life; but made like unto the Son of God; abideth a priest continually.*

Now consider how great this man was, unto whom even the patriarch Abraham gave the tenth of the spoils.

It is expected, in the New Testament, that if you wish to claim the blessing of Abraham, you need to be like him. That means we need to establish the tithe in our lives.

> *Lev 27:30 And all the tithe of the land, whether of the seed of the land or of the fruit of the tree, is the LORD'S: it is holy unto the LORD.*

> *Heb 7:8 And **here men that die receive tithes**; but there he receiveth them, of whom it is witnessed that he liveth.*

We give God the first ten percent of our income and deposit it in whatever ministry He directs, but the act of tithing must between us individually and God Himself. We will be credited on how we tithe, the men that receive our tithes will give an account to God personally as to how they handled our offerings. We do it, each time, as a witness that Jesus rose from the dead, He lives!

*3. He developed raw land for agricultural use.*

*Gen 13:6 And the land was not able to bear them, that they might dwell together: for their substance was great, so that they could not dwell together.7 And there was a strife between the herdmen of Abram's cattle and the herdmen of Lot's cattle: and the Canaanite and the Perizzite dwelled then in the land. And Abram said unto Lot, Let there be no strife, I pray thee, between me and thee, and between my herdmen and thy herdmen; for we be brethren. Is not the whole land before thee? Separate thyself, I pray thee, from me: if thou wilt take the left hand, then I will go to the right; or if thou depart to the right hand, then I will go to the left. And Lot lifted up his eyes and beheld all the plain of Jordan, that it was well watered everywhere, before the LORD destroyed Sodom and Gomorrah, even as the garden of the LORD, like the land of Egypt, as thou comest unto Zoar. Then Lot chose him all the plain of Jordan; and Lot journeyed east: and they separated themselves the one from the other.*

So, Abraham understood the blessing, the anointing, the promise of God, and what it would produce in his life. He willingly chose the more barren land, because he instinctively knew that God, who created the universe, was well able to make his barren land bloom.

*Isa 51:3 For the LORD shall comfort Zion: he will comfort all her waste places; and he will **make her wilderness like Eden**, and her desert like the garden of the LORD; joy and gladness shall be found therein thanksgiving, and the voice of melody.*

*Joe 2:3 A fire devoureth before them; and behind them, a flame burneth:* **the land is as the garden of Eden before them** *and behind them a desolate*
   *wilderness; yea, and nothing shall escape them.*

The Spirit of God, resting upon obedient men and women, will produce a land, as the garden of Eden was back in the creation story. This is a covenant.

This is redemption. This is what your faith should be producing. This is your spiritual birthright in Jesus.

Yet, work was involved.

> *Gen 26:15 For all the wells which his father's servants had digged in the days of Abraham, his father, the Philistines had stopped them and filled them with earth.*

I've dug a few post holes for fences in my day, and a couple of hours on a post hole digger is good old-fashioned work. Digging wells is no picnic, nor is managing, fencing, or shepherding livestock.

Working with the Lord is a whole lot different than working for mere men.

> *1 Cor 15:58 Therefore, my beloved brethren, be ye steadfast, unmovable, always abounding in the work of the Lord, forasmuch as ye know that your labor is not in vain in the Lord.*

Now when I work, it is part of my worship, earning money to provide for my family and to support the work of the Gospel around the world. This work bears eternal consequence and weight and is far more than just a job.

I just noticed an interesting thing. Lot took the better land, but it was near the wicked cities of Sodom and Gomorrah. God is a jealous God and demands 100% devotion to Him. Notice how Lot was enjoying the benefits of the blessing of God but did not appear to know or care about God Himself. No sign anywhere of him praying, seeking, or hearing from God himself. God blessed Abraham for separating himself from Lot. Sometimes you need to bless people and get yourself away from them to experience the blessing of God fully upon your life.

He sowed a seed (the best land), walked in love, and refused strife, and reaped everything! When he did, he immediately built an altar to God and worshipped!

> *Gen 13:14-17 And the LORD said unto Abram, after that Lot was*

*separated from him, Lift up now thine eyes, and look from the place where thou art northward, and southward, and eastward, and westward: For all the land which thou seest, to thee will I give it, and to thy seed forever. And I will make thy seed as the dust of the earth: so that if a man can number the dust of the earth, then shall thy seed also be numbered. Arise, walk through the land in the length of it and the breadth of it, for I will give it unto thee. Then Abram removed his tent and came and dwelt in the plain of Mamre, which is in Hebron, and built there an altar unto the LORD.*

God promised this land to Abram, but Abram had to believe it, receive it, work it, develop it, possess it, and make it a garden of Eden in his generation. If we are to walk in the responsibility of Abraham, we too will be given specific promises of land, vocation, and blessing that, like Abraham, we must believe, receive by faith, work at, develop, possess, and make our particular garden of Eden in this generation.

*4. He raised up an army to secure his land.*

*Gen 13:12 And they took Lot, Abram's brother's son, who dwelt in Sodom, and his goods, and departed. And there came one that had escaped and told Abram the Hebrew, for he dwelt in the plain of Mamre the Amorite, brother of Eshcol, and brother of Aner: and these were confederate with Abram.And when Abram heard that his brother was taken captive, he armed his trained servants, born in his own house, three hundred and eighteen, and pursued them unto Dan. And he divided himself against them, he and his servants, by night, and smote them, and pursued them unto Hobah, which is on the left hand of Damascus. And he brought back all the goods, and also brought again his brother Lot, and his goods, and the women even, and the people.*

Notice, from the very inception of this land now called Israel, there was war. For whatever reason, God knew that man must fight, and He placed a warrior heart in us to protect, defend, and fight for our families and our lands.

This was in the beginning even in the garden of Eden. We read in Gen 2:15:

*And the LORD God took the man and put him into the garden of Eden to dress it and to keep it.*

Strong's Concordance gives a lengthy definition of the Hebrew, shamar, which King James translates as *to keep; to guard, keep watch and ward, protect, save a life.* Even in paradise, Satan, an enemy to defend ourselves against, was in the earth. We were to be vigilant and to protect our family and land from him.

Here, we see Abraham having raised up a trained army of 318 men that went to battle against a hostile force to deliver wayward Lot, his nephew. He pursued his enemies and recovered all.

What is the lesson for us today? There is a fight of faith to be fought in this generation.

Satan is a thief and will not hesitate to steal from us if he can. Hear the Words of Jesus:

*Matt 11:12 And from the days of John the Baptist until now the kingdom of heaven suffereth violence and the violent take it by force.*

*Luke 19:13 And he called his ten servants, and delivered them ten pounds, and said unto them, **Occupy until I come.***

*Matt 16:18 And I say also unto thee, That thou art Peter, and upon this rock, I will build my church; and the gates of hell shall not prevail against it. There is a warrior heart God has placed in every leader to defend and protect that which God has given him. This heart will war to deliver captives and to preserve and deliver the defenseless widows and orphans. If we claim the blessing of Abraham, we need to be willing to fight for what God has given us.*

Here is an exciting thought about Abraham's army:

> *Gen 17:12 And he that is eight days old shall be circumcised among you, every man child in your generations, he that is born in the house, or bought with money of any stranger, which is not of thy seed.*

> *Gen 17:13 He that is born in thy house, and he that is bought with thy money, must needs be circumcised: and my covenant shall be in your flesh for an everlasting covenant.*

All of these had to obey God in coming into covenant with God through circumcision. As Abraham increased and needed more help to manage his estate, he purchased help, which reminds me of employees that I have hired over the years. As long as I paid them, they hung around; otherwise, they had no interest in the vision and promises of God being worked out in our lives.

Yet, Abraham insisted that every one of these come under the covenant of God and become circumcised. Based on this, I do not think it unreasonable to establish godly conditions for employment in our lives and ministries. Conditions that we might consider:

Are you a tither?

Are you a born-again Christian?

Are you willing to come to morning prayer at the company headquarters?

Do you attend a Bible-believing local church?

Are you faithful to your wife?

Are you living a godly, holy life? (criminal background check and drug test)

Are you filled with the Holy Spirit with the evidence of speaking in other tongues?

These conditions seem to me to be much less painful than circumcision.

*5. Abraham was given authority from heaven, in the earth.*

*Gen 14:18 And Melchizedek king of Salem brought forth bread and wine: and he was the priest of the most high God. And he blessed him, and said, Blessed be Abram of the most high God, possessor of heaven and earth: And blessed be the most high God, which hath delivered thine enemies into thy hand. And he gave him tithes of all.*

A lot is going on here. Abraham comes back victorious from battle and meets this strange character named Melchizadek, king of Salem. Well, a little background here, the Hebrew word for 'city of' is Jeru, I am told, and the Hebrew word for 'peace' is *Salem*. Jerusalem is God's chosen capital of the earth, the holy city, from where He will rule.

*1Ki 11:13 Howbeit I will not rend away all the kingdom but will give one tribe to thy son for David my servant's sake, and for Jerusalem's sake, which I have chosen.*

*Jer 3:17 At that time, they shall call Jerusalem the throne of the LORD; and all the nations shall be gathered unto it, to the name of the LORD, to Jerusalem: neither shall they walk any more after the imagination of their evil heart.*

*Mic 4:2 And many nations shall come, and say, Come, and let us go up to the mountain of the LORD, and to the house of the God of Jacob, and he will teach us of his ways, and we will walk in his paths: for the law shall go forth of Zion and the word of the LORD from Jerusalem.*

*Zec 14:16 And it shall come to pass, that every one that is left of all the nations which came against Jerusalem shall even go up from year to year to worship the King, the LORD of hosts, and to keep the feast of tabernacles.*

So, here we have a mysterious king of the city of Salem, or Jerusalem, appearing to Abraham. And he was greater than Abraham because Abraham gave him tithes. The man was a priest of the Most High God, and priests pray and offer sacrifices to God. In this case, this priest brought forth bread and wine (sound familiar, yet) and announced to the earth on behalf of God: 'Blessed be Abram of the Most High God, possessor of heaven and earth.'

Most scholars call this a theophany, a pre-incarnate appearance of the Lord Jesus Christ. There are many books written about this, where scholars argue that the man that appeared to Joshua as captain of the Lord's host. Or the fourth man in the fire with the three Hebrew boys, was Jesus appearing as God the Son, before He began His earthly ministry. *Rev 13:8 And all that dwell upon the earth shall worship him, whose names are not written in the book of life of the Lamb slain from the foundation of the world.*

What I want to focus upon, though, is what He said: Abram, possessor of heaven and earth.'

This is strong language, only understood in light of blood covenant. To fully understand this passage, one needs to understand what happened in the covenant ceremony; when blood was shed, vows were taken, and destinies were joined irrevocably, unto death.

Many excellent books are written on this topic. I like EW Kenyon's mini-book, titled *Blood covenant*, explaining the significance of blood covenants entered into person to person, and more importantly, between man and God. Basically, in a covenant, two parties were saying all I have is yours, your enemies are my enemies, your family is my family, your resources are my resources, and my resources are your resources.

What Melchisedek says here literally is: Abram, because of your covenant with God, all that God has, is at your disposal to be called upon, in honor as you require. This makes you possessor of heaven and earth. The next verse clarifies this.

*Gen 14:20 And blessed be the Most High God, which hath delivered thine enemies into thy hand. And he gave him tithes of all.*

God spoke to Abram covenant talk. You are my covenant representative, and your enemies are my enemies. Because of this, I have delivered them into your hand.

Abram, with his little army of 318 soldiers, challenged four kings and emerged victorious in the conflict. Because of Jesus, the blessing of Abraham are ours. God has given you authority in the earth.

*Isa 45:11 Thus saith the LORD, the Holy One of Israel, and his Maker, Ask me of things to come concerning my sons, and concerning the work of my hands command ye me.*

*Matt 28:18 And Jesus came and spake unto them, saying, All power is given unto me in heaven and in earth. Go ye therefore, and teach all nations, baptizing them in the name of the Father, and of the Son, and of the Holy Ghost:*

He is Lord. He is our high priest. He has established His covenant with us through His shed blood, enacted through the partaking of the bread and the wine. His enemies are our enemies; His resources are our resources. His joy is our joy. His lands are our lands, and His power is available for us to enforce His rule and reign in the earth.

*Gen 15: 5 And he brought him forth abroad, and said, Look now toward heaven, and tell the stars, if thou be able to number them: and he said unto him, So shall thy seed be.*

*And he believed in the LORD, and he counted it to him for righteous- ness.*

So, Abraham had Isaac miraculously in his old age. Through Isaac came the nation of Israel, and we, the church, have been grafted into this Abrahamic covenant by faith in Jesus's death, burial, and resurrection.

This promise of God is our inheritance and is still going on. Each one of us is one of the grains of sand and one of the innumerable stars. Every time we preach the gospel of the kingdom of God, and another person comes into the kingdom and is raised up in the promises of God, this promise God made to Abraham continues to bear fruit in the earth.

> *Gen 22:17-18 That in blessing I will bless thee, and in multiplying I will multiply thy seed as the stars of the heaven, and as the sand which is upon the seashore; and thy seed shall possess the gate of his enemies;*
> *And in thy seed shall all the nations of the earth be blessed; because thou hast obeyed my voice.*

We receive this mighty Abrahamic covenant through faith, and immediately all the promises God made to Abraham become ours through Jesus. Blessing, increase, prosperity, authority, honor, strength, protection, victory, and wisdom become ours the moment we understand this and believe it. Again, in this sin-sick, broken earth, a light shines. A blessing is invoked, and the garden of Eden begins to grow again through each person's obedient life that results from the covenant God made all these years ago through a man named Abraham.

*6. He had to look after at least 400 families.*

We looked at the 318 men that were born in Abraham's house that went to battle to rescue Lot. Then we saw that when God implemented circumcision, there were other servants present that Abraham purchased, whether as slaves or employees is unclear, but required by God to be circumcised to partake of the benefits of Abraham's covenant.  Yet, having owned a company and partnered in another, how well I know the pressure of responsibility of having to make payroll each week.  I remember one particular week when my little daughter, my princess, saw me on the phone attempting to collect money from clients so that I could make sure money was in the bank to issue paychecks that week. She said, 'Dad, the crowd is bigger than you think.' Amid the pressure, I stopped and asked, 'Princess, what did you say?' She repeated, 'Dad, the crowd is bigger than you think." "What do you mean?' I asked. She understood far more than I thought an eight-year-old could. "Dad, you are fighting to get money for your men to give them their paychecks, but there are many more people depending upon you than just them. There are their wives, children, and all of the people they support each week. *"That is a big crowd, Dad, bigger than you think."*

At the time, I had 27 people working for me, plus probably another 20 suppliers and subcontractors that needed to be paid. We made it through that week, and everyone got paid. Thank God!

I think of how that particular dynamic might have looked in the life of Abraham, out in the desert, having to provide leadership to over 400 families. All the relational dynamics that entailed, the wisdom and strength of character it took, and the raw courage to have to see God provide for all of them daily.

It seems everyone wants the blessing of God, but here, I see the responsibility of leadership, very intimately and clearly.

Do you still want the blessing of Abraham? In my mind, it's one of those things that you don't dare live without.

*7. He had a responsibility to believe what God said.*

> *Gen 15:6 And he believed in the LORD; and he counted it to him for righteousness.*
> *Only believe. All things are possible if we only believe.*

And so, we have it in a nutshell, the crux of the matter, faith.

This faith is the entire responsibility of the new covenant; it is the currency of heaven. The difference between heaven or hell in our personal lives is faith, and the sole determinate as to the quality of life we will enjoy here in this earth, in light of eternity, is God's grace received by faith.

> *Matt 8:10-12 When Jesus heard it, he marveled, and said to them that followed, Verily I say unto you, I have not found so great faith, no, not in Israel. And I say unto you, That many shall come from the east and west and shall sit down with Abraham, and Isaac, and Jacob, in the kingdom of heaven. But the children of the kingdom shall be cast out*

*into outer darkness: there shall be weeping and gnashing of teeth.*

*Rom 4:3 For what saith the Scripture? Abraham believed God, and it was counted unto him for righteousness.*

*Gal 3:6 Even as Abraham believed God, and it was accounted to him for righteousness.*

*Gal 3:7 Know ye therefore that they which are of faith, the same are the children of Abraham.*

*Gal 3:8 And the scripture, foreseeing that God would justify the heathen through faith, preached before the gospel unto Abraham, saying, In thee shall all nations be blessed.*

*Gal 3:9 So then they which be of faith are blessed with faithful Abraham.*

*Gal 3:14 That the blessing of Abraham might come on the Gentiles through Jesus Christ, that we might receive the promise of the Spirit through faith.*

*Gal 3:16 Now to Abraham and his seed were the promises made. He saith not, And to seeds, as of many, but as of one, And to thy seed, which is Christ. Gal 3:18 For if the inheritance be of the law, it is no more of promise: but God gave it to Abraham by promise.*

*Gal 3:29 And if ye be Christ's, then are ye Abraham's seed, and heirs according to the promise.*

*James 2:23 And the scripture was fulfilled which saith, Abraham believed God, and it was imputed unto him for righteousness: and he was called the Friend of God.*

*Ep 2:8-19 For by grace are ye saved through faith; and that not of yourselves: it is the gift of God: Not of works, lest any man should boast. For we are his workmanship, created in Christ Jesus unto good works, which God hath before ordained that we should walk in them. Wherefore remember, that ye being in time past Gentiles in the flesh, who are called Uncircumcision by that which is called the Circumcision in the flesh made by hands; That at that time ye were without Christ, being aliens from the commonwealth of Israel, and strangers from the covenants of promise, having no hope, and without God in the world: But now in Christ Jesus ye who sometimes were far off are made nigh by the blood of Christ. For he is our peace, who hath made both one, and hath broken down the middle wall of partition between us; Having abolished in his flesh the enmity, even the law of commandments contained in ordinances; for to make in himself of twain one new man, so making peace; And that he might reconcile both unto God in one body by the cross, having slain the enmity thereby: And came and preached peace to you which were afar off, and to them that were nigh. For through him we both have access by one Spirit unto the Father. Now therefore ye are no more strangers and foreigners but fellow citizens with the saints, and of the household of God; And are built upon the foundation of the apostles and prophets, Jesus Christ himself being the chief cornerstone; In whom all the building fitly framed together groweth unto a holy temple in the Lord: In whom ye also are built together for a habitation of God through the Spirit.*

*Heb 8:10 For this is the covenant that I will make with the house of Israel after those days, saith the Lord; I will put my laws into their mind, and write them in their hearts: and I will be to them a God, and they shall be to me a people: And they shall not teach every man his neighbor, and every man his brother, saying, Know the Lord: for all shall know me, from the least to the greatest.*

This reminds me of that children's cartoon, 'The Lion King' and its circle-of-life illustration. Abraham believed, and the Jewish people were birthed through all their generations until Jesus the Messiah, the fulfillment of all the promises and prophecies came into the earth. And through His death, burial, and resurrection, He opened a new and better way to Jew and Gentile alike, a way to come directly to God through His shed blood and to be grafted into this Abrahamic covenant, which is based upon new and better promises. A new covenant God has made with humanity for whosoever would believe. And all the promises become yes, and Amen, in Jesus!

God no longer lives with us, but through acceptance of Jesus, literally comes to live within us. No longer do we worship a God that is far off, but One who draws near. Though God our Father forever sits enthroned in the heavens, and Jesus sits at His right hand as God the Son. He sent His Holy Spirit to the earth to fill us and give us a heavenly tongue to empower, equip, and direct our lives. Now we walk by faith; we are not alone. He can literally say, 'I will never leave you nor forsake you.' So, the circle of life goes on from generation to generation, as we go from faith to faith, strength to strength, and glory to glory. We are designed by God to be fruitful and robust. We are called to establish and replenish the earth as the increase of His government grows within us and through us as we progressively submit and enforce Jesus's Lordship everywhere we go. How does faith come?

> *Rom 10:17 So then faith cometh by hearing and hearing by the word of God.*

Daily we need to hear the Word of God. We need to daily feed and grow our inner man, our spirit, in the things of God.

How is faith exercised? Primarily by words.

> *2 Cor 4:13 We having the same spirit of faith, according as it is written, I believed, and therefore have I spoken; we also believe, and therefore speak.*

What are the works of faith?

*James 2:17 Even so faith, if it hath not works, is dead, being alone.*

*James 2:24 Ye see then how that by works a man is justified and not by faith only.*

*Gal 5:6 For in Jesus Christ neither circumcision availeth anything, nor uncircumcision, but faith which worketh by love.*

There are many works of faith.  Primarily, we believe and speak, setting the authority of heaven in motion in our lives. Yet, God is love. And after we have believed, His love beating in our breast will compel us to do some things to help suffering people.  We will work, build, teach, equip, train, send, spend, sing, and bless, to name a few - anyone that would name the name of Jesus.

It all comes down to our day to day relationship with Jesus through the Holy Spirit and His Word. He is still speaking to people today. Our job is ever to seek Him and obey. Like Mary said, before Jesus's first miracle, 'Whatever He says, DO IT!'

# 11

# Teamwork Makes the Dream Work

*1 Corinthians 12:27 Now you are the body of Christ, and each one of you is a part of it.*

Teams make you better than you are, multiply your value, enable you to do what you do best, allow you to help others do their best, and give you more time,

Teams provide you with companionship, help you fulfill the desires of your heart, and compound your vision and effort. John C. Maxwell

Jesus spent His most precious time, with 12 leaders in training.

They changed the world. Teamwork makes it all happen.

Every year in Alaska, a 1000-mile dogsled race is run called the Iditarod, a run for prize money and prestige, that commemorates an original "race" run to save lives. Back in January of 1926, six-year-old Richard Stanley showed symptoms of diphtheria, signaling the possibility of an outbreak in the small town of Nome. When the boy passed away a day later, Dr. Curtis Welch began immunizing children and adults with an experimental but effective anti-diphtheria serum. But it wasn't long before Dr. Welch's supply ran out, and the nearest serum was in Nenana, Alaska–1000 miles of frozen wilderness away. Amazingly, a group of trappers and prospectors volunteered to cover the distance with their dog teams! Operating in relays

61

from trading post to trapping station and beyond, one sled started from Nome while another, carrying the serum, started from Nenana. Oblivious to frostbite, fatigue, and exhaustion, the teamsters mushed relentlessly until, after 144 hours in minus 50-degree winds, the serum was delivered to Nome. As a result, only one other life was lost to the potential epidemic. Their sacrifice had given an entire town the gift of life.

Who is your team?

There are no benchwarmers or second-class citizens in the kingdom of God. Jesus made every one of us a player.

Let's Pray:

*'Jesus, put us in the game of life. Use us to empower, heal, bless, or save someone today. Amen.'*

# 12

# Even Miracles and Gods Presence Will Use A Person to Repent

The Presence of God and gifts of the spirit will not change a human heart. Let's look at an example of this from Scripture:

*1 Sam 19:19 And it was told Saul, saying, Behold, David is at Naioth in Ramah. And Saul sent messengers to take David: and when they saw the company of the prophets prophesying, and Samuel standing as appointed over them, the Spirit of God was upon the messengers of Saul, and they also prophesied. 21 And when it was told Saul, he sent other messengers, and they prophesied likewise. And Saul sent messengers again the third time, and they prophesied also. Then went he also to Ramah, and came to a great well that is in Sechu: and he asked and said, Where are Samuel and David? And one said, Behold, they be at Naioth in Ramah. And he went thither to Naioth in Ramah: and the Spirit of God was upon him also, and he went on, and prophesied, until he came to Naioth in Ramah. 24 And he stripped off his clothes also, and prophesied before Samuel in like manner, and lay down naked all that day and all that night. Wherefore they say, Is Saul also among the prophets?*

Admittedly, we see a divine encounter with the kingdom of God here. Let's think about what is going on here.

Saul disobeyed God, and the kingdom was stripped from him. The anointing of God was taken from him and given to David. And an evil spirit came upon Saul. Saul hates David because he sees in him that which he lacks in himself: courage, bravery, excellence of spirit, purity of heart, and a heart that is in love with God Himself.

Even though Saul has been throwing spears at him and hunting him to kill him, David, on the run, refuses to take Saul's life. He continually cries out to God on behalf of Saul. Yet, Saul determines to keep the kingdom, so he continuously sends soldiers to attempt to kill David. David can avoid them every time by hearing the voice of God and obeying.

Why did God allow David all those years in the wilderness running from Saul? I think it is because David had to hear God accurately in life or death situations if he was ever going to be fit to be king.

In this account, David has run for refuge from Saul to Samuel's house, and they have a revival meeting where the gifts of the Holy Spirit are very much in operation. So much so that when Saul's soldiers come chasing David there, they are arrested by the Spirit of God and find themselves prophesying under the anointing of God.

Saul does not want to hear this, so he sends two more sets of messengers to Ramah. Each time, the messengers also succumb to the power of God and find themselves prophesying by the Spirit of God and unable to apprehend David.

So, Saul Himself goes down to Samuel's revival meeting, and what happens is v 24, And he stripped off his clothes also, and prophesied before Samuel in like manner, and lay down naked all that day and all that night.

Wherefore they say, Is Saul also among the prophets?

So, you would think, after the Holy Spirit so humbled Saul, that he would repent and begin again to serve the Lord and leave David alone.

Yet, what did he do?

He went home and again began to plot again how to murder king David!

Even after the presence of God had caused him to prophesy naked for a day and a night at the feet of Samuel!

In Luke 16, we read the account of the rich man and Lazarus. Notice here that this is not an allegory or parable but a true story Jesus is recounting. The rich man went to hell, and the poor beggar went to Abraham's bosom or paradise (Jesus had not yet risen from the dead, so heaven was not open yet).

We see this rich man in hell, seeing father Abraham and crying out that someone be sent to his family, that they do not end up in the same place.

Yes, people in hell are praying that we share the gospel with their families!

Let's pick it up here:

*Luke 16:29 Abraham saith unto him, They have Moses and the prophets; let them hear them. And he said, Nay, father Abraham: but if one went unto them from the dead, they will repent. And he said unto him, If they hear not Moses and the prophets, neither will they be persuaded, though one rose from the dead.*

Notice what Abraham, in the afterlife, said: that it is more important for people to hear the word of God and repent than to see miracles. The implication here is strong: That if someone will not hear the word of God, even if they saw someone raised from the dead telling them of what was to come, they would not change!

So, what is the moral of the story?

The gifts of the Holy Spirit, and the presence of God, will not change a human heart unless that heart is willing to be changed.

I have heard it said that **the only thing greater than the power of God in the earth is the free will of man.**

Saul might have been able to repent here and be of some use to King David in his future reign had he humbled himself, but he refused!

It eventually cost him his life and the life of his son, and many others.

The only safe prayer I see in all of this is the repeated theme of my life and ministry:

'Father, please grant me purity of heart and purpose. Please open my eyes and deliver me from my own delusions of grandeur, my will, and my way. Jesus, You are the way.  Please become my way with no other agenda, no compromise. May I serve and fully obey You, in spirit and in truth, whatever the cost, for Your name and honor's sake, Amen.'

# 13

# Conscience

**Meditation on conscience**

- 4893 suneidesis soon-i'-day-sis
- the consciousness of anything
- the soul as distinguishing between what is morally good and evil, prompting to do the former and shun the latter, commending one, condemning the other

*Tim 1:1 Paul, an apostle of Jesus Christ by the commandment of God our Savior, and Lord Jesus Christ, which is our hope; unto Timothy, my own son in the faith: Grace, mercy, and peace, from God our Father and Jesus Christ our Lord. As I besought thee to abide still at Ephesus, when I went into Macedonia, that thou mightest charge some that they teach no other doctrine, Neither give heed to fables and endless genealogies, which minister questions, rather than godly edifying which is in faith: so do. Now the end of the commandment is charity out of a pure heart, and of a good conscience, and of faith unfeigned: From which some having swerved have turned aside unto vain jangling; Desiring to be teachers of the law; understanding neither what they say, nor whereof they affirm.*

*John 8:9 And they which heard it, being convicted by their own conscience, went out one by one, beginning at the eldest, even unto the last: and Jesus was left alone, and the woman standing in the midst.*

*Acts 23:1 And Paul, earnestly beholding the council, said, Men and brethren, I have lived in all good conscience before God until this day.*

*Acts 24:16 And herein do I exercise myself, to have always a conscience void of offense toward God, and toward men.*

*Romans 2:15 Which shew the work of the law written in their hearts, their conscience also bearing witness, and their thoughts the mean while accusing or else excusing one another;)*

*Romans 9:1 I say the truth in Christ, I lie not, my conscience also bearing me witness in the Holy Ghost,*

*Romans 13:5 Wherefore ye must needs be subject, not only for wrath, but also for conscience sake.*

*1 Corinthians 8:7 Howbeit there is not in every man that knowledge: for some with conscience of the idol unto this hour eat it as a thing offered unto an idol; and their conscience being weak is defiled.*

*1 Corinthians 8:10 For if any man see thee which hast knowledge sit at meat in the idol's temple, shall not the conscience of him which is weak be emboldened to eat those things which are offered to idols;*

*1 Corinthians 8:12 But when ye sin so against the brethren, and wound their weak conscience, ye sin against Christ.*

*1 Corinthians 10:25 Whatsoever is sold in the shambles, that eat, asking no question for conscience sake; If any of them that believe not bid you to a feast, and ye be disposed to go; whatsoever is set before you, eat, asking no question for conscience sake.*

*1 Corinthians 10:27-29 But if any man say unto you, This is offered in sacrifice unto idols, eat not for his sake that shewed it, and for conscience sake: for the earth is the Lord's, and the fulness thereof: Conscience, I say, not thine own, but of the other: for why is my liberty judged of another man's conscience?*

*2 Corinthians 1:12 For our rejoicing is this, the testimony of our conscience, that in simplicity and godly sincerity, not with fleshly wisdom, but by the grace of God, we have had our conversation in the world, and more abundantly to you-ward.*

*2 Corinthians 4:2 But have renounced the hidden things of dishonesty, not walking in craftiness, nor handling the word of God deceitfully; but by manifestation of the truth commending ourselves to every man's conscience in the sight of God.*

*1 Timothy 1:5 Now the end of the commandment is charity out of a pure heart, and of a good conscience, and of faith unfeigned: Conscience tells us that we ought to do right, but it does not tell us what right is—that we are taught by God's word.*

*Hebrews 5:14 But strong meat belongeth to them that are of full age, even those who by reason of use have their senses exercised to discern both good and evil.*

*1 Peter 4:5 Who shall give account to him that is ready to judge the quick and the dead.*

Did you know that ever since 1811 (when someone who had defrauded the government anonymously sent $5 to Washington D.C.), the U.S. Treasury has operated a Conscience Fund? Since that time, almost $3.5 million has been received from guilt-ridden citizens. Swindoll, *The Quest For Character*, Multnomah, p. 70.

> *Rom 13:1 Let every soul be subject unto the higher powers. For there is no power but of God: the powers that be are ordained of God. Whosoever therefore resisteth the power, resisteth the ordinance of God: and they that resist shall receive to themselves damnation. For rulers are not a terror to good works, but to the evil. Wilt thou then not be afraid of the power? do that which is good, and thou shalt have praise of the same: For he is the minister of God to thee for good. But if thou do that which is evil, be afraid; for he beareth not the sword in vain: for he is the minister of God, a revenger to execute wrath upon him that doeth evil. Wherefore ye must needs be subject, not only for wrath, but also for conscience sake. For for this cause pay ye tribute also: for they are God's ministers, attending continually upon this very thing. Render therefore to all their dues: tribute to whom tribute is due; custom to whom custom; fear to whom fear; honor to whom honor.*

Here's a quote from *"Book II: Admonitions Concerning the Inner Life:"*

> *"The glory of a good person is the testimony of a good conscience. A good conscience can bear very much and is very cheerful in adversities. An evil conscience is always fearful and unquiet, never rejoicing except when you have done well." (Thomas à Kempis; The Imitation of Christ The Harvard Classics. 1909–14.)*

You shall rest sweetly if your heart does not accuse you. Sinners never have true joy or feel inward peace because 'there is no peace for the wicked,' says the Lord (Isaiah 57:21).

The glory of the good is in their consciences and not in the tongues of others. The gladness of the just is of God and in God, and their joy is of the truth. A person will easily be content and pacified whose conscience is pure. If you consider what you are within, you will not care what others say concerning you. People consider the deeds, but God weighs the intentions. To be always doing well and to esteem little of one's self is the sign of a humble soul. For not he who commends himself is approved, but whom the Lord commends,' says Paul (2 Corinthians 10:18).

To walk inwardly with God and not to be kept abroad by any outward affection is the state of a spiritual person. Conscience is that faculty in me that attaches itself to the highest that I know and tells me what the highest I know demands that I do. It is the eye of the soul that looks out either toward God or toward what it regards as the highest authority. If I am in the habit of steadily facing toward God, my conscience will always introduce God's perfect law and indicate what I should do. The point is, will I obey? I have to make an effort to keep my conscience so sensitive that I walk without offense. I should be living in such perfect sympathy with God's Son that, in every circumstance, the spirit of my mind is renewed. The one thing that keeps the conscience sensitive to Him is the habit of being open to God on the inside. When there is any debate, quit.

*"There is no debate possible when conscience speaks."* C.F.H. Henry, Christian Personal Ethics, Eerdmans, 1957, p. 509ff.

How complicated the legal profession can make simple matters of right and wrong. The Holy Spirit is, first of all, holy and reveals absolute truth. Prayer and the presence of God in legal issues would make short work of many cases, consider the following:

*"The great attorney, orator, and statesman Daniel Webster was such*
*an imposing figure in court that he once stared a witness out of the*
*courtroom. Apparently, Webster knew the man was there to deliver*
*false testimony, so he fixed his "dark, beetle-browed" eyes on the*
*man and searched him. According to the story, later in the trial,*

*"Webster looked around again to see if [the witness] was ready for the inquisition. The witness felt for his hat and edged toward the door. A third time Webster looked on him, and the witness could sit no longer. He seized his chance and fled from the court and was nowhere to be found."* (Today in the Word, Moody Bible Institute, January 1992, p.31.)

God loves justice, and those of us who serve Him know His character and unchanging nature. Hear the heart of Abraham, here, in his prayer to God:

*Genesis 18:25 That be far from thee to do after this manner, to slay the righteous with the wicked: and that the righteous should be as the wicked, that be far from thee: Shall not the Judge of all the earth do right?*

He knows God and knows He is just. God cannot lie nor change. The heart of all justice is truth at all costs then mercy and grace wherever possible. Mercy is not possible when based on lies because there is no acknowledgment of wrongdoing; hence, there is no remorse or intent to change behavior. Only truth, no matter how ugly, can find true mercy through the shed blood of Jesus.

**More verses:**

- John 8:9 And they which heard it, being convicted by their own conscience, went out one by one, beginning at the eldest, even unto the last: and Jesus was left alone, and the woman standing in the midst.
- Acts 23:1 And Paul, earnestly beholding the council, said, Men and brethren, I have lived in all good conscience before God until this day.
- Acts 24:16 And herein do I exercise myself, to have always a conscience void of offense toward God, and toward men.
- Romans 2:15 Which shew the work of the law written in their hearts, their conscience also bearing witness, and their thoughts the mean while accusing or else excusing one another;)

- Romans 9:1 I say the truth in Christ, I lie not, my conscience also bearing me witness in the Holy Ghost,
- Romans 13:5 Wherefore ye must needs be subject, not only for wrath, but also for conscience sake.
- 1 Corinthians 8:7 Howbeit there is not in every man that knowledge: for some with conscience of the idol unto this hour eat it as a thing offered unto an idol; and their conscience being weak is defiled.
- 1 Corinthians 8:10 For if any man see thee which hast knowledge sit at meat in the idol's temple, shall not the conscience of him which is weak be emboldened to eat those things which are offered to idols;
- 1 Corinthians 8:12 But when ye sin so against the brethren, and wound their weak conscience, ye sin against Christ.
- 1 Corinthians 10:25 Whatsoever is sold in the shambles, that eat, asking no question for conscience sake:
- 1 Corinthians 10:27 If any of them that believe not bid you to a feast, and ye be disposed to go; whatsoever is set before you, eat, asking no question for conscience sake.
- 1 Corinthians 10:28 But if any man say unto you, This is offered in sacrifice unto idols, eat not for his sake that shewed it, and for conscience sake: for the earth is the Lord's, and the fulness thereof:
- 1 Corinthians 10:29 Conscience, I say, not thine own, but of the other: for why is my liberty judged of another man's conscience?
- 1 Corinthians 1:12 For our rejoicing is this, the testimony of our conscience, that in simplicity and godly sincerity, not with fleshly wisdom, but by the grace of God, we have had our conversation in the world, and more abundantly to you-ward.
- 2 Corinthians 4:2 But have renounced the hidden things of dishonesty, not walking in craftiness, nor handling the word of God deceitfully; but by manifestation of the truth commending ourselves to every man's conscience in the sight of God.
- 1 Timothy 1:5 Now the end of the commandment is charity out of a pure heart, and of a good conscience, and of faith unfeigned:
- 1 Timothy 1:19 Holding faith, and a good conscience; which some having

put away concerning faith have made shipwreck:
- Timothy 3:9 Holding the mystery of the faith in a pure conscience.
- 1Timothy 4:2 Speaking lies in hypocrisy; having their conscience seared with a hot iron;
- Timothy 1:3 I thank God, whom I serve from my forefathers with pure conscience, that without ceasing I have remembrance of thee in my prayers night and day;
- Titus 1:15 Unto the pure all things are pure: but unto them that are defiled and unbelieving is nothing pure, but even their mind and conscience is defiled.
- Hebrews 9:9 Which was a figure for the time then present, in which were offered both gifts and sacrifices, that could not make him that did the service perfect, as pertaining to the conscience;
- Hebrews 9:14 How much more shall the blood of Christ, who through the eternal Spirit offered himself without spot to God, purge your conscience from dead works to serve the living God?
- Hebrews 10:2 For then would they not have ceased to be offered? because that the worshippers once purged should have had no more conscience of sins.
- Hebrews 10:22 Let us draw near with a true heart in full assurance of faith, having our hearts sprinkled from an evil conscience, and our bodies washed
- with pure water.
- Hebrews 13:18 Pray for us: for we trust we have a good conscience, in all things willing to live honestly.
- 1 Peter 2:19 For this is thankworthy, if a man for conscience toward God endure grief, suffering wrongfully.
- 1 Peter 3:16 Having a good conscience; that, whereas they speak evil of you, as of evildoers, they may be ashamed that falsely accuse your good conversation in Christ.
- 1 Peter 3:21 The like figure whereunto even baptism doth also now save us (not the putting away of the filth of the flesh, but the answer of a good conscience toward God,) by the resurrection of Jesus Christ:

# 14

# Adversity and Character

It is easy when the day of promotion and favor rests upon you to obey God and serve Him.  It is when the hand of authority is against you, and your character is under attack, that it takes the supernatural strength of God to prevail, and not give up. Stand upon what He speaks, no matter what people or circumstances may scream. Your faith and the purity of your heart will win the day, and God will be glorified in your obedience. Never allow smaller hearts or visions to dictate your greatness! Jesus is a great and mighty king, and you are high and mighty in Him. Refuse to compromise, but fully obey, remain humble, and He will exalt you in good season!

# 15

# Eagles Still Go to Church

*Luke 17:37 And they answered and said unto him, Where, Lord? And he said unto them, Wheresoever the body is, thither will the eagles be gathered together.*

I like to think about this verse literally. Eagles fly alone in general, except when they find their mate, for life.

Yet, here God calls a people to Himself, the Body of Christ, and here in the church, the Bride of Jesus, eagles gather.

You are a unique, privileged child of the King with a specific individual destiny and calling in Him. We hear the voice of God and soar high on the winds of His grace. The Holy Spirit leads us into higher and higher levels of truth in the Word of God in our business and our family.  Revelation often separates us unto God Himself, for only He who gave the insight truly understands the incredibly complex creation that we are and the intricacies of our lives.

Yet, we are not called to fly alone. We are part of the body of Christ. Though much of our week may be alone in our unique calling, where the Body is, we gather. Leaders go to church.

*Rom 15:1 We then that are strong ought to bear the infirmities of the weak, and not to please ourselves. Let every one of us please his neighbor for his good to edification.  3 For even Christ pleased not himself; but, as it is written, The reproaches of them that reproached thee fell on me.*

Jesus is Lord, the ultimate leader, yet He comes to church!

*Hebrews 2:12 Saying, I will declare thy name unto my brethren. In the midst of the church, I will sing **praise** unto thee.*

*Heb 10: 25 Not forsaking the assembling of ourselves together, as the manner of some is; but exhorting one another: and so much the more, as ye see the day approaching.*

The days of lone ranger Christianity are gone.  You were not designed to walk alone. You are part of the Body of Christ, and where the Body is, eagles gather.

Let's pray:

*'Father, show me the areas I need to fly alone in life, the unique individual plans You have for me in this life. Yet, despite my uniqueness, You have called me to the Body of Christ and given me a place there. Help me to find my place and help others around me. In Your name, I pray, Lord Jesus, Amen.'*

# 16

# The Spirit of the Leader is the Spirit of the House

*Numbers 11:16-17 And the LORD said unto Moses, Gather unto me seventy men of the elders of Israel, whom thou knowest to be the elders of the people, and officers over them; and bring them unto the tabernacle of the congregation, that they may stand there with thee. And I will come down and talk with thee there: and **I will take of the spirit which is upon thee**, and will put it upon them, and they shall bear the burden of the people with thee, that thou bear it not thyself alone.*

*Numbers 11:24-29 And Moses went out, and told the people the words of the LORD, and gathered the seventy men of the elders of the people, and set them round about the tabernacle.*

*And the LORD came down in a cloud, and spake unto him, and took of the spirit that was upon him, and gave it unto the seventy elders: and it came to pass, that, when the spirit rested upon them, they prophesied, and did not cease.*

*But there remained two of the men in the camp, the name of the one was Eldad, and the name of the other Medad: and the spirit rested upon them; and they were of them that were written, but went not out unto the tabernacle, and they prophesied in the camp.*

*And there ran a young man, and told Moses, and said, Eldad and Medad do prophesy in the camp.*

*And Joshua, the son of Nun, the servant of Moses, one of his young men, answered and said, My lord Moses, forbid them.*

*And Moses said unto him, Enviest thou for my sake? Would God that all the LORD'S people were prophets and that the LORD would put his spirit upon them!*

Have you noticed that certain leaders set the very culture of the organizations they lead by their personalities? Notice in this passage that God came down in a cloud and **took of the spirit that was on Moses** and placed that spirit or anointing on 70 elders. In the case of Moses, there must have been a strong prophetic anointing upon his life because first 68 of the elders began to prophesy, without ceasing, then the other two, busy with responsibilities in the camp, also received the anointing, and they too began to prophesy.

Moses did not get offended at this but spoke a prophetic utterance:

*Num 11:29 "And Moses said unto him, Enviest thou for my sake? Would God that all the LORD'S people were prophets and that the LORD would put his spirit upon them!"*

This is still the heart of God today:

*1 Cor 14:1 Follow after charity, and desire spiritual gifts, but rather that ye may prophesy.*

Now, rather than give you a long teaching, I will let Graham Cooke do it. Read *Developing Your Prophetic Gifting* by Graham Cooke.

Yet, I want to continue in this line of reasoning for a minute. Could it be that the spirit of the house comes from the anointing on the leader in the house? If the leader is an influential evangelist, vigorous evangelism comes from the ministry. If the leader is a tremendous mentor, pastor, shepherd, and counselor, then tremendous pastors, counselors, shepherds get raised up. If the leader is a church planter that blasts, builds, and plants churches, and ministries in the earth. Afterward, the ministry elders partake of the spirit of the building. Blasting, and planting churches and ministries. Things in the kingdom reproduce after their own kind. While all this is great, wise leaders learn to 'cross-pollinate' their ministries, bringing in ministry gifts that can produce in the disciples of the ministry, the character of Jesus, rather than being limited to merely the gift of the senior minister.

> *Rom 8:29 For whom he did foreknow, he also did predestinate to be conformed to the image of his Son.*

Our job as leaders is to make people more like Jesus, not us.

> *Eph 4:13 Till we all come in the unity of the faith, and of the knowledge of the Son of God, unto a perfect man, unto the measure of the stature of the fulness of Christ: that he might be the firstborn among many brethren.*

If the church you are leading is not able to do this, avail yourself of books, videos, and teaching materials from other ministry gifts that can bring your people to a level that you cannot. In the meantime, you will grow on the journey!

If you are in a ministry where that is not happening, grow anyway. You go ahead and find the ministry supplies that will cause you to grow in Christ. The only thing limiting your spiritual growth is you, not your pastor. Grow!

Let's Pray:

> *"Father, send into my life, ministry supplies that will cause me to grow in You. Feed me, Father, a right word in season, that I might be a blessing to this hurting world. In your name, I pray, Lord Jesus, Amen."*

# 17

# Who is Watching You?

They watched Him. Who is watching You?

> *Luke 14:1 And it came to pass, as he went into the house of one of the chief Pharisees to eat bread on the sabbath day, **that they watched him.***

So, as usual, in the earthly ministry of Jesus, people were watching his every move. Would He break with tradition? Or worse yet, their limited understanding of the Word of God?

Sure enough, often on purpose, Jesus loved to mess with their mess and live outside of their mental boxes of what they thought God in the flesh could look like.

Well, I have some good news for you. People, especially religious people, would love to keep you in check through the tyranny of tradition and unspoken rules that, if you get in touch with the living God, you, like Jesus, will have to break on purpose.

Why? To be obnoxious and to rebel against the status quo? No, to be an active disciple.

I saw a custom license plate on a beautiful Hummer in front of me at a red light that caused me to break out laughing. It read: 'BOW UP!'. Now, for those of you in other countries that do not understand red-neck righteousness or colloquial American terminology, the term 'BOW UP' means to rebel, to reject the status quo, to break out of the box.

Now, real rebellion and hardness of heart tend to anarchy, and this was not the message I received from that license plate. Nope, that person had a beautiful ride on a bright sunny day. Perhaps they were a combat veteran, and the message I received from that plate was to be strong, be honorable, be honest, but do not bow down to complacency, compromise, or the mere status quo. Chickens travel in flocks, eagles can soar alone, while their lifelong mates tend the nest.

The person in that Hummer was a leader, and I hope an honorable one.

*Matt 5:5 Blessed are the meek: for they shall inherit the earth.*

My definition of meek is 'strength under pressure.' My picture of an egg in a vice is that bench vise is made of case-hardened steel and can easily crush the egg in its jaws, but because its character is meek, not weak, it carefully holds the egg without breaking it.

We should be as strong as that vise yet gentle. Holding delicate things like the hearts of our wives and children with tenderness and tears, but strong enough to crush rocks or hold on a God-given vision with unbreakable force.

The man of God gives his anger, frustration, and tears to God and can say, like King David:

*2 Sam 22:36 Thou hast also given me the shield of thy salvation: and* **thy gentleness hath made me great.**

Then, by the fruit of the Holy Spirit, and the love of God:

Isa 40:11 He shall feed his flock like a shepherd: he shall gather the lambs with his arm, and carry them in his bosom, and shall gently lead those that are with young.

Wives are loved and confident around him. Children run into his safe, strong arms for hugs because, deep in their hearts, they know he will never hurt them, secure that his great strength is given by God to work and to protect them. Influential leaders continually grow in strength, both physically, mentally, and spiritually, not so that they can merely strut their stuff, but to be an example to those they are called to lead. When we serve, it is not because we have no power or authority; it takes more strength to serve than to dominate or control a situation.

*2 Thes 3:9 Not because we have not power, but to make ourselves an ensample unto you to follow us.*

*Luke 22: 26 And there was also a strife among them, which of them should be accounted the greatest. And he said unto them, The kings of the Gentiles exercise lordship over them; and they that exercise authority upon them are called benefactors. But ye shall not be so: but he that is greatest among you, let him be as the younger, and he that is chief, as he that doth serve. For who is greater, he that sitteth at meat, or he that serveth? Is not he that sitteth at meat? But I am among you as he that serveth.*

*Luke 14:33 So likewise, whosoever he be of you that forsaketh not all that he hath, he cannot be my disciple.*

One of the things we need to forsake is concern about what other people might think.

There are times when we need to assault their stinking thinking, control tactics, and limited understanding of what God may be saying to us. They are watching, and God is moving. Though people may not fully understand why we are doing things the way we are at present, the Holy Spirit is teaching us obedience.

Yet, when we fully obey God in walking in love in truth, and though we offend them today in moving outside of their mental box, God is faithful, and we may well be of some use to them in years to come.

Let's pray:

*Father, speak to us, grow us, strengthen us. Make us firm in You, Lord, and the power of Your might. Cause us, Lord, to express Your gentle, tender, wise, rock-crushing strength. Strengthen our ability to grasp, maintain, and stand upon Your specific vision and mandate for our lives and families. Give us the courage to think, speak, and act outside of society's box, by following Your Word and Your Holy Spirit, that I might be the example of red-hot, radical obedience this generation desperately needs. In Your name, I pray. Lord Jesus. Amen!*

# 18

# Leadership Process Servant Kingship

*1 Cor 4:8-9 Now ye are full, now ye are rich, ye have reigned as kings without us: and I would to God ye did reign, that we also might reign with you. For I think that God hath set forth us the apostles last, as it were appointed to death: for we are made a spectacle unto the world, and to angels, and to men.*

How life changes as we grow up! We first come to Jesus, and the whole world lights up. The sun seems brighter, the flowers more beautiful, the sky clear. And we want to love the entire world. Jesus loves me; this I know, for the Bible tells me so. He loves me; He loves me. He loves me!

May this love ever burn in our hearts! May this love compel us to action!

Yet, quickly we also discover that there is great evil in the world. Fallen men, empowered by their sin nature and devils, do abominable things! Babies killed, abused, wars, carnage, greedy people raping others, the land, for their own selfish carnal desires to be met.

Then, someone teaches us that we have authority over the devil! That we have something to say in this world! We can exercise God's authority on the earth because we have read:

*Rev 1:5 And from Jesus Christ, who is the faithful witness, and the first begotten of the dead and the prince of the kings of the earth. Unto him that loved us, and washed us from our sins in his own blood, And hath made us kings and priests unto God and his Father; to him be glory and dominion forever and ever. Amen.*

*Rev 5:10 And hast made us unto our God kings and priests: and we shall reign on the earth.*

Indeed, we are kings before Him and priests of the Most High God offering acceptable sacrifices of prayer, praise, worship, and service through Jesus shed blood!

*1 Pet 2:9 But ye are a chosen generation, a royal priesthood, an holy nation, a peculiar people; that ye should shew forth the praises of him who hath called you out of darkness into his marvelous light.*

We have been given authority over the works of darkness, positionally, and we begin to walk it out!

*Luke 10:19-20 Behold, I give unto you power to tread on serpents and scorpions, and over all the power of the enemy: and nothing shall by any means hurt you. Notwithstanding in this rejoice not, that the spirits are subject unto you; but rather rejoice, because your names are written in heaven.*

We are those who hear His voice, and we get filled with the Holy Spirit and experience His power in our lives. Signs and wonders start to happen daily in our life!

*Mark 16:17-18 And these signs shall follow them that believe; In my name shall they cast out devils; they shall speak with new tongues; They shall take up serpents, and if they drink any deadly thing, it shall not hurt them; they shall lay hands on the sick, and they shall recover. We pray, and heaven opens, and we see visions, experience living revelation from a very living God.*

*Act 2:17 And it shall come to pass in the last days, saith God, I will pour out of my Spirit upon all flesh: and your sons and your daughters shall prophesy,and your young men shall see visions, and your old men shall dream dreams: And on my servants and on my handmaidens I will pour out in those days of my Spirit; and they shall prophesy: And I will shew wonders in heaven above, and signs in the earth beneath; blood, and fire, and vapor of smoke: The sun shall be turned into darkness, and the moon into blood, before that great and notable day of the Lord come: And it shall come to pass, that whosoever shall call on the name of the Lord shall be saved.*

Yet, after some years, God decides on a specific calling for our lives, something for us to do individually. He speaks to us and sends us.

The word apostle means: 'sent one.'

Now, I can send my children to the refrigerator for milk, making them the apostle of milk.

This is not what Paul is talking about here. There is fivefold ministry in the earth, set in place by the hand of God, to govern His church.

*1 Cor 12:28 And God hath set some in the church, first apostles, secondarily prophets, thirdly teachers, after that miracles, then gifts of healings, helps, governments, diversities of tongues.*

*1 Cor 12:29 Are all apostles? Are all prophets? Are all teachers? Are all workers of miracles?*

*Eph 4:11 And he gave some, apostles; and some, prophets; and some, evangelists; and some, pastors and teachers;*

These offices are the government of God in the earth that have the authority, power, and grace from God to accomplish what He needs to be established.

I am led to share about the journey from a revelation position and spiritual authority, to practical authority, responsibility, and seasoned leadership, in authentic five-fold ministry gifts operating in the earth now.

Paul discovered himself initially in his early years of ministry to be great in the kingdom, called of God, with both spiritual and earthly authority. He was a king, priest and lord, subject only to the King of all Kings, the High Priest we confess, and the Lord of all Lords!

> *2 Cor 11:5 For I suppose I was not a whit behind the very chiefest apostles. What caused the apostle Paul to call himself the 'very chiefest of apostles'?*

He had a revelation from heaven, and it was incredibly high!  Yet, the character of the Master must become the character of the servant. By the end of his life, we read the same apostle Paul:

> *1 Tim 1:15 This is a faithful saying, and worthy of all acceptation, that Christ Jesus came into the world to save sinners; of whom I am chief.*

The journey of his life was from chief apostle to chief of all sinners to king and priest and power.

> *1 Cor 4:9 For I think that God hath set forth us the apostles last, as it were appointed to death: for we are made a spectacle unto the world, and to angels, and to men.*

Did his identity change? Did God demote him?

> *Rom 11:29 For the gifts and calling of God are without repentance.*

God promoted him so much so that he wrote over half of the New Testament. God did not change, but Paul did! Consider these words of Jesus carefully:

*Luke 22:25-30 And he said unto them, The kings of the Gentiles exercise lordship over them; and they that exercise authority upon them are called benefactors. But ye shall not be so: but he that is greatest among you, let him be as the younger, and he that is chief, as he that doth serve. For whether is greater, he that sitteth at meat, or he that serveth? Is not he that sitteth at meat? But I am among you as he that serveth. Ye are they which have continued with me in my temptations. And I appoint unto you a kingdom, as my Father hath appointed unto me; That ye may eat and drink at my table in my kingdom, and sit on thrones judging the twelve tribes of Israel.*

What I want you to see is that your eternal rank, privilege, and reward are given to you by God Himself **AS A SERVANT!**

*Rom 8:29 For whom he did foreknow, he also did predestinate to be conformed to the image of his Son, that he might be the firstborn among many brethren.*

I have discovered this as a missionary, first back to Canada, my home country, and now to Tulsa, Oklahoma, to the United States of America and the nations. That is my heavenly office, authority, and position.

Yet, in the natural order of life in my day to day walk, I have become a spectacle unto the world, a laughing stock from my family, colleagues from college, and former business leadership friends where I am, at best, misunderstood.

Even angels that minister to me, my family, and the nations through me are probably amazed at what I put up with and undergo to obey God intimately daily. Even my fellow brothers and sisters at my church probably question my sanity (I must admit, I doubt it some days too!) Again, Jesus leads me far outside my comfort zone, as my more deep-seated insecurities and need for control and position are stripped away so that the love of the kingdom of God, demonstrated through pure motives, might shine through me.

If you are called to lead, He is doing the same thing in you, too.

The great violinist, Niccolo Paganini, willed his marvelous violin to the city of Genoa on condition that it must never be played. "The wood of such an instrument while used and handled wears only slightly but set aside, it begins to decay. Paganini's lovely violin has today become worm-eaten and useless except as a relic. A Christian's unwillingness to serve may soon destroy his capacity for usefulness." *J.K. Laney, Marching Orders, p. 34.*

I am not sure who this is for, but the very call of God upon you to greatness has produced the deeper workings of the cross in your life as you seek to obey Him intimately.

Dreams and visions that did not come to pass in your timing produce a quiet peace and trust that He will make everything beautiful in His time. He has eternity on His mind and a people on the other side of your obedience.

Obedience is the Word of the day for if you are truly called of God, there is no other way to get from here to where you know you need to be otherwise.

*1 Cor 15:31 I protest by your rejoicing which I have in Christ Jesus our Lord, I die daily. Have a Happy Death!*

*Gal 4:19 My little children, of whom I travail in birth again until Christ be formed in you.*

Let's pray:

*Father, I embrace the cross. I receive Your process and provision for the process, as I quietly hear and obey your voice today. Jesus, You are my good Shepherd. May I hear Your voice, and fully obey You, today. Amen.*

# 19

# Don't Imitate Others, Follow Jesus

*2 Corinthians 10:12 For we dare not make ourselves of the number, or* **compare** *ourselves with some that commend themselves: but they measuring themselves by themselves, and comparing themselves among themselves, are not wise.*

Two people try to do the same thing before God. One has a word from the Lord, and Jesus does miracles for them. The other does not have a word from the Lord, and they crash and burn and cause great heartbreak to the Lord, their families, and everyone around them. He will pay for and bless only what He gives voice to. He will not bless our imitation of others. Honestly, it is life or death – accurately hearing Him.

*John 2:5 – Whatever HE says, do it!*

I usually sign all my books with this verse.

*John 10:27 (KJV)My sheep hear my voice, and I know them, and they follow me.*

When we have fully committed to His Lordship and direction in our lives, He will speak. And great blessing will result.

Let's Pray:

> *Father, I choose to follow Jesus today and submit to His plan for my life. Lord Jesus, please speak to me what to do today.*

# 20

# Trust But Verify

Trust but verify is a form of advice given that recommends that, while a source of information might be considered reliable, one should perform additional research to verify that such information is accurate or trustworthy. The term was a signature phrase adopted and made famous by U.S. President Ronald Reagan. Reagan frequently used it when discussing U.S. relations with the Soviet Union. The phrase was originated by Russian leader Vladimir Lenin.[citation needed] The phrase was learned by Reagan from Suzanne Massie, a writer on Russia. She told Reagan, *"The Russians like to talk in proverbs. It would be nice of you to know a few. You are an actor – you can learn them very quickly."* The original Russian proverb is a short rhyme which states, "Доверяй, но проверяй (doveryai, no proveryai)."

After Reagan used the phrase at the signing of the INF Treaty. His counterpart Mikhail Gorbachev responded: *"You repeat that at every meeting,"* To which Reagan answered, *"I like it."*

In Joshua chapter 9, we read the account of how the Gibeonites disguised themselves to avoid being conquered and killed. I can't say that I blame them, but Joshua missed it. He forgot to seek the Lord and gave his word to these people. When Joshua discovered their deception, he employed them as laborers in the camp of Israel. However, 'he should have sought the LORD!'.

It would have been nice had they had a New Testament:

*Ephesians 4:14 That we henceforth be no more children, tossed to and fro, and carried about with every wind of doctrine, by the sleight of men, and cunning **craftiness, whereby they lie in wait to deceive;***

Clever people are great at presenting facts that look wonderful, but as we proceed forward, we can find ourselves caught in their web of iniquity. We should not rely on mere sense knowledge alone in our decision-making abilities.

We are a covenant people, supernatural, led by the Holy Spirit. We are not orphans, but sons and daughters of the Most High God, who hear His voice.

Are you facing a decision today, Leader, that looks too good to be true?

It probably is not true. It is easy to check it out. Check references. Check financial statements, and above all else, PRAY!

I heard a story that made me chuckle along these lines:

* * *

Two hunters chartered a plane to fly into the Canadian wilderness. Two weeks later, when the pilot came to pick them up, he saw the two animals they had bagged and said, *"I told you fellows I could only take you and one moose. You'll have to leave the other behind."*

*"But we did it last year in a plane this size,"* protested one of the hunters, *"and the other pilot let us take two moose."*

*"Well, okay,"* said the pilot. *"If you did it before, I guess we can do it again."*

So, the two moose and the hunters were loaded in, and the plane took off. Because of the heavyweight, it rose with difficulty and was unable to clear an obstructing hill. After the crash, the men climbed out and looked around.

One hunter said to the other, *"Where are we, anyway?"*

His companion surveyed the scene. *"I think we got about half a mile farther than we got last year."* Source Unknown.

* * *

There are countless promises in the Word of God where He promises to speak to you and give you wisdom. He will bear witness to the truth. It all comes down to the same thing in every decision: Am I doing it my way or His?

Let's Pray:

*Father God, I come to you right now asking you for clarity, strength, and direction in every decision of life. Speak to me and give me wisdom on all my business dealings. In Jesus's name. Amen.*

# 21

# Our Mission The Great Commission

*The Call*
*The Command*
*The Commission*
*The Reception*

**The Call:**

**Isaiah**

*Isaiah 6 In the year that king Uzziah died I saw also the Lord sitting upon a throne, high and lifted up, and his train filled the temple.*

*Above it stood the seraphim: each one had six wings; with twain he covered his face, and with twain he covered his feet, and with twain, he did fly.*

*And one cried unto another, and said, Holy, holy, holy, is the LORD of hosts: the whole earth is full of his glory.*

*And the posts of the door moved at the voice of him that cried, and the house was filled with smoke.*

*Then said I, Woe is me! For I am undone; because I am a man of unclean lips, and I dwell in the midst of a people of unclean lips: for mine eyes have seen the King, the LORD of hosts.*

*Then flew one of the seraphim unto me, having a live coal in his hand, which he had taken with the tongs from off the altar:*

*And he laid it upon my mouth, and said, Lo, this hath touched thy lips; and thine iniquity is taken away, and thy sin purged.*

*Also I heard the voice of the Lord, saying,* **Whom shall I send, and who will go for us?** *Then said I, Here am I; send me.*

*And he said, Go, and tell this people, Hear ye indeed, but understand not; and see ye indeed, but perceive not.*

*Make the heart of this people fat, and make their ears heavy, and shut their eyes; lest they see with their eyes, and hear with their ears, and understand with their heart, and convert, and be healed.*

## Samuel

*Sam 3 And the child Samuel ministered unto the LORD before Eli. And the word of the LORD was precious in those days; there was no open vision.*

*And it came to pass at that time, when Eli was laid down in his place, and his eyes began to wax dim, that he could not see;*

*And ere the lamp of God went out in the temple of the LORD, where the ark of God was, and Samuel was laid down to sleep;*

*That the LORD called Samuel: and he answered, Here am I.*

*And he ran unto Eli, and said, Here am I; for thou calledst me. And he said, I called not; lie down again. And he went and lay down.*

*And the LORD called yet again, Samuel. And Samuel arose and went to Eli, and said, Here am I; for thou didst call me. And he answered, I called not, my son; lie down again.*

*Now Samuel did not yet know the LORD, neither was the word of the LORD yet revealed unto him.*

*And the LORD called Samuel again the third time. And he arose and went to Eli, and said,* **Here am I; for thou didst call me.** *And Eli* *perceived that the LORD had called the child.*

*Therefore Eli said unto Samuel, Go, lie down: and it shall be, if he call*

*thee, that thou shalt say, Speak, LORD; for thy servant heareth. So Samuel went and lay down in his place.*

*And the LORD came, and stood, and called as at other times, Samuel, Samuel. Then Samuel answered, **Speak; for thy servant heareth.***

***And the LORD said** to Samuel, Behold, I will do a thing in Israel, at which both the ears of every one that heareth it shall tingle.*

## Paul

*Acts 9 And Saul, yet breathing out threatenings and slaughter against the disciples of the Lord, went unto the high priest,*

*And desired of him letters to Damascus to the synagogues, that if he found any of this way, whether they were men or women, he might bring them bound unto Jerusalem.*

*And as he journeyed, he came near Damascus: and suddenly there shined round about him a light from heaven:*

*And he fell to the earth, and heard a voice saying unto him, Saul, Saul, why persecutest thou me?*

*And he said, Who art thou, Lord? And the Lord said, I am Jesus whom thou persecutest: it is hard for thee to kick against the pricks.*

***And he trembling and astonished said, Lord, what wilt thou have me to do? And the Lord said unto him, Arise, and go into the city, and it shall be told thee what thou must do.***

Three men, all servants of God, were suddenly faced with the presence or voice of God Himself. Isaiah, Samuel, and Saul all obeyed, and they each went on to do great exploits for God.

The Scripture is our guide. Yet, as great as these records of the call of God upon these men's lives are, it's your turn now. God is calling you specifically, and He will reveal to you the reason you were born, the high calling you are destined to live!

In the eleventh century, King Henry III of Bavaria grew tired of court life and the pressures of being a monarch. He made an application to Prior Richard at a local monastery asking to be accepted as a contemplative and spend the rest of his life in the monastery.

*"Your Majesty,"* said Prior Richard, *"do you understand that the pledge here is one of obedience? That will be hard because you have been a king."*

*"I understand,"* said Henry. *"The rest of my life, I will be obedient to you, as Christ leads you."*

*"Then I will tell you what to do,"* said Prior Richard. *"Go back to your throne and serve faithfully in the place where God has put you."*

When King Henry died, a statement was written: *"The King learned to rule by being obedient."* When we tire of our roles and responsibilities, it helps to remember God has planted us in a particular place and told us to be a good accountant or teacher or mother, or father. Christ expects us to be faithful where he puts us, and when he returns, we'll rule together with him.

Some think that the only way we can genuinely serve Jesus is in the vocation of ministry, yet ministry means: 'to serve.' We can all obey Jesus and serve in whatever vocation He calls and commissions us.

## The Command

*Mark 16:15 And he said unto them, **Go** ye into all the world, and preach the gospel to every creature. He that believeth and is baptized shall be saved; but he that believeth not shall be damned. And these signs shall follow them that believe; In my name shall they cast out devils; they shall speak with new tongues; They shall take up serpents; and if they drink any deadly thing, it shall not hurt them; they shall lay hands on the sick, and they shall recover. So then after the Lord had spoken unto them, he was received up into heaven, and sat on the right hand of God. And they went forth, and preached everywhere, the Lord working with them, and confirming the word with signs following. Amen.*

*Matt 28:18 And Jesus came and spake unto them, saying, All power is given unto me in heaven and in earth. **Go** ye therefore, and teach all nations, baptizing them in the name of the Father, and of the Son, and of the Holy Ghost: Teaching them to observe all things whatsoever I have commanded you: and, lo, I am with you alway, even unto the end of the world. Amen.*

This is the great commandment that we call the great commission. All of us are called into this work, and it is the last days:

Pack, pay for someone else to go, or pray fervently for those of us who have already gone!

## The Commission

Heaven and Hell are real. Hell is real. Lazarus made heaven; the rich man burns in hell to this day. He prayed that someone is sent to tell his family about Jesus so that they would not come to Hell (Luke 16). People in Hell are praying for you to go to their families and bring the gospel to them!

*1 Tim 2:1 I exhort therefore, that, first of all, supplications, prayers, intercessions, and giving of thanks, be made for all men;*

For kings, and for all that are in authority; that we may lead a quiet and peaceable life in all godliness and honesty.

For this is good and acceptable in the sight of God our Savior;

**Who will have all men to be saved, and to come unto the knowledge of the truth?**

For there is one God, and one mediator between God and men, the man Christ Jesus.

*Eph 2:8 For by grace are ye saved through faith; and that not of yourselves: it is the gift of God: Not of works, lest any man should boast.*

*Romans 10:8 But what saith it? The word is nigh thee, even in thy mouth, and in thy heart: that is, the word of faith, which we preach; That if thou shalt confess with thy mouth the Lord Jesus, and shalt believe in thine heart that God hath raised him from the dead, thou shalt be saved.*

For with the heart, man believeth unto righteousness; and with the mouth, confession is made unto salvation.

**Salvation:** you must believe (that God raised Jesus from the dead), confess (out loud)

Jesus is Lord (not just the Lord, but your Lord, must put Him in charge of your life). For the scripture saith, "Whosoever believeth on him shall not be ashamed." You also must believe **and** speak.

For there is no difference between the Jew and the Greek: for the same Lord over all is rich unto all that call upon him.

*Rom 10:13-16 For whosoever shall **call** upon the name of the Lord shall be saved. How then shall they call on him in whom they have not **believed**? and how shall they **believe** in him of whom they have not **heard**? and how shall they **hear** without a preacher? And how shall they **preach**, except they be **sent**? As it is written, How beautiful are the feet of them that preach the gospel of peace and bring glad tidings of good things! But they have not all obeyed the gospel. For Esaias saith, Lord, who hath believed our report? **So then faith cometh by hearing, and hearing by the word of God.** But I say, Have they not heard? Yes verily, their sound went into all the earth, and their words unto the ends of the world.*

This is the process of the gospel.

- People must hear the voice of God and be sent.
- They must obey and go.
- Once they go, they must preach.

- The people they preach to must-hear.
- When they hear, they must believe.
- When they believe, they must Call upon the name of the Lord.

There will be a glorious echo from heaven, and all who call upon the name of the Lord, will be saved! Can people believe and not speak? Yes, but they will not be saved. Silent prayer will not cut it.

> *John 12:36 While ye have light, believe in the light, that ye may be the children of light. These things spake Jesus, and departed, and did hide himself from them. But though he had done so many miracles before them, yet they believed not on him: That the saying of Esaias the prophet might be fulfilled, which he spake, Lord, who hath believed our report? and to whom hath the arm of the Lord been revealed?*
>
> *Therefore they could not believe, because that Esaias said again, He hath blinded their eyes, and hardened their heart; that they should not see with their eyes, nor understand with their heart, and be converted, and I should heal them.*
>
> *These things said Esaias, when he saw his glory, and spake of him. Nevertheless among the chief rulers also **many believed on him; but because of the Pharisees they did not confess him,** lest they should be put out of the synagogue: For they loved the praise of men more than the praise of God.*
>
> *Jesus cried and said, He that believeth on me, believeth not on me, but on him that sent me. And he that seeth me seeth him that sent me. I am come a light into the world, that whosoever believeth on me should not abide in darkness.*
>
> *And if any man hear my words, and believe not, I judge him not: for I came not to judge the world, but to save the world.*
>
> *He that rejecteth me, and receiveth not my words, hath one that judgeth him: the word that I have spoken, the same shall judge him in the last day.*
>
> *Can someone hear and not believe?*

*Matt 13:11-12 And he said unto them, Unto you it is given to know the mystery of the kingdom of God: but unto them that are without, all these things are done in parables: that seeing they may see, and not perceive; and hearing they may hear, and not understand; **lest at any time** they should be converted, and their sins should be forgiven them.*

*Mark 4:14 And in them is fulfilled the prophecy of Esaias, which saith, By hearing ye shall hear, and shall not understand; and seeing ye shall see, and shall not perceive: For this people's heart is waxed gross, and their ears are dull of hearing, and **their eyes they have closed; lest at any time** they should see with their eyes, and hear with their ears, and should understand with their heart, and should be converted, and I should heal them.*

*But blessed are your eyes, for they see: and your ears, for they hear.*

God's side is that anyone, anywhere, at any time who turns to Him and calls upon the name of Jesus shall be saved.

Can people be around Christians and not hear? Yes. Many of us go into our day to day worlds, and we do not preach. People are going to hell around us simply because we refuse to tell them about God's plan of salvation. We must preach.

Are there Christians who don't go? Obviously! How many of us will go to the person next to us at work and tell them about Jesus? If we won't go to the person next to us at work, how can God ever send us to China or the uttermost parts of the earth?

*Acts 1:8 But ye shall receive power, after that the Holy Ghost is come upon you: and ye shall be witnesses unto me both in Jerusalem, and in all Judaea, and in Samaria, and unto the uttermost part of the earth.*

Can anyone say that God has not sent them? Not after tonight! Jesus, King of glory, your Lord and Master, sends you to tell others about Him.

*Matt 10:6-7 But **go** rather to the lost sheep of the house of Israel. And as ye go, preach, saying, The kingdom of heaven is at hand. Heal the sick, cleanse the lepers, raise the dead, cast out devils: freely ye have received, freely give. Now all of this is going to take the Holy Ghost to accomplish anything.*

## The Reception:

*Acts 10:1 There was a certain man in Caesarea called Cornelius, a centurion of the band called the Italian band,*

*A devout man, and one that feared God with all his house, which gave much alms to the people, and prayed to God always.*

*He saw in a vision evidently about the ninth hour of the day an angel of God coming in to him, and saying unto him, Cornelius.*

*And when he looked on him, he was afraid and said, What is it, Lord? And he said unto him, Thy prayers and thine alms are come up for a memorial before God.*

*And now send men to Joppa, and call for one Simon, whose surname is **Peter:** He lodgeth with one Simon a tanner, whose house is by the seaside: he shall tell thee what thou oughtest to do.*

Angels are not instructed to preach the gospel but assist us in our responsibility in preaching it. All over the world are Cornelius' type people. People are honestly seeking God that God is visiting and drawing to Himself.

God may well be speaking to them about you!

*Acts 8:27-31 And he arose and went: and, behold, a man of Ethiopia, an eunuch of great authority under Candace queen of the Ethiopians, who had the charge of all her treasure, and had come to Jerusalem for to worship. Was returning, and sitting in his chariot read Esaias the prophet. **Then the Spirit said** unto Philip, Go near, and join thyself to this chariot.*

*And Philip ran thither to him, and heard him read the prophet Esaias, and said, Understandest thou what thou readest?*

*And he said, How can I, except some man should guide me? And he desired Philip that he would come up and sit with him.*

The place of the scripture which he read was this, *"He was led as a sheep to the slaughter; and like a lamb dumb before his shearer, so opened he not his mouth"* Isaiah 53:7 KJV

In his humiliation, his judgment was taken away: and who shall declare his generation? for his life is taken from the earth.

*Acts 8:34 And the eunuch answered Philip, and said, I pray thee, of whom speaketh the prophet this? of himself, or of some other man*

Then Philip opened his mouth and began at the same scripture and preached unto him Jesus.

This Ethiopian was already reading the Bible, seeking God. God sent Philip to Him. There are Ethiopian-type people all over this region who are seeking God. God wants to send you to them.

*Acts 16:6 Now when they had gone throughout Phrygia and the region of Galatia, and were forbidden of the Holy Ghost to preach the word in Asia, 7 After they were come to Mysia, they assayed to go into Bithynia: but the Spirit suffered them not.*

**Go!**

Ever tried to steer a parked car? It's hard

Have you ever try to steer a docked ship? It's impossible VVehicles need to MOVE to be directed

You, too, need to move and have faith that God will direct you to the right people, places, and situations that are ready for Him and you!

*Acts 5:32 And we are his witnesses of these things; and so is also the*

*Holy Ghost, whom God hath given to them that obey him.*

As you obey, He will show Himself strong on your behalf.

*Daniel 11:32 And such as do wickedly against the covenant shall he corrupt by flatteries: but the people that do know their God shall be strong, and do exploits.*

I believe in you here that you are a people of destiny, a doer of daring deeds, a history maker, and a nation shaker designed to make an eternal impact with your life!

I want to pray tonight a prayer of commission for you. It will be a fire send-off, if you will, to be an endowment of power from heaven for your life:

*Act 4:29 And now, Lord, behold their threatenings: and grant unto thy servants, that with all boldness they may speak thy word,*

By stretching forth thine hand to heal; and that signs and wonders may be done by the name of thy holy child Jesus.

And when they had prayed, the place was shaken where they were assembled together; and they were all filled with the Holy Ghost, and they spake the word of God with boldness.

Let's pray:

Father, speak to me about my part in the Great Commission. Fill me with the Holy Spirit, and grant me all boldness to speak Your word with signs following, bearing witness that You, Father, raised Jesus from the dead. Amen'

# 22

# Relationships

**Who are you hanging out with?**

I was speaking with a minister one day about a particular business deal I was considering that involved a lot of money. I asked him about a specific leader, and he said to me something profound: *"Chris, I am not too sure about the character of that man, but always remember you will be labeled by the people you associate with."*

I am going to show you that who you hang around will determine your success in this life, that you need to come out from sin and things of this world to receive all that God has for you. You need to develop godly friendships.

Here is a picture of the Saturday morning men's prayer group I have attended since 2009 at Victory Christian Center here in Tulsa, OK. They are an incredible group of men of God who are doing great things in business and ministry around the world.

*Psalm 1:1 Blessed is the man that walketh not in the counsel of the ungodly, nor standeth in the way of sinners, nor sitteth in the seat of the scornful. But his delight is in the law of the LORD; and in his law doth he meditate day and night. And he shall be like a tree planted by the rivers of water, that bringeth forth his fruit in his season; his leaf also shall not wither; and whatsoever he doeth shall prosper.*

Now, for those of you who have been around this for a while, you know that the word 'blessed' means: empowered to prosper. That God is a good God, and if you want better for your children than you had, how much more God our heavenly father who loves you more than you love yourself. V1 **counsel** means advice. From whom are you receiving your advice?

The Bible says in *Proverbs 13:20 He that walketh with wise men shall be wise: but a companion of fools shall be destroyed.*

This verse tells us about three ways to be blessed by God.

The Bible says here that the person is blessed and given power from God to get ahead in life if first, you don't listen to the counsel of the ungodly.

Jesus said, *"By their fruits you shall know them."* So, when someone comes to speak into my life, the first question I ask myself is this: Are they saved?

What is their walk like with the Lord? Does what they are suggesting agree with the Word of God? Does it bring peace to my heart? What is coming out of their mouth? For out of the heart, the mouth will speak!

Now Jesus is a friend to sinners and tax collectors. He did not pray that we be taken out of this world, but that we are in it and not of it. We need to live and work with those who are not yet born again, but that does not permit us to talk like they talk or do what they do. We are to be a witness, something they need to look up to.

This verse says not to stand in the way of sinners. Someone is going partying, or to the Casino, or for a smoke break. What do we do? Get out of their way. Jesus is your way, and don't get into some sloppy Agape kind of limp-wristed version of love. Gently say, *"I'm a Christian, and I can't go down that road with you. I love you, but I've got a family that needs me, a church that loves me, and my mindset is on heavenly things."*

So, you are a good witness at work and are growing in your love walk and the fruit of the spirit. And you are seeking to win souls for you have read in your search for wisdom.

*Proverbs 11:30 The fruit of the righteous is a tree of life; and he that winneth souls is <u>wise</u>. But those around you begin to scoff and mock the things of God.*

Jesus said to seek and save the lost, not chase down the rebellious. No, what does our verse teach us here? When those around you begin to mock the things of God, what are you to do? Leave!

While I was studying for the ministry, I drove a school bus and picked up extra hours working at a bus depot washing buses. The Bus wash and the mechanic shop were part of the yard. I used to eat lunch with the guys, and they would ask questions about Jesus and the Bible. At first, they were friendly. After a while, they began to mock God and His Word deliberately. I would see how perverted and gross the conversation could get. I began eating lunch in my car because the guys had become scoffers. I spent my lunch hour listening to some good praise and worship music and talking to Jesus.

Let's ask God to show us people in our lives that we have become too familiar with and ask Him for the grace to spend the time with Him and in the study of His word instead of hanging around foul speech.

*Eph 5:16 Redeeming the time because the days are evil.*

*Col 4:5 Walk in wisdom toward them that are without, redeeming the time.*
*Separate Yourself unto God!*

*Joshua 24:5 I sent Moses also and Aaron, and I plagued Egypt, according to that which I did among them: and afterward I* **brought you out.** *And I brought your fathers out of Egypt: and ye came unto the sea; and the Egyptians pursued after your fathers with chariots and horsemen unto the Red sea. And when they cried unto the LORD, he put darkness between you and the Egyptians, and brought the sea upon them, and covered them; and your eyes have seen what I have done in Egypt: and ye dwelt in the wilderness a long season. And I* **brought you into the land** *of the Amorites, which dwelt on the other side Jordan; and they fought with you: and I gave them into your hand, that ye might possess their land; and I destroyed them from before* *you.*

Now Egypt is a type of the world's system that God hates. It represents your old, sinful lifestyle. Everyone says, "He brought me out to bring me in."

> *2 Corinthians 6:17 Wherefore come out from among them, **and be ye separate,** saith the Lord, and touch not the unclean thing; and **I will receive you,**18 And will be a Father unto you, and ye shall be my sons and daughters, saith the Lord Almighty.*

- 873 aforizw aphorizo af-or-id'-zo from 575 and 3724; TDNT-5:454,728; v
- AV-separate 8, divide 1, sever 1; 10
- **1) to mark off from others by boundaries, to limit, to separate**
- 1a) in a bad sense: to exclude as disreputable
- 1b) in a good sense: to appoint, set apart for some purpose

The word of God, preached as it is under the anointing of the Holy Spirit, is designed to impregnate your very spirit with the life of God. It is food, and it is the way God has designed to make you a success. Jesus said His words are spirit and life, and Hebrews 12:9 *"Furthermore, we have had fathers of our flesh which corrected us, and we gave them reverence: shall we not much rather be in subjection unto the Father of spirits, and live?"*

If Jesus is your Lord, the way He prefers to correct you is by His word, not in chastening after the flesh. Yet, if you continue to act in the flesh, He will correct you in the flesh. With children, we call this applying the board of instruction to the seat of higher learning!

I have been asked why I teach so much and why I spend hours pouring the Word of God into people. Well, I am instructed as a man of God to teach the word in season and out of season to feed the flock of God among us.

Yet, I'm no fool; I've spent the hours and hours counseling people and walking with people from tragedy to trial to tears. Finally, the Holy Spirit showed me a better way.

The Bible says that by these promises, we have everything we need for life and godliness. God sent His word and healed them and delivered them from all their destruction.

The answer to your problem is in the word of God. So, what does a shepherd do? He goes before God in prayer on your behalf, then God answers. He speaks his Word and knows this: God always backs up His word with His power. He cannot lie.

> *Psalms 138:2 I will worship toward thy holy temple and praise thy name for thy lovingkindness and for thy truth:* **for thou hast magnified thy word above all thy name.**

God is your rock, and He has sent ministry into your life to lead you deeper into His plan for your life. I am simply an act of God's mercy and compassion in your life. He knows not all of you have five hours a day or ten years to study in God's word. The ministry gifts are delivery boys who help you to understand and apply His word in your lives.

The package I deliver is God's word. Unwrap it and apply it to your life, and it will produce a blessing every time. God's way is His word, and His word spoken from here will manifest His power to meet your need. Your answer is the Word of God. I spend many, many hours each day praying for YOU!

Certain people would wear me out! They would constantly call me in crisis, asking me to come to pray for them, to go to the hospital, to come over for dinner. They were usually very polite when I came. Yet, I noticed that those that often took significant amounts of my time and rarely attended services. They loved to hear the Word of God, but they missed God's order in attending church.

> *Heb 10:25 Not forsaking the assembling of ourselves together, as the manner of some is; but exhorting one another: and so much the more, as ye see the day approaching. Finally, God set me free from chasing*

*these people.*

*1 Pet 5:2 Feed the flock of God **which is among you**, taking the oversight thereof, not by constraint, but willingly; not for filthy lucre, but of a ready mind;*

I realized that if they were not among us in regular attendance at church, my responsibility to feed, lead, and counsel them ended.

*John 16:13 Howbeit when he, the Spirit of truth, is come, he will guide you into all truth: for he shall not speak of himself; but whatsoever he shall hear, that shall he speak: and he will shew you things to come.*

What's the point? While we must love all people, some must be given reduced access to our lives if we are going to be people of impact. They will drain our critical energies and finances if we let them, and it is our fault. Sometimes the best we can do for them is NOT return their calls while fervently praying for them. We are not God. Jesus is Lord. It is wrong to do for people that which they have the responsibility to do for themselves.

Perhaps they have some unmet emotional need and need sympathy, so they go to another meeting and ask another group of Christians to pray. And surprise surprise, God tells them to do the same thing. I've met Christians who have been involved with codependent relationships and sin issues, and they refuse to sever ties to those sins. If you quit drinking, you pour whatever alcohol is in your house down the sink. When you learn about the presence of God that comes in worship and Christian music, you probably need to go through your CDs and cassettes and pitch the ones that do not bring the presence of God into your world. Video's, magazines, and even TV shows that glorify sin need to be removed from your life. He's bringing you out so that He can bring you in.

John Hagee calls television *"that little god in your living room"* for *"do not many prostrate themselves before it and spend more time with it than in the word and prayer?"*

> *3 John 1:2 Beloved, I wish above all things that thou mayest prosper and be in health, even as thy soul prospereth.*

I am a prosperity preacher because prosperity is in the word. Yet, as a shepherd, I need to bring you out so that I can bring you in. Notice in this verse, we studied that God wants you to prosper and be in health **as your soul prospers.**

> *2 Corinthians 6:17-18 Wherefore come out from among them, **and be ye separate,** saith the Lord, and touch not the unclean thing; and I will receive you, **And will be a Father unto you**, and ye shall be my sons and daughters, saith the Lord Almighty.*

God is a good God and loves you more than you love yourself. He wants to prosper you more than your wildest dreams, but it must be done His way.

Your soul is your mind, will, and emotions. Many of you have been through hell emotionally, and your mind is a full mixture of the world and the devil's thoughts with a little bit of God. So, your day to day decisions wobble due to your pain and mixed-up reasoning. God has more than that for you. He wants you to come out of the things that are causing you pain and that dishonor His name. Why? So that He can take you in His arms and pour into you love, acceptance, affirmation, healing, comfort, strength, and confidence. All the things you never got growing up, God wants to restore to you. He is a father to the fatherless, but you must spend time with Him. You can't say you love Him and then serve His enemy. Draw near to Him, and He will do things for you and cause you to avoid situations that would have caused you much grief. His presence is prosperity; it's the drug we all need. He brought you out of sin so that you may fall into His arms.

Well, my last point is short and sweet; God has a place for you in His kingdom specifically for you - a place where you can grow and develop godly relationships.

*Acts 4:23 And being let go, **they went to their own company** and reported all that the chief priests and elders had said unto them.*

God has a company for you, a company of believers in your home, in your workplace, at your school, and in a local church where you are celebrated, not merely tolerated.

*2 Peter 1:1 Simon Peter, a servant and an apostle of Jesus Christ, to them that have obtained like precious faith with us through the righteousness of God and our Savior Jesus Christ: I want to be around people that have a like-precious faith, people that are quick to pray and believe God on purpose.*

For several years, I ran a construction company here in Tulsa, Oklahoma. The church I attend, Victory Christian Center, is big on developing small group Bible studies, called connect groups, where we study the word of God together and get to know folks. For several years, I attended three of these, some weekly, others bi-weekly, that each had a different focus. The three I attended have been the business owners, the men's group, and the married with children group.

In the business owners' group, we deliberately have sought God for wisdom to run our respective companies and have networked and prayed in confidence for each other's needs. The pressures, responsibilities, and crises we often faced as business owners grew us tremendously over the five years that we met. God used that group to disciple and to help us grow strong as men of God. We did this for seven years. Then, I stopped for a couple of years while I traveled as a missionary. As soon as I came back to Tulsa, I was asked by several men to restart the group, and I have: http://chrisaomministries.com/2016/01/19/contractors-bible-study/

Like precious faith!

*Daniel 11:32 And such as do wickedly against the covenant shall he corrupt by flatteries: **but the people that do know their God shall be***

***strong, and do exploits.***

***Prov 13:20 He that walketh with wise men shall be wise: but a companion of fools shall be destroyed.***

Deliberately seek out and cultivate relationships with those who are maturing in the Lord and doing exploits for the kingdom.

The converse of this is also true; ungodly people will betray you and will corrupt you. The mighty apostle Paul realized this truth, as immoral people lied about him, conspired against him, had him falsely accused, beaten, and imprisoned. He realized relationships are critical to success in life and ministry. Hear his heart:

> *2 Thes 3:2 And that we may be delivered from unreasonable and wicked men: for all men have not faith.*

Just as there are relationships of honor, integrity, wisdom, strength, and like precious faith, there are treacherous people in this world that will betray you and siphon the very life and power of God from you, if you let them.

These people need to leave your life!

> *2 Thessalonians 3:2 and that we may be delivered from* **unreasonable** *and wicked men: for all men have not faith.*

Today I have tried to show you that who you hang around will determine your success in this life, that you need to come out from sin and things of this world to receive all that God has for you. God wants you to develop godly friendships with people of honor, integrity, and precious faith!

I've asked you to consider leaving relationships with ungodly counselors and, instead, spending the time talking to God in His word with prayer and worship. I've asked you to leave the trappings of sin. Leave the things of this world so that He can bring you into His presence and prosperity. I've challenged you to develop godly friendships on purpose to cultivate relationships with those influential in the Lord and have the power of His might that are doing exploits for Him.

I read this little story that I find appropriate here. Perhaps you have already read it but bear with me. It might encourage you to hear it again.

* * *

"People always come into your life for a reason, a season, and a lifetime. When you figure out which it is, you know what to do.

When someone is in your life for a **REASON**, it is usually to meet a need you have expressed outwardly or inwardly. They have come to assist you through a difficulty or to provide you with guidance and support to aid you physically, emotionally, or even spiritually. They may seem like a god-send to you, and they are. They are there for a reason, and you need them to be. Then, without any wrongdoing on your part or at an inconvenient time, this person will say or do something to bring the relationship to an end. Sometimes they die. Sometimes they walk away. Sometimes they act up or out and force you to take a stand. What we must realize is that our need has been met and our desire fulfilled. Their work is done. The prayer you sent up has been answered, and it is now time to move on.

When people come into your life for a **SEASON**, it is because your turn has come to share, grow, or learn. They may bring you an experience of peace or make you laugh. They may teach you something you have never done. They usually give you an unbelievable amount of joy. Believe it! It is real! But, only for a season. And like spring turns to summer and summer to fall, the season eventually ends.

**LIFETIME** relationships teach you a lifetime of lessons; those things you must build upon to have a solid emotional foundation. Your job is to accept the experience, love the person/people (anyway), and put what you have learned to use in all other relationships and areas in your life. It is said that love is blind, but friendship is clairvoyant. Thank you for being part of my life." *Reason, Season, or a Lifetime?* by Brian A. "Drew" Chalker

* * *

Now God needs to demonstrate this word so that you can know that God is alive and in the house. Maybe some of you don't know Jesus yet. Today is your day. He is not I was, not I will be. His name is I AM. Now Faith is. You need to give Him your life. He is Lord, and you need to sell out to Him totally, no compromise. He rose from the dead, and He wants to forgive you and save you, adopting you into His great family. He wants to show you the reason He created you and the place He has called you to serve Him in.

Let's Pray:

*Father, I come before You, deciding to place Jesus as Lord of my life. I believe that because You love me, You will not fail me. Your plan for my life is better than what I have planned. I receive You, Lord Jesus, as my Savior, personal Pastor, Shepherd, and Counselor. Jesus, add to me people of faith, honor, wisdom, strength, and integrity. And like Paul, I pray "that we may be delivered from unreasonable and wicked men." Help me to carve time out of my day, to listen to and meditate on Your Word and worship. In Your name, I pray, Lord Jesus. Amen.*

# 23

# He that is Spiritual, Restore

He that is spiritual, restore:

*Galatians 6:1 Brethren, if a man be overtaken in a fault, ye which are spiritual, **restore** such a one in the spirit of meekness; considering thyself, lest thou also be tempted. Some time ago, I had a discussion with a friend of mine about the topic of a person being restored to fellowship in the local church after they had been removed from that church through the church disciplinary process.*

*2 Cor 2:7-11 So that contrariwise ye ought rather to forgive him, and comfort him, lest perhaps such a one should be swallowed up with overmuch sorrow. Wherefore I beseech you that ye would confirm your love toward him. For to this end also did I write, that I might know the proof of you, whether ye be obedient in all things. To whom ye forgive anything, I forgive also: for if I forgave any thing, to whom I forgave it, for your sakes forgave I it in the person of Christ; Lest Satan should get an advantage of us: for we are not ignorant of his devices.*

In this extended discussion, Pastor Richard Lyons taught me a beautiful truth about forgiveness and restoration. In this case, the apostle Paul was asked to render judgment upon a problematic case. A man had committed an abominable sin. He had been removed from the church and turned over to Satan, that his flesh is destroyed, though his spirit is eternally saved.

> *Cor 5:1-4 It is reported commonly that there is fornication among you, and such fornication as is not so much as named among the Gentiles, that one should have his father's wife. And ye are puffed up, and have not rather mourned, that he that hath done this deed might be taken away from among you. For I verily, as absent in body, but present in spirit, have judged already, as though I were present, concerning him that hath so done this deed, In the name of our Lord Jesus Christ, when ye are gathered together, and my spirit, with the power of our Lord Jesus Christ, To deliver such an one unto Satan for the destruction of the flesh, that the spirit may be saved in the day of the Lord Jesus. Your glorying is not good. Know ye not that a little leaven leaveneth the whole lump?*

Incest! Ugh! Paul, judging by the Holy Spirit, had the man thrown out of the church so that the church would not be defiled.

Yet, now, after a passage of time (not sure how much time you theologians can surely tell me), Paul is asking this same church to restore this same man.

In the natural, it's not possible, but in Christ, all things are possible.

Ever wondered how to forgive? What might the process look like? Let's look at a few key points:

> *2 Cor 2:10 To whom ye forgive any thing, I forgive also: for if I forgave any thing, to whom I forgave it, for your sakes forgave I it in the person of Christ.*

## ONLY IN THE PERSON OF THE ANOINTED ONE AND HIS ANOINTING, CAN WE FORGIVE THE UNFORGIVABLE!

This was brought home to me as I ministered among the people of Rwanda. Both victims of the genocide were in church, worshipping God with the very perpetrators that had slaughtered their families.

The Holy Spirit had done such a profound work of forgiveness that there was an honest love among them, both sides, from the repentant and forgiven to the restored and forgivers. There could be seen no distinction; they were both sides lost in the presence of God in sincere worship, brokenness, humility, and servanthood, loving and serving one another in the love of Jesus. Only the presence of God could make this miracle happen. Only Jesus could perform such a profound work of mercy, forgiveness, and reconciliation.

Before someone who had been removed from fellowship could be restored, the apostolic authority has to hear God, judge, and in the presence of Jesus, decide to restore them.

How was this to be done?

*1 Cor 2:7 So that contrariwise ye ought rather to forgive him, and comfort him, lest perhaps such a one should be swallowed up with overmuch sorrow. Wherefore I beseech you that ye would confirm your love toward him.*

We see three steps here:

1. They must be forgiven. Here is where life becomes tricky, individual, and very specific because only the Holy Spirit knows the heart of the person who has been removed from fellowship. Only He can tell us the state of the person's heart, whether or not they have truly repented or are only exhibiting 'worldly sorrow.'
2. They must be comforted. I believe both from the Body of Christ through prayer and the ministry of the Holy Spirit.
3. They must be confirmed in our love for them. For a time, they must be continuously encouraged, established, blessed, strengthened.

There is much more to be said about how to do these things practically, and I, like you, need to grow and learn some things here. What are your thoughts on church discipline?  What is the process in your particular assembly by which discipline is decided upon and executed?  How do you discern if a person has genuinely repented and therefore needs to be restored to fellowship?

Let's pray:

> *Father, show us how to restore broken people. I pray for those of us in leadership that you grant us strength and discernment to know when to bar someone from fellowship and when to restore them. Help us to forgive them in the presence of the Holy Spirit, truly to comfort them, and to confirm them in their restoration into their gift and calling. In Your name, I pray, Lord Jesus.*

24

# Levels Of Intimacy For Leaders

I have been thinking about levels of intimacy in relationships, especially in leadership. Looking at Jesus for our example, I see He had different levels of intimacy with those He was called to lead.

This is a basic thought on some things, and I will tell you why: Jesus was the only Son of God on the earth when He lived here. Today, Jesus is Lord of Lords and King of Kings, and He has many great leaders on the earth today. How they are to relate with honor in this generation is something I will address at the end of this line of thinking.

1.) The first and greatest intimacy Jesus shared was and always is with His (and our) Heavenly Father.

> *Matt 6:6 But thou, when thou prayest, enter into thy closet, and when thou hast shut thy door, pray to thy Father which is in secret; and thy Father which seeth in secret shall reward thee openly.*

> *John 10:30 My Father and I are one.*

> *John 5:19 Then answered Jesus and said unto them, Verily, verily, I say unto you, The Son can do nothing of himself, but what he seeth the Father do: for*

*what things soever he doeth, these also doeth the Son likewise.*

*John 5:20 For the Father loveth the Son, and sheweth him all things that himself doeth: and he will shew him greater works than these, that ye may marvel.*

That is a powerful verse. Jesus experienced such a beautiful intimacy with Father God that Father God would show Him what He wanted to do. And Jesus went and did the mighty miracles that we read about in the Word of God.

*John 5:30 I can of mine own self do nothing: as I hear, I judge: and my judgment is just; because I seek not mine own will, but the will of the Father which hath sent me.*

*Isa 50:4 The Lord GOD hath given me the tongue of the learned, that I should know how to speak a word in season to him that is weary: he wakeneth morning by morning, he wakeneth mine ear to hear as the learned.*

Here are Jesus and our morning regiment and devotion, seeking heaven for direction and His Word for the day. Then we walk out what He has shown us.

Jesus's most excellent relationship is with His heavenly Father. He is our example. He died and rose again to reconcile us to our heavenly Father. Our greatest relationship must also be with our heavenly Father, enjoying His presence and seeking Him daily for His direction for our lives.

2.) John was His right-hand man. Jesus trusted John with even the care of His mother after He died on the cross. He told him about Judas's betrayal, while others did not understand it. Could it be that Jesus used John to restore Peter, and keep him on track?

3.) Peter, James, and John.

*Matt 17:1 And after six days Jesus taketh Peter, James, and John, his brother, and bringeth them up into a high mountain apart, And Jesus was transfigured before them: and his face did shine as the sun, and his raiment was white as the light.*

*Matt 26:37 And he took with him Peter and the two sons of Zebedee and began to be sorrowful and very heavy.*

*Mark 5:37–41 And he suffered no man to follow him, save Peter, and James, and John, the brother of James. And he cometh to the house of the ruler of the synagogue, and seeth the tumult, and them that wept and wailed greatly. And when he was come in, he saith unto them, Why make ye this ado, and weep? The damsel is not dead but sleepeth. And they laughed him to scorn. But when he had put them all out, he taketh the father and the mother of the damsel, and them that were with him, and entereth in where the damsel was lying. And he took the damsel by the hand, and said unto her, Talitha cumi; which is, being interpreted, Damsel, I say unto thee, arise.*

*Mark 13:3 And as he sat upon the mount of Olives over against the temple, Peter and James and John and Andrew asked him privately,*

*Luke 9:28 And it came to pass about an eight days after these sayings, he took Peter and John and James and went up into a mountain to pray.*

*Luke 22:8 And he sent Peter and John, saying, Go and prepare us the Passover, that we may eat.*

4.) The 12 disciples.

5.) The 120 that came from the multitudes that followed Him.

6.) The multitudes.

7.) The world that He loves.

We need to think about how leaders are to relate, all serving Him together.

# 25

# Set Yearly Goals, Work for Them

I am a disciple of Jesus Christ! The word disciple means: 'disciplined one.' My aim, my passion, my destiny, my calling, is to fully obey Him and make a radical, eternal impact upon this world through my obedience and love.

I read this quote, and it encourages me today:

**"Time is the inexplicable raw material of everything. With it, all is possible; without it, nothing. The supply of time is truly a daily miracle, an affair genuinely astonishing when one examines it. You wake up in the morning, and lo! Your purse is magically filled with twenty-four hours of the unmanufactured tissue of the universe of your life! It is yours. It is the most precious of possessions... No one can take it from you. It is not something that can be stolen. And no one receives either more or less than you receive. Moreover, you cannot draw on its future. Impossible to get into debt! You can only waste the passing moment. You cannot waste tomorrow; it is kept for you. You cannot waste the next hour; it is kept for you.**

**You have to live on these twenty-four hours of daily time. Out of it, you have to spin health, pleasure, money, content, respect, and the evolution of your immortal soul. Its right use, its most**

**effective use, is a matter of the highest urgency and of the most thrilling actuality. It all depends on that.**

**Your happiness — the elusive prize that you are all clutching for, my friends — depends on that.**

**If one cannot arrange that an income of twenty-four hours a day shall exactly cover all proper items of expenditure, one does muddle one's whole life indefinitely. We shall never have any more time. We have, and we have always had, all the time there is."** *Arnold Bennett, Bits & Pieces, March 4, 1993, p. 18-20*

We begin New Year's resolutions cyclically. Many of us put together a battle plan to get where we need to be. It is a great day to reflect on where we are and to rethink perhaps if we are spending time doing the critical. Or have we allowed ourselves to become so busy that we have drifted off course from our dreams and God-given vision? I see this here in Paul's letter to the Corinthian church:

*1 Cor 16:6 And it may be that I will abide, yea, and winter with you, that ye may bring me on my journey whithersoever I go. For I will not see you now by the way; but I trust to tarry a while with you, if the Lord permit. But I will tarry at Ephesus until Pentecost.*

Notice here Paul was planning out his year, scheduling what he would do, and what he would not do.

*Proverbs 16:9 A man's heart deviseth **his** way: but the Lord **directeth his steps**.*

*Jer 10:23 O LORD, I know that the way of man is not in himself: it is not in man that walketh to direct his steps.*

*"Time is the coin of your life. It is the only coin you have, and you alone can determine how it will be spent. Be careful lest you let other*

*people spend it for you"—Carl Sandburg.*

In January, I pray, fast, and set yearly goals for the next 12 months. So far, so good. The Lord has honored my faith. I am on track pretty much for what I set out to accomplish in the previous year. Truthfully, I missed a couple of fitness goals because I did not rest enough, so we learn, adjust, implement, and move forward.

Jesus is welcome to change any of my plans or schedule at any point. But for now, I am walking out and working toward my goals, trusting Him to do the impossible daily. It has been said that it is better to shoot for the stars and only hit the moon than to aim at nothing and hit nothing. Or, you can shoot for the moon, overshoot, and land among the stars. Set measurable concrete goals now. Plan your work, and work your plan, daily reviewing your plan to keep yourself on track.

Then, each time I complete a project or portion, I can go back to the blueprint for the year and begin focusing on the next level of excellence I need to achieve.

Millions long for immortality who do not know what to do with themselves on a rainy Sunday afternoon. Susan Ertz.

*"As if you could kill time without injuring eternity."—Henry David Thoreau*

How well I have learned the truth of these verses:

*James 4:13 Go to now, ye that say, Today or tomorrow we will go into such a city, and continue there a year, and buy and sell, and get gain. Whereas ye know not what shall be on the morrow. For what is your life? It is even a vapor, that appeareth for a little time, and then vanisheth away. For that ye ought to say, **If the Lord will, we shall live,** and do this, or that.*

When we began our company, we produced a 400-page business plan on what we thought we would do with our business. For grins and giggles, 2-3 years into it, we would read it for humor. What we actually HAD to do, to feed our families daily, was a far cry from our fantasy dream. Then, we produced a 60-page business plan birthed in prayer and real-life experience. It worked, and our company grew from doing 150K a year to 550K in a couple of years.

Then we studied. My business partner took his business degree, and we had a team of MBA students doing a competitive business analysis of our company. They produced a 300-page booklet for us that was awesome, setting a realistic path to grow us to 5 million/year over the next five years. We grew it to 1.1 million over the next two years. From the time we started the business, it took eight years to accomplish this. Then, at my office one night, I had an 'open-heaven' experience where Jesus clearly called me to walk away from the company to do ministry full-time, and I have obeyed. Yet, I am convinced that had we continued on the business plan we set out, we would have made it to the 5 million/year mark, as long as we, the leaders, were willing to continue to grow and learn how to survive and effectively manage the growth.

Yet the principle remains. For our organizations to grow, we must improve. We must always be bigger on the inside than whatever challenges life throws at us. This takes faith.

I would love to say this was my idea, but I heard it taught both at Victory and again at Tom Leding's meetings. Faith without works is dead.

*Psalm 90:12 Teach us to number our days aright, that we may gain a heart of wisdom.*

Let's Pray:

*Father, You have a perfect plan for each of us this year. Please show us clearly what that is and help us to align ourselves with what You desire for us, then stay the course, and faithfully work at what You have shown us to do, in Your name, I pray, Lord Jesus. Amen.*

# 26

# Approvers of Excellence

*Dan 5:12 Forasmuch as an excellent spirit and knowledge, and under-standing, interpreting of dreams and shewing of hard sentences and dissolving of doubts, were found in the same Daniel, whom the king named Belteshazzar: now let Daniel be called, and he will shew the interpretation.*

*Phil 1:9 And this I pray, that your love may abound yet more and more in knowledge and in all judgment; That ye may APPROVE THINGS THAT ARE EXCELLENT; that ye may be sincere and without offense till the day of Christ; Being filled with the fruits of righteousness, which are by Jesus Christ, unto the glory and praise of God.*

*Phil 3:13 Brethren, I count not myself to have apprehended: but this one thing I do, forgetting those things which are behind, and reaching forth unto those things which are before, I press toward the mark for the prize of the high calling of God in Christ Jesus. May we continue to pursue Jesus today, growing in our gift and calling without compromise!*

Let's Pray:

*Father, place within us a spirit of excellence. In Your name, we pray, in Jesus's name, Amen.*

# 27

# Not By Works - It's All About Love

Let's unmask performance orientation.

*Eph 2:8 For by grace are ye saved through faith; and that not of yourselves: it is the gift of God.*

**Not of works,** lest any man should boast.

For we are his workmanship, created in Christ Jesus unto good works, which God hath before ordained that we should walk in them. **Not of works**, yet created **unto good works**, Hm!

Well, fasten your seat belts, folks! Here we go.

In my old-time evangelistic preaching, I used to proclaim Jesus is the way, the truth, and the life. He wants a personal relationship with you. You can know Him, and He will forgive you and grant you not only eternal life but life and life more abundantly, here and now.

Religion has always been man's works, his rules, and his regulations. It is where you work, and work, and work, trying to earn the acceptance and approval of God.

Jesus is God's way to reach humanity.

None of us can ever earn our way into heaven. No matter how hard we work, salvation is a gift granted to us by God upon the cross, and our job is to receive it simply.

*John 1:12 (AKJV) But as many as received him, to them gave he power
to become the sons of God, even to them that believe on his name.*

Jesus, God the Son, came, not to make bad people good, nor good people better, but rather to make dead people alive!

We who know Him are unlike any other species on planet earth. We have literally become new creations in Him. God lives in our hearts; our bodies have become His temple.

It is the stewardship and obedience to this life we have received that is the sole focus of heaven. Neither can we earn any particular grace or blessing from God.

First, we must believe we receive something, according to either the written or revealed Word of God, and then, our works of faith will keep in step with the specific leadings and promptings of the Holy Spirit.

Here is the problem: God loves us individually more than the work we do. He is a jealous God and desires intimacy with us. We are designed to be loved, and from the overflow of the love we receive, we love and work to create a better world.

*1 Corinthians 15:58 Therefore, my beloved brethren, be ye steadfast,
unmovable, always abounding **in** the work of the Lord, forasmuch as
ye know that your labor is **not in vain in** the Lord.*

The problem is most of the earthly love we have ever received, that is, human love is conditional.

If you do this, then I will love and reward you. If you do not, I will reject you and turn my back upon you.

When a baby is born, how much can it do to protect itself? Provide for itself? Feed itself? Care for itself?

Yet, that baby is designed to receive love, care, provision, protection.

Because of this messed up world we live in, most children are not loved well.

So, the child grows up and learns that to be loved and accepted. They have to perform, often like a circus dog, jumping through death-defying feats, hoops of fire, and incredible hardship, just to get that treat and pat on the head from its master.

God is not that way!

God is a loving Father, and He created us. He did it because He wanted a family. He wants children to love and care for, to protect and provide for. Like any father, He wants to be loved back. He longs for a relationship, and, from that relationship of love, He creates lovely works for us to walk in, works specifically and individually designed, for our unique and individual personalities, gifts, and characters. Are we going to be provided for? YES.

When He brings us into the earth He created for our life, He already made provision for us.

Yet, we are taught that we must work for that provision. This is a half-truth, and the problem with half of the truth is you are not quite sure which half you got.

Yes, there are principles and laws of seedtime and harvest in the earth that people have operated by and become wealthy. Yet, working WITH the Lord in His blessing and grace will bring increase and prosperity:

*Isaiah 65:23 They shall **not** labor **in vain**, nor bring forth for trouble; for they are the seed of the blessed of the Lord, and their offspring with them.*

Yet, I am dealing with a specific heart condition here. Wealthy does not equal Godly prosperity.

Prosperity, God's way, means having the love, presence, and provision of God to meet any human need.

I have met wealthy Christians who prospered by God's hand. In general, they are people of integrity, honor, wisdom, and great love and strength.

I have also met wealthy people who either were godless, or worse yet, religious. These folks are mean or often depraved. What do I mean by depraved?

All money will do is make more of YOU. If you like wine, women, and songs, well, more money will produce more wine, more women, and more music and sound systems.

Whatever you like, money will make more of it. I have been in homes with exquisite media rooms, watched wealthy doctors do a line of cocaine upon entry into their homes, or immediately mix a whiskey on the rocks to start the evening. Others, on their second or third marriage, are in bondage to lust, pornography, and sex looking for love in all the wrong places.

What if, though, you love Jesus? What if you honestly love people and seek to better the human condition?

More money for you is going to build healthy churches, Bible schools, orphanages, food to the poor, evangelism, prison outreaches, clothing and humanitarian aid, disaster relief, and works of compassion into the earth.

Here is what the Lord is dealing with me.

**Mark: Type 'A'; Mover and Shaker dude.**

It seems that much of what I used to do was based upon my own initiatives, desires, and motivations.

As the owner of a construction company, I've been a getter-done kind of guy. Most men are.

Although I have been a Christian, I would simply 'throw one up there' prayers in the morning, and then turn on the computer and the phone, and GO!

I used 6000 mins/month on my cell phone and spent way too much money buying meals for clients, selling work, and making things happen.

I would spend money on things I didn't like to impress people I sometimes didn't like, and who often did not like me because of my walk with the Lord.

While spirit-led works are Biblical, flesh and soulish practices produce no eternal consequence. In this life, these soulish works will self-destruct. Why? God loves us and wants a relationship!

When I have run, and run, and run, and worked and organized, agonized, managed, financed, pushed, and pressed with all of my might, and finally fall at His feet, exhausted, poured out, cored out, at a level of fatigue only another leader can genuinely understand: He will meet with me.

If I am wise, I will rest and allow Him to pour in His Word and teaching and refreshing. God will impart the love, strength, comfort, wisdom, and gentle grace that only He can give. You can then gently arise and walk with Him in a beautiful relationship — peace, love, and joy in the Holy Spirit.

*Isa 30:15 For thus saith the Lord GOD, the Holy One of Israel; In returning and rest shall ye be saved; in quietness and in confidence shall be your strength: and ye would not. 16 But ye said, No, for we will flee upon horses; therefore shall ye flee: and, We will ride upon the swift; therefore shall they that pursue you be swift.*

*One thousand shall flee at the rebuke of one; at the rebuke of five shall ye flee: till ye be left as a beacon upon the top of a mountain, and as an ensign on a hill.*

*And therefore will the LORD wait, that he may be gracious unto you, and therefore will he be exalted, that he may have mercy upon you: for the LORD is a God of judgment: blessed are all they that wait for him.*

*Leviticus 26:20 and your strength shall be spent **in vain**: for your land shall **not** yield her **in**crease, neither shall the trees of the land yield their fruits.*

If I refuse, I have learned, through much pain:

*Isa 40:31 But they that wait upon the LORD shall renew their strength; they shall mount up with wings as eagles; they shall run, and not be weary; and they shall walk, and not faint.*

If mere hard work, organization, discipline, and zeal were all that was required, Hitler, Napoleon, Kublai Khan, and Stalin would have succeeded in their quest to rule the world. Yet, they forgot God.

Here, where I live, the motto of the state of Oklahoma is 'Labor Omnia

Vincit,' which is Latin for "Hard work conquers all."

Well, I am all for hard work.

Nothing is so satisfying as your head hitting the pillow after a productive day. The Oklahoma motto is a reference to the early pioneers of the Oklahoma territory.

Now, perhaps I am unique, but as God has grown and gifted me. I am prone to overdo some things.

Balance is not always one of my most durable qualities. I like to get stuff done.

I understand 'make something happen.' I have loved faith teaching that amplifies this thought of 'grab hold of the promises and go for it.' I understand GO!

Yet, God is a very living God, and there are other commands He can give. How about "STOP!"?

How about "Wait!"

How about "NO!"

How about "Sit down over there and let me teach you a few things!"

Remember Mary and Martha? I have seen more executives with high blood pressure, heart attacks, and various health conditions because things got out of balance, or dare I say, away from God's will for their lives over into self-will?

Most of you know my testimony, working some 14-16 hour days for years without a day off until I found myself blacked out from a mini-stroke at the wheel of my truck in the median in the middle of Highway 75, coming up from Glenpool. When I finally got to the emergency room, my blood pressure was 200/150, and I had to work to regain my health. It took a couple of years of radical life changes (exercise, diet, sleep, reduced hours at work, and yes, even a couple of vacations!). Now, I am in a different type of press:

*Phil 3:14 I press toward the mark for the prize of the high calling of God in Christ Jesus.*

What does this look like in my life?

I spend much more time in prayer, Bible study, journaling with a firm determination to hear accurately what I believe God is saying to me. Then I, gently and quietly, let Him open doors for my gift and calling instead of my previous method of kicking down any doors that appeared closed.

Now, I have learned that just because God speaks to me clearly about some things HE wants me to do that I might need to learn a few things about how He wants them done. Perhaps, so do you.

How many times do I hear of folks experiencing brutal circumstances or health conditions that could have been completely averted if they had accurately heard and obeyed God?

> *Matthew 11:29 Take my yoke upon you and **learn of me**, for I am **me**ek and lowly in heart: and ye shall find rest unto your souls.*

He loves you. He does. You are not an orphan, and you do not need to work to receive His love.

Yet, Jesus sees past the 'what' you are doing, to the 'why,' and I hear Him weeping for many of you today, as you, like a hamster on a treadmill, are running hard but going nowhere.

One day of God's favor, one instance of His power demonstrated, one glimpse of His glory, is higher than the total of all the work you have ever done or will do.

Think about it for a second: He is the one who flung the stars into being and created the universe.

It is my prayer that right now, wherever you are, you hear this word and take a second to look up into His face and say hello quietly. He told me to write this, and He's going to show up, and speak, reveal, and demonstrate to you His great love for you, His child.

Now, what are you going to do about it?

Are you willing to let Him run your show?

Will you, like me, make a radical decision that, if He does not tell you personally to do something in His timing, that you will refuse to do it?

Or, are you going to run some more?

Are you serving the tyranny of unfulfilled expectations from your own passions and pride? Are you serving the pride and passions of those around you and your family?

Or will you determine to discover the life you were born to live? Will you serve the one created for you from before the foundation of the world?

I think of the revival now known as 'The Toronto Blessing.' This was the message that changed my life forever. I have learned that I have a Father in heaven that loves me and will meet with me and love out my deepest pains, fears, and questions. From this place of intimacy with Him, I get something to give to a hurting world.

**Psalm 37:4 Delight thyself also in the Lord, and he shall give thee the desires of thine heart.**

If you willingly learn to allow Him to love you, He will change even the desires of your heart and give you peace instead of tyranny.

Soaking up His love and presence like a sponge, I am one who has been and who is still being changed to become more like Jesus.

I study. I learn. I pray. I work. And I grow.

This commitment to intimacy and growth is the greatest thing I can do for God and my fellow man. I hazard to guess; it's yours too. The first commandment is to love God with ALL of our hearts, mind, soul, and strength. It precedes the second – to love our neighbor as ourselves.

You see, when we genuinely love Him, He will reach back into us into the deepest unmet hunger and emotional needs in our hearts and meet them with Himself. His passion, intimacy, and presence are like a drug from which there is no high that satisfies. To this, I am an addict, and as I receive my daily 'fix,' I can work with Him to fix this broken Creation.

I am not you, and you are not me. You are unique, and your gift and calling are different than anyone else's on the planet.

Yet, you will never find satisfaction in the Creation until you intimately know Him, your Creator. There is a place of intimacy He is calling you to....

now!

> *2 Corinthians 6:16–18 and what agreement hath the temple of God with idols? For ye are the temple of the living God; as God hath said, I will dwell in them and walk in them; and I will be their God, and they shall be my people. Wherefore come out from among them, and be ye separate, saith the Lord, and touch not the unclean thing; and I will receive you, and will be a Father unto you, and ye shall be my sons and daughters, saith the Lord Almighty.*

I know it seems weird to slow down so that you can speed up — schedule time where you sit at His feet. Maybe you can play the audio Bible like I do and go into 'soaking' mode, allowing Holy Spirit to go deep inside your soul and minister to your deepest hunger. Honestly, the fate of the world rests upon it!

Let's Pray:

> *'Father, meet with me. I need You, show me my need, my hunger, passions, longings, that You alone can satiate. Visit me, speak to me, reveal to me Your love, Your presence, Your passion, Your purpose for my life, for I come to Your throne only by Your shed blood, Lord Jesus. Amen.'*

**For prayer, comments, or to donate online, email me at chris.aomministries@gmail.com**

# 28

# Freely Give

*1 Corinthians 9:11 If we have sown [the seed of] spiritual good among you, [is it too] much if we reap from your material benefits?*

*1 Corinthians 9:14 [On the same principle], the Lord directed that those who publish the good news (the Gospel) should live (get their maintenance) by the Gospel.*

Paul goes on to say that he did not use his position as a minister of the gospel to take up offerings, but instead, he worked to make tents to support himself.

You might notice here that Paul was not married, nor did he have children. Family responsibilities take time, and just as you bust a move on your job to provide for your family, I work every bit as hard, doing this, faithful to the Lord in prayer and the ministry of His Word to you.

I will never charge for this: it is my responsibility to God. Freely I have been given; now I freely give.

As you give, hear Holy Spirit what to give and honestly expect God to reward you for your giving.

*Matt 10: 41-42 He who receives and welcomes and accepts a prophet because he is a prophet shall receive a prophet's reward, and he who receives and welcomes and accepts a righteous man because he is a righteous man shall receive a righteous man's reward. And whoever gives to one of these little ones [in rank or influence] even a cup of cold water because he is My disciple, surely I declare to you, he shall not lose his reward.*

I am a five-fold ministry gift and office – this is my life – I pray, I hear, I write, and wonderful things happen. You have your job description. I have mine – this is mine.

I have 'see-through' faith for you in this: Gal 3:9 *So then they which be of faith are blessed with faithful Abraham.*

I believe I have a responsibility before God to be like Jesus in every offering I receive. I receive it with thanksgiving, just like Jesus received the little boy's lunch. Then, because I walk and live by faith according to the blessing of Abraham, I believe that God will take your seed sown, and multiply it, according to what the blessing of Abraham promises:

*Genesis 22:17 In blessing, I will bless you and in multiplying I will multiply your descendants like the stars of the heavens and like the sand on the seashore. And your Seed (Heir) will possess the gate of His enemies.*

It has been a joy to me to see the hand of the living God act in the lives of those who have supported us this year!

Many have seen the tremendous blessing come into your households, and for this, we give thanks and give Jesus all the glory!

# 29

# The Sabbath

*Colossians 2:16 Let no man, therefore, judge you in meat, or in drink, or in respect of a holy day, or of the new moon, or of the sabbath days:*

*Ex 31:13-17 Speak thou also unto the children of Israel, saying, Verily my sabbaths ye shall keep: for it is a sign between me and you throughout your generations; that ye may know that I am the LORD that doth sanctify you. Ye shall keep the sabbath therefore; for it is holy unto you: every one that defileth it shall surely be put to death: for whosoever doeth any work therein, that soul shall be cut off from among his people.*

*Six days may work be done; but in the seventh is the sabbath of rest, holy to the LORD: whosoever doeth any work in the sabbath day, he shall surely be put to death. Wherefore the children of Israel shall keep the sabbath, to observe the sabbath throughout their generations, for a perpetual covenant.*

*It is a sign between me and the children of Israel forever: for in six days the LORD made heaven and earth, and on the seventh day he rested and was refreshed.*

So, the Sabbath is from sundown on Friday to sunset Saturday. If my schedule permits, I love to rest during this time to honor the eternal record forever established in the heavens.

Yet, we see hospital workers, retail, police, etc., all having to work Saturdays in this society. It is probably not God's best. It would be good for us to all rest one day per week as a society.

J. Vernon McGee tells this story about a man who wanted to argue about the Sabbath.

* * *

The man said, *"I'll give you $100 if you show me where the Sabbath day has been changed."*

McGee answered, *"I don't think it has been changed. Saturday is Saturday; it is the seventh day of the week, and it is the Sabbath day. I realize our calendar has been adjusted and can be off a few days, but we won't even consider that point. The seventh day is still Saturday, and it is still the Sabbath day."*

He got a gleam in his eye and said, *"Then why don't you keep the Sabbath day if it hasn't been changed?"*

McGee answered, *"the DAY hasn't changed, but I have been changed. I've been given a new nature now; I am joined to Christ; I am a part of the new creation. We celebrate the first day because that is the day He rose from the grave."*

* * *

That is what it means that the ordinances have been nailed to the cross (Colossians 2:14).

Now, we have theologians arguing about whether weekly worship services should be on Saturday or Sunday.

> *Mark 2:27 He said unto them, The* **sabbath** *was made* **for man**, *and not* **man for** *the* **sabbath.**

The Sabbath is Saturday, but the spirit of the Sabbath is the love of God. Rest sometimes!

Take a day off a week and relax! Recreation is RE-Creation. Come back to your Creator and experience times of refreshing in His presence. Too simple for most, I guess.

Let's Pray:

*Father, help us to rest, completely, one day/week. In Your name, I pray, Lord Jesus, Amen.*

# 30

# A Shepherd's Heart's True Intercession

A shepherd's heart is faithful intercession.

*Ex 32: 30 And it came to pass on the morrow, that Moses said unto
the people, Ye have sinned a great sin: and now I will go up unto
the LORD; peradventure I shall make an atonement for your sin. And
Moses returned unto the LORD, and said, Oh, this people have sinned
a great sin, and have made them gods of gold. Yet now, if thou wilt
forgive their sin−; and if not, blot me, I pray thee, out of thy book
which thou hast written. And the LORD said unto Moses, Whosoever
hath sinned against me, him will I blot out of my book.*

*Php 4:3 And I entreat thee also, true yokefellow, help those women
which labored with me in the gospel, with Clement also, and with
other my fellow-laborers, whose names are in the book of life.*

*Rev3:5 He that overcometh, the same shall be clothed in white raiment;
and I will not blot out his name out of the book of life, but I will confess
his name before my Father, and before his angels.*

We see here real ministry through leaders who recognize that what they do
holds eternal consequence. Moses, when he rebuked the people, they came

to him. He approached God, willing to die, eternally, on behalf of the people God gave into his care in sacrificial. This is an example of eternal love.

God heard him and received his prayer. God spared his life, both temporally and eternally, with His reply: *v33 And the LORD said unto Moses, Whosoever hath sinned against me, him will I blot out of my book.*

**Free will has eternal consequences.**

So the apostle Paul recognized the same as sacrificial servants who worked with him in the gospel. He spoke by revelation of an actual event that he understood to have occurred in the heavenlies. Their names were written in the Book of Life, a genuine book, before the throne of God, that keeps an eternal record of who might enter heaven and what their reward might be forever.

In Revelation, we see a judgment occurring upon Christians implies that some had their names removed or blotted out from the book of life for failing to overcome. The eternal question the Holy Spirit commands me to ask you today is this:

Is **your** name written in the Book of Life?

Have you made Him your Lord? Or do you merely pay lip service to a dead church, full of dead traditions and rituals, void of the presence of God in His holiness and power?

Let's Pray:

*Father, reveal Yourself to my friend reading this! Show them the reality of who You are. May help come to them now in this sanctuary as this very Word enters the earth. May they bow to your Lordship, Jesus, and serve and seek You daily, without compromise. Amen.*

# 31

# Where I Will Meet You...

These are the words that come alive from the pages of Scripture today!

> *Ex 29:42 This shall be a continual burnt offering throughout your generations at the door of the tabernacle of the congregation before the LORD:* **where I will meet you**, *to speak there unto thee.  43 And there I will meet with the children of Israel, and the tabernacle shall be sanctified by my glory. After all of our works of obedience and love, this truth remains: He will meet with us!*

We must remember Who HE is!

Sovereign God of all creation, the One who spoke the universe into being. He will meet with us and speak to us.

> *Ex 29:42 This shall be a continual burnt offering throughout your generations at the door of the tabernacle of the congregation before the LORD:* **where I will meet you**, *to speak there unto thee. And there I will meet with the children of Israel, and the tabernacle shall be sanctified by my glory.*

He first speaks with His leaders; then, He meets with the people and brings comfort, direction, order, grace to them in a way we never could.

My thought of the day is that the highest truth in all the Word of God is that God Almighty looks down from heaven and sees us. He takes time to speak to us individually and corporately in a place called 'there,' the particular area of our obedience.

Let's pray:

*Father, show us our place of obedience, the place we each get to offer our lives as a living sacrifice to You, that You might meet us, and speak to us and, in that meeting, and Your glory be revealed. In Your name, I pray, Lord Jesus. Amen.*

# 32

# Kingdom Business Outreach

Some years ago, when I was running hard keeping our construction company going, we filmed these testimonies of business owners who have trusted Jesus to build successful companies.

From what I understand, these were translated into Urdu and aired in Pakistan.

We have not copy-written them. Feel free to use them as you see fit for the glory of God.

### Give In Faith

*1 Corinthians 9:11 If we have sown [the seed of] spiritual good among you, [is it too] much if we reap from your material benefits?*

*1 Corinthians 9:14 [On the same principle], the Lord directed that those who publish the good news (the Gospel) should live (get their maintenance) by the Gospel.*

Paul goes on to say that he did not use his position as a minister of the gospel to take up offerings; instead, he worked at making tents to support himself. You might notice here that Paul was not married, nor did he have children. Family responsibilities take time, and just as you bust and move on your job to provide for your family, I work every bit as hard doing this and remain faithful to the Lord in prayer and the ministry of His Word to you.

I will never charge for this; it is my responsibility to God. It is my calling. Freely I have been given, now, I freely give.

As you give, listen to the Holy Spirit as to what to give and honestly expect God to reward you for your giving.

> *Matt 10:41 He who receives and welcomes and accepts a prophet because he is a prophet shall receive a prophet's reward; he who receives and welcomes and accepts a righteous man because he is a righteous man shall receive a righteous man's reward. 42 And whoever gives to one of these little ones [in rank or influence] even a cup of cold water because he is My disciple, surely I declare to you, he shall not lose his reward.*

I am a five-fold ministry gift and office. This is my life. I pray, I hear, I write, and wonderful things happen. You have your job description; I have mine – this is mine.

I have 'see-through' faith for you in this:

> *Gal 3:9 So then they which be of faith are blessed with faithful Abraham.*

I believe I have a responsibility before God to be like Jesus in every offering I receive. I receive it with thanksgiving just like Jesus received the little boy's lunch. Then, because I walk and live by faith according to the blessing of Abraham, I believe that God will take your seed sown and multiply it, according to what the blessing of Abraham promises:

> *Genesis 22:17 In blessing, I will bless you and in multiplying I will multiply your descendants like the stars of the heavens and like the sand on the seashore.*

And your Seed (Heir) will possess the gate of His enemies

It has been my joy to see the hand of the living God act in the lives of those of you who have supported us this year!

Many have seen the tremendous blessing come into your households, and for this, we give thanks and give Jesus all the glory!

# 33

# True Grace

The only right living we will ever experience is ONLY by the grace of God.

*Titus 2:11-12 For the grace of God that bringeth salvation hath appeared to all men.* **Teaching us** *that, denying ungodliness and worldly lusts, we should live soberly, righteously, and godly, in this present world;*

It is grace that **teaches us** to live right and grace alone.

Here's the way Jesus has worked this out in my life: I do certain things with good intentions that, in many cases, fall short of excellence due to my immaturity and lack of knowledge. As I go to the Lord to try and figure out why certain ventures did not turn out the way I had planned, often, He shows me a much higher way of doing the thing that demands far greater excellence of moral character.

So, I cry out to Him for **GRACE** to excel, to improve, to learn, to love, to walk in truth, that I can live a more righteous life.

Yes, I know that, positionally, before the throne of God, I am loved, accepted, forgiven and that because of the blood of Jesus, I cannot ever become more holy than Jesus has already made me. Yet, the throne of God is called 'the throne of grace,' the place where His power comes to teach me in love and how to live the extraordinary moral life I long to live.

Some have forgotten this truth, that God is holy, and they preach a false grace, saying we can do as we please because God loves us.

*Jude 1:4 For there are certain men crept in unawares, who were before of old ordained to this condemnation, ungodly men, turning the grace of our God into lasciviousness, and denying the only Lord God, and our Lord Jesus Christ.*

When Jesus forgave the woman caught in adultery, hear His words:

*John 8:10-11(NLT) Then Jesus stood up again and said to the woman, 'Where are your accusers? Didn't even one of them condemn you?''No, Lord,' she said. And Jesus said, 'Neither do I. Go and sin no more.'"*

*John 8:11 (BRG) She said, No man, Lord.  And Jesus said unto her, Neither do I condemn thee: go, and sin no more.*

What a fascinating account that reveals the love and power of God!

In love, Jesus forgave this woman about to be stoned. If this were all He did, it would be a beautiful story; yet, as Lord of the universe, Whose eternal words carry the power of God, He did something else. He said: **GO AND SIN NO MORE.**

In those words came not only His manifest forgiveness but also His power to leave her life of sin. Grace, the power of God, is the ONLY thing that can free us from a sinful lifestyle. The law will never accomplish this.

It is only those that hunger and thirst for righteousness that will be filled.

Let's pray:

*Father, I know you love me and have only good for my life. Teach me to live pure and holy with excellence before You.  Show me the next level of honor that You would have me to walk in and then give me the grace to do it. I ask this, knowing I am heard and answered, for I ask in Your name, Lord Jesus. Amen.*

# 34

# The Discipline of Silence

*Matt 27: 12 And when he was accused of the chief priests and elders, he answered nothing.*

A great strength of the heart is needed to be quiet and trust the Lord when you are falsely accused. If we can guard our hearts and say nothing, even when people are raging, we see the power of God to deliver as long as we do not bow to their pressure. When you have spoken the Word of God over your circumstance, the power of God is always working to deliver you out of the hand of man, all men, no matter what people try to get you to agree to. Refuse to speak when anything you say will obviously be twisted and used against you.

"During his years as premier of the Soviet Union, Nikita Khrushchev denounced many of the policies and atrocities of Joseph Stalin.

Once, as he censured Stalin in a public meeting, Khrushchev was interrupted by a shout from a heckler in the audience.

*"You were one of Stalin's colleagues. Why didn't you stop him?"*

*"Who said that?"* roared Khrushchev.

An agonizing silence followed as nobody in the room dared move a muscle.

Then Khrushchev replied quietly, *"Now you know why."* (*Today in the Word,*

July 13, 1993)

It had been a rather stormy board meeting, and some disconcerting things had been said. One man—always highly respected and unusually wise in his judgments—had said nothing throughout the proceedings. Suddenly one of the leaders in the argument turned to him,

*"You have not said a word. I am sure we would all like to hear your opinion about this matter."*

*"I have discovered,"* replied the quiet one, *"that there are many times when silence is an opinion." (Bits & Pieces*, September 1989)

Let's Pray:

> *Father, set a watch upon my lips before my enemies. Give me the strength to trust You and never betray You with my words. In your name, I pray, Lord Jesus. Amen.*

* * *

> *Matt 27: 12 And when he was accused of the chief priests and elders, he answered nothing.*

> *1 Peter 2:23 Who, when he was **reviled, reviled** not again; when he suffered, he threatened not; but committed himself to him that judgeth righteously:*

Notice here, that silence is not agreement with another's evil, and that in this case, you are not doing anything by not speaking. What you are doing is aggressively, on purpose, trusting in our Father, Creator of the Universe, to do right in our case, and to act as He pleases. Yet, there is a time to speak too.

What would you do here when speaking out would probably cost you your very life?

Only you and the Holy Spirit can make that decision.

God is love, and sometimes the most loving thing He does is not speaking.

Why? Because He is also holy, and sometimes when someone is far from Him doing things contrary to His nature and His Word, if He were to speak, the only thing He could say would be a word of judgment. Rather than judge (for with His judgments, come the execution of those judgments), He remains silent for a time:

> 2 Peter 3:9 *The Lord is not slack concerning his promise, as some men count slackness; but is **longsuffering** to us-ward, not willing that any should perish, but that all should come to repentance.*

God is love, and Jesus's mission remains the same, to seek and save the lost, not condemn them.

Yet, just because He is longsuffering does not mean He ever condones evil; we cannot mistake His silence for His permission.

# 35

# The Weightier Matter of Life

*Matt 23:23 Woe unto you, scribes and Pharisees, hypocrites! For ye pay tithe of mint and anise and cumin, and have omitted the **weightier matters of the law, judgment, mercy,** and faith: these ought ye to have done, and not to leave the other undone.*

As I read this passage of Scripture, the words 'Weightier Matters' jumped off the page at me, making me think carefully about the weightier matters of life. So, I looked up this verse in several other versions.

**Matthew 23:23** *Amplified Bible (AMP) Woe to you, scribes and Pharisees, pretenders (hypocrites)! For you give a tenth of your mint and dill and cumin and have neglected and omitted the weightier (more important) matters of the Law—right and justice and mercy and fidelity. These you ought [particularly] to have done without neglecting the others.*

**Matthew 23:23** *The Message (MSG) "You'Rev hopeless, you religion scholars and Pharisees! Frauds! You keep meticulous account books, tithing on every nickel and dime you get, but on the meat of God's Law, things like fairness and compassion and commitment—the absolute*

158

*basics! —you carelessly take it or leave it. Careful bookkeeping is commendable, but the basics are required. Do you have any idea how silly you look, writing a life story that's wrong from start to finish, nitpicking over commas, and semicolons?*

## Justice, Mercy, and Faith

What a topic! This land of the free and home of the brave is where we strive for freedom, liberty, and justice for all.

If we can't get it right in the church house, there is no hope for the White House!

*1 Peter 4:17 For the time is come that **judgment** must begin at the house of God: and if it first begin at us, what shall the end be of them that obey not the gospel of God?*

Let's look at Webster's simple definition of 'Justice.'

- Justice is the process or result of using laws to judge and punish crimes and criminals fairly: a judge in a court of law
- **Justice** —used as a title for a judge (such as a judge of the U.S. Supreme
- *1a*: the maintenance or administration of what is just especially by the impartial adjustment of conflicting claims or the assignment of merited rewards or punishments: judges: the administration of law; *especially*: the establishment or determination of rights according to the rules of law or equity
- *2a*: the quality of being just, impartial, or fair *(1)*: the principle or ideal of just dealing or right action *(2)*: conformity to this principle or ideal: righteousness: the quality of conforming to the law
- *3*: conformity to truth, fact, or reason: correctness

I am not an attorney, legislator, nor judge. Yet, as a man of God, determined to walk in holiness and integrity, I am required to look at justice, mercy, and faith. We see *Lady Justice* with scales in one hand and a sword in the other. How well I knew it all after finishing Bible school, full of the Word of God, determined to make a difference in our generation, a man on fire for Jesus, filled with spiritual power, loving my enemies, walking by faith, knowing that the Word of God held every answer to humanity's needs, for it is written:

> *2 Peter 1:2 Grace and peace be multiplied unto you through the knowledge of God, and of Jesus our Lord,*

According to as his divine power hath given unto us **all things** that pertain unto life and godliness, through the knowledge of him that hath called us to glory and virtue:

Whereby are given unto us exceeding great and precious promises: that by these ye might be partakers of the divine nature, having escaped the corruption that is in the world through lust.

I still believe that, that Jesus is the answer, and that through His promises, we can overcome any difficulty this world throws at us, for

> *1 Cor 15:57 But thanks be to God, which giveth us the victory through our Lord Jesus Christ.*

> *1 John 5:4 For whatsoever is born of God overcometh the world: and this is the victory that overcometh the world, even our faith.*

If we walk in love and stand bold in faith, we will see victory in this life in every arena!

Then, I realized that not everyone sees it that way. Some people are not ever going to see it and receive the love of God, nor will they decide to walk in faith.

God gave people free will, and it has amazed me over the years how firmly people will hold on to their will over the will of God!

The United States has three branches of government, while the kingdom of God only has two:

The political government of the country and the authority of God invested in His Church. Where these two meets is an interesting dynamic.

Let's give a couple of examples:

As a pastor, I have performed marriages and marriage counseling for church members. Yet, what about the divorcee? What does a child custody agreement need to look like?

Or how about our outreach to folks struggling with an addiction? People are broken, battered, and abused by their helplessness to stop the insatiable cravings for their drug of choice.

Let me tell a story:

* * *

Several years ago, a community that I pastored in had a drug problem. It was a government housing project, and one night in a drug raid, they arrested 70 people! They shut down seven crack houses in a day! Glory to God, right?

Yet, God directed me to open an alcohol drug program for those hopelessly addicted, and suddenly our life became interesting!

I promised to love and walk with the 22 addicts that joined my program, through whatever they got themselves into, on one condition: they had to be willing to take a 6-month, 26-lesson course.

I had to mediate unpaid drug debts, go to hospitals to visit sick or overdosed folks, attend family court with those who had children, and regularly go to the local jails and prisons to visit people.

Some of these court sessions were brutal yet enlightening and sometimes comical.

Here's another story from The Book of Blunders:

"Supreme Court Justice Horace Gray once informed a man who had appeared before him in a lower court and had escaped conviction on a technicality, *'I know that you are guilty, and you know it. I wish for you to remember that one day you will stand before a better and wiser Judge and that there you will be dealt with according to justice and not according to law.'*

Surprised while burgling a house in Antwerp, Belgium, the thief fled out the back door, clambered over a nine-foot wall, dropped down the other side, and found himself in the city prison." (*Oops: The Book of Blunders,* 1980)

As a pastor, I always stood in love with the person in my care, but as a man of God, I could never lie nor agree with sinful choices they had made.

Sometimes the courts had mercy. Other times, folks went to jail, but here I stood in love, compassion, and faith believing the best for the addict, while the courts read the muck and mire they had been involved in.

Brokenness and tears were my portions during that season, crying out to God for mercy and deliverance for these suffering souls, and by His grace, 21 of the 22 folks who went through the program remain alcohol and drug-free ten years later.

This whole season was not a formula, but a vital living relationship with the Holy Spirit, seeking Him for wisdom as to how to help people and for the judges to know what to do also.

Love with skin on.

> *John 1:14 And the **Word** was made **flesh** and dwelt among us (and we beheld his glory, the glory as of the only begotten of the Father) full of grace and truth.*

How easy it would have been to become cold and clinical, detached, and to say to those broken people: well, you did the crime, now do the time.

This appears to be the position of these religious leaders in Jesus's day. They knew the letter of the law but had not experienced God personally so that their example had become cold, sterile, lifeless, and devoid of love and power.

How easy it is for us in caregiving positions to become this way!

Doctors, nurses, counselors, health care, senior care, we must break before Him, often daily, or quietly die inside. If you have died inside, here's good news:

> *Ezekiel 36:26 A new **heart** also will I give you, and a new spirit will I put within you: and I will take away the **stony heart** out of your flesh, and I will give you a **heart** of flesh.*

Pray for tears that He again break your heart with the things that are breaking His.

Thank God for the eternal standard of the Word of God and His holiness that we all seek to emulate! Holiness is simply another word for LOVE...

> *1 Cor 13:1 Yet, without love, we are clanging gongs and have not charity; I have become as sounding brass or a tinkling cymbal.*

### Freedom, Liberty, And Justice For All

Jesus said, knowing Him and Him alone will produce true freedom.

> *John 8:32 And ye shall know the truth, and the truth shall make you free.*

Then there is a walk of faith and intimacy with God, where the Holy Spirit is given preeminence that will produce liberty.

> *2 Cor 3:17 Now the Lord is that Spirit: and where the Spirit of the Lord is, there is liberty.*

Yet, mercy is what we all need, forgiveness at the feet of a holy God.

> *Romans 15:9 And that the Gentiles might glorify God for his mercy; as it is written, for this cause, I will confess to thee among the Gentiles, and sing unto thy name.*

> *James 2:13 For he shall have judgment without mercy, that hath*

*shewed no mercy; and mercy rejoiceth against judgment.*

* * *

A mother once approached Napoleon seeking a pardon for her son. The emperor replied that the young man had committed a specific offense twice, and justice demanded death.

*"But I don't ask for justice,"* the mother explained. *"I plead for mercy."*

*"But, your son does not deserve mercy,"* Napoleon replied.

*"Sir,"* the woman cried, *"it would not be mercy if he deserved it, and mercy is all I ask for."*

*"Well, then,"* the emperor said, *"I will have mercy."*

And he spared the woman's son. (Luis Palau, *Experiencing God's Forgiveness,* Multnomah Press, 1984)

* * *

Let's Pray:

*Father, we recognize that people make wrong choices. There are sure consequences to those choices. Father, for those of us in leadership, empower us to do what we must to restrain evil in our generation, always operating in Your love for people. Have mercy on us today and give us the courage to continue to care, love, and pursue You in purity of heart before You. May we continue to trust and obey You. May the strong muscles of our faith break every chain that would attempt to hold us back from the destiny You have created us to walk. In Your name I pray, Lord Jesus. Amen.*

# 36

# Are All Politicians Liars

*Matt 24:7 For nation shall rise against nation, and kingdom against kingdom:*

So, we are living in the last days, and if we were to base our faith upon what we see in the news media, life would be constant turmoil and stress, for *Prov 23:7 For as he thinketh in his heart, so is he.*

No, as Christians, we must be people of the Word. *For Psalm 119:165 Great peace have they which love thy law: and nothing shall offend them.*

Our thoughts must be pure.

*Phil 4:8 Finally, brethren, whatsoever things are true, whatsoever things are honest, whatsoever things are just, whatsoever things are pure, whatsoever things are lovely, whatsoever things are of good report; if there be any virtue, and if there be any praise, think on these things.*

So, what happens to a man in politics? I believe that many a person enters the political arena with pure intentions, sincere in their desire to contribute to a better nation, determined to do right and provide honest leadership to countries that are often facing some degree of chaos or another. The job of leadership is to bring order out of chaos, and influential leaders should honestly be trying to do what is best for all the people they are called to serve, both rich and poor alike.

Yet, let's consider this thought: What if a leader makes a sincere decision that they believe is right for the country, but that is not entirely in line with the Word or Spirit of God for that nation?

What happens?

Well, no matter what government you live under politically, there are always two forms of government under God, the political one and the Church of our Lord Jesus Christ exercising God's authority through prayer.

So, we have the nations of man rising up in conflict with one another, influenced in many cases by demonic principalities and powers, and Holy Spirit then alerts intercessors to pray and stop evil works in the earth.

Kingdom arises against Kingdom!

The Kingdom of God arises against satanic rule and oppression.

So, what about the politicians?

Well, after the church prays, and smashes mind blinding spirits from their lives, God pours out His spirit on all flesh, and we discover that *Prov 21:1 The king's heart is in the hand of the LORD, as the rivers of water: he turneth it whithersoever he will.*

After the Church prays for the political leaders, God deals with the leaders' hearts. And they realize that though they may have been sincere, they may have been sincerely wrong.

If they are wise, they humble themselves before God and change their minds, and set a correct course for their leadership before a holy God.

When it looks like they have changed their mind, generally, the media screams 'Liar, liar, pants on fire!' but those that are rational fear not the press, nor any man, but God alone to Whom each of us must one day give an account.

*"My concern is not whether God is on our side; my greatest concern is to be on God's side, for God is always right." Abraham Lincoln*

## ARE ALL POLITICIAN LIARS

*"I'm a success today because I had a friend who believed in me, and I didn't have the heart to let him down."* Abraham Lincoln

We who know Jesus have a true friend who will never let us down.

*Prov 18:24 A man that hath friends must shew himself friendly, and there is a friend that sticketh closer than a brother.*

Jesus is that friend that sticks closer than a brother, the one who truly loves and understands us.  He is the one we must ultimately be faithful to, no matter what other men say or do!

So, to answer my own question: 'Are all politicians, liars?'

My answer is this: It depends only upon their motive of the heart. If they have a sincere desire to do right and are humble, they will remain teachable before God and will be willing to change their minds when they discover the error of their ways.

In my mind, this does not make them liars; rather, men and women of God.

What do you think?

Let's Pray:

*Father, help me to do right and to pray for every person holding any position in government, political, military, or judicial office, that You might lead them and guide them in all truth. Grant us light, integrity, courage, strength, health, and wisdom to live fully for You and Your interests in our nation, bringing your kingdom in righteousness, peace, and joy in the Holy Spirit. Amen.*

# 37

# Your Heavenly Calling

Take your place and lead!

*Psalm 20:6 Now know I that the LORD saveth his anointed; he will
hear him from his holy heaven with the saving strength of his right
hand.*

A time and season come in the life of a Christian when one can no longer
sit back and watch others lead, preach, teach, serve, and do exploits for the
kingdom of God. You can no longer be a fan nor a bench-warmer on God's
team. It's time to enter the game!

Birth can be a bloody, painful, messy, even traumatic event, but after
the baby is born, it cries, smiles, and begins to nurse. Then, all the pain is
forgotten.

Like a sporting event, you may participate in every aspect. There you are
about to step onto the field of play, with adrenaline pumping, butterflies in
your gut, but ready to play and determined to win!

As you begin to step up to the battle, you may well discover that folks you
thought were your friends have become enemies. These are people who are
a little too familiar with who **they** think you are. They haven't been up in the
night in anguished prayer; they have not heard the things God has spoken
to you, and they want to pigeon hole you into a nice little compartment in

their mind.

Your heavenly calling and destiny have spoken, and you embrace the life you were born to live!

Suddenly, people you thought you knew, oppose you. Even Jesus faced it.

*John 6:42 And they said, Is not this Jesus, the son of Joseph, whose father and mother we know? How is it then that he saith, I came down from heaven?*

It was okay for Jesus to be a carpenter, son of Joseph, but Messiah, Son of God? NO WAY, they say.

You, too, have come down from heaven into the kingdom for such a time of this. You were anointed, and now it is time to step out in obedience to Holy Spirit, for you are being appointed by God for position, rank, privilege, and power in the kingdom for such a time as this.

And your enemies rage, rail, insinuate, assassinate your character, and seek to undermine your heart, your message, your motive, and your mission, simply because they do not understand you.

People are generally creatures of comfort, determined to destroy anything they find threatening or that threatens their understanding. In this case, that is you!

Yet, you pray, and the call is sure, and you tentatively begin to move forward, and it seems like all hell breaks loose! Allegations, accusations, innuendos, misunderstandings come from others, simply because they have not heard God concerning you.

They need to be spending as much time praying for you as talking about you! So, what are you going to do?

Are you tempted to lash back in anger and blast them with the Word?

It doesn't work. Been there, done that.

*James 1:20 For the **wrath of man** worketh not the righteousness **of** God.*

Here is what you must do:

1. Guard your heart and be careful who you disclose precious secrets from heaven to.
2. Determine to stay out of strife, gossip, offense, or bitterness.
3. Pray often and fervently for the perfect will of God; let God deal with them.
4. Move forward in the call of God, hear Holy Spirit, and go for it!

> *Isaiah 49:2 And he hath made my mouth like a sharp **sword**; in the shadow of his hand hath he hid me, and made me a polished shaft; in his quiver hath he hid me;*

If you do these things, misunderstanding and persecution will drive you to your knees in prayer and deeper into the word of God. It will sharpen you, not stop you.

Here a couple of verses I have found comfort in:

> *Prov 16:7 When a man's ways please the LORD, he maketh even his enemies to be at peace with him. Eventually, people will get it, but not today.*

> *Rom 12:21 Be not overcome of evil but overcome evil with good.*

> *Matt 5:44 But I say unto you, Love your enemies, bless them that curse you, do good to them that hate you, and pray for them which despitefully use you, and persecute you;*

> *Psalm 5:12 For thou, LORD, wilt bless the righteous; with favor wilt thou compass him as with a shield.*

> *Rom 12:17 Recompense to no man evil for evil. Provide things honest in the sight of all men.*

*2 Thes 1:6 Seeing it is a righteous thing with God to recompense tribulation to them that trouble you;*

*Psalm 31:20 Thou shalt hide them in the secret **of** thy presence from the pride **of** man: thou shalt keep them secretly in a pavilion from the **strife of tongues**.*

*Heb 10:30 For we know him that hath said, Vengeance belongeth unto me, I will recompense, saith the Lord And again, The Lord shall judge his people.*

*Isa 54:17 No weapon that is formed against thee shall prosper; and every tongue that shall rise against thee in judgment thou shalt condemn. This is the heritage of the servants of the LORD, and their righteousness is of me, saith the LORD.*

I heard Kenneth E Hagin say regarding persecution: *"No attack, no defense."*

When persecuted, he determined to walk in love and refused to attack his persecutors back. When he moved in God and preached cutting-edge sermons straight from the heart of God and folks got upset over them, he refused to defend himself but kept on obeying God.

I heard another minister say this about Isa 54:17, how the Lord showed him that as he prayed this very verse that in the realm of the Spirit was a two-edged sword. On one side, the folks that loved him and prayed for him received a blessing such as anointing, grace, prosperity, healing, and every good thing.

Yet the other side of the sword, the judgment of God was upon devils and the people that tried to stop him.

He said it this way: *"Fear God, Folks. You may not like me, but do not get in my way. If you don't like me, pray for me, and God will bless you. If you don't, you will discover that the other side of this sword will cut you and deliver me, and you can join the rest of the pile of bodies at my feet."*

Let's Pray:

*Father, as I step out in your calling, I see enemies arrayed against me. I honestly love them and want to help them according to Your Word. Father, I forgive them. I pray that your goodness and love might lead them to repentance. I lift up your Word, and believe that You surround me with favor as with a shield, and that no weapon formed against me shall prosper, and every tongue risen up against me might be silenced. In your name, I pray, Lord Jesus. Amen.*

# 38

# By Them Is Thy Servant Warned

*Psalm 19:9-11 The fear of the Lord is clean, enduring forever: the judgments of the Lord are true and righteous altogether. More to be desired are they than gold, yea, than much fine gold: sweeter also than honey and the honeycomb. Moreover by them is thy servant warned: and in the keeping of them there is great reward.*

People make choices in life that have brutal consequences. After praying fervently, the only thing to do is to love them and let the chips fall where they may. There are always consequences to violations of the Word of God.

I heard a minister say: *"Every person in life is either encouragement or an illustration of what not do. We can learn from all people, as long as we gauge our lives by the Scripture."*

If we are alert, we can see these consequences in the lives of others and avoid the pain similar decisions would cause us. In the meantime, we are called to love people and trust Jesus to do miracles. He delights to forgive, show mercy, and restore broken people and lives.

Let's Pray:

*Father, open our eyes to the consequences of our decisions. Help us to see clearly in the lives of others. Help us see Your Word working either in deliverance or judgment upon their sin. Cause us to pursue and walk in purity and holiness and to run from evil. For those around us who violate Your Word, help us to be the answer, not the critic in their lives. Give us authentic love for them and help us to be quick to restore them after they have repented. I ask this, knowing that You heard me for I ask in Your name, Lord Jesus. AMEN.*

39

# Negotiations - Not Every Offering Is Acceptable

*2 Kings 5:26 Is it a time to receive money?*

I remember this verse well, but to begin, let's look at the account of Abraham searching for a burial place for his beloved wife, Sarah.

*Gen 23: 4 I am a stranger and a sojourner with you: give me a possession of a burying place with you, that I may bury my dead out of my sight.*

*And the children of Heth answered Abraham, saying unto him, 6 Hear us, my lord: thou art a mighty prince among us: in the choice of our sepulchres bury thy dead; none of us shall withhold from thee his sepulchre, but that thou mayest bury thy dead.*

*And Abraham stood up, and bowed himself to the people of the land, even to the children of Heth.*

*And he communed with them, saying, If it be your mind that I should bury my dead out of my sight; hear me, and entreat for me to Ephron, the son of Zohar, that he may give me the cave of Machpelah, which he hath, which is in the end of his field; for as much money as it is worth, he shall give it to me for a possession of a burying place amongst you.*

*And Ephron dwelt among the children of Heth: and Ephron the Hittite answered Abraham in the audience of the children of Heth, even of all that went in at the gate of his city, saying, nay, my lord, hear me: the field give I thee, and the cave that is therein, I give it thee; in the presence of the sons of my people give I it thee: bury thy dead. And Abraham bowed down himself before the people of the land.*

*And he spake unto Ephron in the audience of the people of the land, saying, But if thou wilt give it, I pray thee, hear me: I will give thee money for the field; take it of me, and I will bury my dead there.*

*And Ephron answered Abraham, saying unto him, My lord, hearken unto me: the land is worth four hundred shekels of silver; what is that betwixt me and thee? bury therefore thy dead. And Abraham hearkened unto Ephron, and Abraham weighed to Ephron the silver, which he had named in the audience of the sons of Heth, four hundred shekels of silver, current money with the merchant.*

Notice the heart of Abraham here. He could have received this gravesite cave as a gift, but his heart wholly belonged to God full of honor.

He knew that, in the long run, not paying full price for this burial plot would have caused conflict between him and Ephron, and there is no honor in conflict. How? Think about it for a minute. The people in the community would say: Abraham is wealthy, yet he took some of our land to bury his wife. He could have paid for it, but he took advantage of 'Uncle' Ephron's kindness...You know how all that can go.

Reminds me of the heart of Elisha after Naaman was healed of leprosy, yet he did not receive an offering from him.

*2 Kings 5:15 And he returned to the man of God, he and all his company, and came, and stood before him: and he said, Behold, now I know that there is no God in all the earth, but in Israel: now therefore, I pray thee, take a blessing of thy servant. But he said, As the LORD liveth, before whom I stand, I will receive none.*

*And he urged him to take it, but he refused. And he said unto him, Went not mine heart with thee, when the man turned again from his chariot to meet thee? Is it a time to receive money, and to receive garments, and olive yards, and vineyards, and sheep, and oxen, and menservants, and maidservants?*

As we study church history, we have seen great abuses of spiritual authority in this area.

The great healing evangelists who would see the power of God open many deaf ears, or raise cripples miraculously from deathbeds or wheelchairs, only to announce: *'Now, let's honor God by taking up an offering!'*

As if one can buy the miraculous power of God!

*Matthew 10:8 Heal the sick, cleanse the lepers, raise the dead, cast out devils: freely ye have received, freely give.*

Not every offering is acceptable before God, and though folks may offer us money, gifts, great deals, not every offering is acceptable before God.

I remember how the Lord dealt with me along these lines while I attended Bible school at Rhema back in the '90s.

I had prayed for some new suits, and while at a revival meeting, a man approached me and told me that God told him to give me three new suits that he had just purchased. We went to his house after the meeting, and they were beautiful suits and exactly my size! I went home praising God, thanking Him for this blessing, but had a gentle nudge down in my heart that something wasn't quite right. I wasn't sure quite what yet.

The next morning, in devotions, the Lord showed me the motives of this man's heart that had given me the suits, and they were not right before him.

*Matt 9:4 And Jesus knowing their thoughts said, Wherefore think ye evil in your hearts?*

The man was extremely bitter against Rhema and was in gross rebellion towards God Himself. I prayed about what to do, and the Lord told me to return the suits that very minute to the man. So I jumped in my car and drove across town and left them on the doorknob of his house with a note on them. I never saw the man again, but God ignited my heart with joy, and I knew that I had done the right thing.

The heart of any faithful minister of God is to receive offerings in faith, just like Jesus received the little boy's lunch. When people give to us, we should not be merely grateful that OUR needs are being met, but more importantly, that they honored God in their giving. We could, with the faith of Abraham, believe God would multiply their gift exponentially so that THEIR needs are met. This is the heart of the apostle Paul in the famous verses, often misquoted at offering time that he wrote in his letter to the Philippians.

*Phil 4:16 For even in Thessalonica, ye sent once and again unto my necessity. Not because I desire a gift: but* I desire fruit that may abound to your account.

But I have all and abound: I am full, having received of Epaphroditus the things which were sent from you, an odor of a sweet smell, a sacrifice acceptable, well-pleasing to God.

But my God shall supply all your need according to his riches in glory by Christ Jesus.

Paul saw before the throne of God how God Himself was honoring the offerings of the Philippian church, and 'fruit was being added to their account' so that he could state clearly that God would become personally involved in their finances and would supply all of their needs according TO HIS RICHES IN GLORY by Christ Jesus.

I hope this helps someone today who trying to walk in their calling and to keep their heart right before the Lord.

Let's pray:

*Father God, I come before You right now, trusting You alone for all my provision. Show me where to give and where to receive. Give me* strength of heart to never be bought or compromised in our vital, living relationship. In your name, I pray, Lord Jesus, Amen.

# 40

# Increase Your Ability Before Investing

*Matt 25:15 And unto one, he gave five talents, to another two, and to another one; to every man according to his several ability; and straightway took his journey.*

You know the story of a man, a nobleman, who invested in his employees some investment capital before he went on a journey to become king.

He did this according to their ability!

Therefore ability precedes investment capital.

*Use what talents you possess: The woods would be very silent if no birds sang there except those that sang best.* Henry Van Dyke, Bits & Pieces, *March 31, 1994, p. 16.*

You know the rest of the story. One received five cities, the other ten because they were faithful with the ability they had been given.

What are we doing today to increase our abilities to lead? Because the welfare of the people we are called to influence in the cities we are to exercise our gifts in depends upon it.

I ask again, what are you doing today to increase your abilities?

Let's pray:

*Father God, increase my ability today. Teach me, help me to read the right books, articles, and Scripture to grow in my gift and calling today in your name. I pray, Lord Jesus. Amen.*

# 41

# Elihu - A Word For Young Leaders

Elihu did not get rebuked by God nor called on the mat to have Job pray for him. While Job's other three unwise counselors did, the Lord showed me why. Although Elihu was a younger man, he spoke by revelation, not information.

> *Job 28:12 But where shall wisdom be found? And where is the place of understanding? Man knoweth not the price thereof;* ***neither is it found in the land of the living.***

He revealed something incredibly powerful, the cross of Jesus Christ and the righteousness of God. Let's look at it.

> *Job 32:2 Then was kindled the wrath of Elihu, the son of Barachel the Buzite, of the kindred of Ram: against Job was his wrath kindled because he justified himself rather than God. Now Elihu had waited till Job had spoken because they were elder than he.*
>
> *And Elihu, the son of Barachel the Buzite, answered and said, I am young, and ye are very old; wherefore I was afraid, and durst not shew you mine opinion I said, Days should speak, and a multitude of years should teach wisdom. But there is a spirit in man: and the* ***inspiration of the Almighty*** *giveth them understanding.*

Out of the heart, the mouth speaketh, and Elihu had heard Job say…

> *Job 33:8 Surely thou hast spoken in mine hearing, and I have heard the voice of thy words, saying, I am clean without transgression. I am innocent; neither is there iniquity in me.*

Job, in his heart, is trusting in His works, not in the forgiveness, the cross, and the righteousness of God.

> *Job 1:5 And it was so, when the days of their feasting were gone about, that Job sent and sanctified them and rose up early in the morning and offered burnt offerings according to the number of them all: for Job said that it may be that my sons have sinned and cursed God in their hearts. Thus, did Job continually.*

*"88% of Catholics and a majority of Presbyterian and Methodist Evangelists [those who actively try to share their "faith"] believe that "if people are generally good, or do enough good things for others during their lives, they will earn a place in heaven."* (National & International Religion Report, August 23, 1993)

Elihu figured it out. Only the cross and the shed blood of Jesus can provide forgiveness for any man's sin.

> *Eph 2:8-9 For by grace are ye saved through faith; and that not of yourselves: it is the gift of God: Not of works, lest any man should boast.*

See it? Job was trusting in his good works.

> *Job 34: 11 For the work of a man shall he render unto him and cause every man to find according to his ways.*

We know this is what he believed for Jesus explained.

*Matt 12:34 for out of the abundance of the heart the mouth speaketh.*

Job had been blessed by God for his good works but was not righteous before God for them. In the holiness of God, all of us have sinned and fallen short of his glory. All of us need to be cleansed by the blood of Jesus; all of us must be cleansed for our sin.

*1 Cor 1:17 For Christ sent me not to baptize, but to preach the gospel: not with wisdom of words, lest the cross of Christ should be made of none effect.*

*1 Cor 1:18 For the preaching of the cross is to them that perish foolishness, but unto us which are saved it is the power of God*

*Php 3:18 For many walk, of whom I have told you often, and now tell you even weeping, that they are the enemies of the cross of Christ.*

*Job 35:1 Elihu spake moreover, and said, Thinkest thou this to be right, that thou saidst, My righteousness is more than God's? For thou saidst, What advantage will it be unto thee? And, What profit shall I have if I be cleansed from my sin?*

Churches are full of people without this revelation. Many people are working industriously to earn acceptance and approval before a holy God that will never be given apart from the cross of Jesus. People full of guilt and shame for their sin are trying to work it off before God, never fully able to accept His love because they have not yet received the justification that only comes through the cross.

I see them in the pews with fear and brokenness on their faces; they have no boldness, confidence, or love poured out because they have not yet received that liberating truth of the cross. It is that Jesus died for sinners and that He did it because He loves them. This understanding will produce joy, humility, gratefulness, and a holy boldness in the resurrection power of Jesus.

At the end of the book of Job, God shows up before him, in His wisdom and holiness.

> *Job 42:3 Who is he that hideth counsel without knowledge? Therefore have I uttered that I understood not; things too wonderful for me, which I knew not.*

Hear, I beseech thee, and I will speak: I will demand of thee and declare thou unto me.

I have heard of thee by the hearing of the ear: but now mine eye seeth thee. Wherefore I abhor myself and repent in dust and ashes.

Job got it. He repented. He humbled himself before a holy God. Yet then God began to deal with Job's counselors, and notice:

> *Job 42:7-10 And it was so, that after the LORD had spoken these words unto Job, the LORD said to Eliphaz the Temanite, My wrath is kindled against thee, and against thy two friends: for ye have not spoken of me the thing that is right, as my servant Job hath.*
>
> *Therefore take unto you now seven bullocks and seven rams, and go to my servant Job, and offer up for yourselves a burnt offering, and My servant Job shall pray for you: for him will I accept: lest I deal with you after your folly, in that ye have not spoken of me the thing which is right, like my servant Job.*
>
> *So Eliphaz the Temanite and Bildad the Shuhite and Zophar the Naamathite went and did according as the LORD commanded them: the LORD also accepted Job.*
>
> *And the LORD turned the captivity of Job when he prayed for his friends: also the LORD gave Job twice as much as he had before.*

Notice here that God did not rebuke Elihu, nor require him to repent before Him. Well, for the next generation of preachers out there, this is great news.

*1 Tim 4:12 Let no man despise thy youth; but be thou an example of the believers, in word, in conversation, in charity, in spirit, in faith, in purity.*

Preach the cross. This is the central message of the gospel and the only thing that will set people free from their sins.

Preach by revelation, not information. Be a voice for God, not merely an echo.

Respect, but do not fear those older in years. If you have heard God, go on and obey Him, no matter what people think or say.

Let's Pray:

*Father, reveal to me the areas where I, like Job, am trying to please You in my own strength, with MY own works, instead of acts of obedience that flow from Your love. The Word from heaven that will set this generation free. Light me on fire, and make me a voice for You, never merely an echo, a parrot of other preachers. Cause me to hear and obey. You perfect Your will for my life and the people You have called me to reach. In your name, I pray, Lord Jesus. Amen!*

# 42

# Prosperity - Power With God

The man at Gate Beautiful:

*Acts 3:5 And he gave heed unto them, expecting to receive something
of them.*

*Then Peter said, Silver and gold have I none; but such as I have to
give I thee: In the name of Jesus Christ of Nazareth rise up and walk. 7
And he took him by the right hand and lifted him up: and immediately
his feet and ankle bones received strength.*

*And he leaping up stood, and walked, and entered with them into
the temple, walking, and leaping, and praising God.*

Let's read a couple more verses:

*Ex 16:18 And when they did mete it with an omer, he that gathered
much had nothing over, and he that gathered little had no lack; they
gathered every man according to his eating*

*Psalm 34:10 The young lions do lack and suffer hunger: but they that
seek the LORD shall not want any good thing.*

*Prov 28:27 He that giveth unto the poor shall not lack: but he that hideth his eyes shall have many a curse.*

This beggar knew something about the people of God:

**They gave to the poor.**

**They did not lack for anything.**

**God's covenant operating in their life supplied not only their individual needs but enough for the people around them.**

> *Deut 8:18 But thou shalt remember the LORD thy God: for it is he that giveth thee power to get wealth, that he may establish his covenant which he sware unto thy fathers, as it is this day.*

What this beggar did not yet understand is that God's covenant gives the POWER to get wealth. This guy was crippled and thought he needed money, but what he really needed was the power of God to heal him so he could get up and go to work.

God's prosperity is not just financial but rather the power of God to meet every human need, freely available, only through Jesus the anointed one!

Let's Pray:

> *Father God, I ask You to release Your prosperity into my life today. In Your name, Lord Jesus. Amen.*

# 43

# The Invisible Kingdom

*Act 12:21 And upon a set day, Herod, arrayed in royal apparel, sat upon his throne and made an oration unto them.*

And the people gave a shout, saying, It is the voice of a god, and not of a man.

And immediately the angel of the Lord smote him, because he gave not God the glory: and he was eaten of worms, and gave up the ghost.

But the word of God grew and multiplied.

If we believe that the kingdom of God is simply the rule and authority of God in heaven and the earth, then we must understand that the most important thing for us as Christians is how to fully walk in the kingdom of God, even when the political system of the day may be directly opposed to the righteous and holy reign of Jesus.

God only has two authority structures on the earth: The political system (Rom 13:1-5; 1 Tim 2:1-4), and His Church, which rules and reigns with Him (Eph 2:6).

In the above passage, we see how an earthly kingdom collided with the kingdom of God. Here is an example of the thoughts and kingdoms of men colliding with the kingdom of God.

Herod, king of Judea, overstepped his earthly authority in proclaiming himself to be a god. Just like the old adage: *"See the writing on the wall."*

Somewhere in that generation was a church on fire for God praying for God's power and authority to be released. And it was! God sent an angel and struck Herod dead that it might be known there is only one true God in heaven and earth, and that Jesus is Lord to the glory of the Father.

Like the old worship song, we sing: *"Kings and kingdoms will all pass away, but there's something about that name."*

Greece, Rome, the Ottoman empire have all passed away, but the kingdom of God still stands. America will, too, as long as she stands with the Word of God and Jesus, but if she depart, she also would end up in the boneyard of history, another testimony to the unchanging, all-powerful invisible reign of Jesus amongst men.

So, we pray that each of us, from the least to the greatest, might meet Jesus personally and serve him fully in holiness and in the unique and high calling each of us was created to fulfill.

I find myself in the kingdom using every available resource, influence, and moment of my life to build, establish, and enforce the kingdom of God on the earth. Jesus is the answer for every situation and every problem, for its nature is love.

He loves you, too, and has an incredible plan for your life. If we only had eyes to see and ears to hear, we would know the Kingdom of God in the sense of holiness, goodness, and beauty that is as close as breathing and is crying out to born both within ourselves and within the world. We would know that the Kingdom of God is what we all hunger for above all other things even when we don't know its name or realize that it's what we're starving to death for. The Kingdom of God is where our best dreams come from and our sincerest prayers. We glimpse at it in those moments when we find ourselves being better than we are and wiser than we know. We catch sight of it when, at some moment of crisis, strength seems to come to us that is greater than our own strength.

*"The Kingdom of God is where we belong. It is home; and whether we realize it or not, I think we are all homesick for it."* Frederick Buechner

Let's pray:

*Father, You have said that I am to be in this world, but not of it. Bring me to my place in Your kingdom and teach me Your way of walking through this life. May I not waste time on other things, but may I settle for nothing less than the high calling You have placed upon my life. Reveal Your Kingdom to our lives, our nation, our families. Amen.*

# 44

# Tried? You Are Being Tested

Ah, the story of Joseph is an excruciatingly, comforting yet painful confirmation of the faithfulness of God to perform what He said. To anyone out there walking through a Joseph experience, know that you are not alone nor misunderstood. God is with you, and many, many leaders have had to walk through similar things. Don't give up on your dream, and whatever your circumstance, continue to pray and do what you can to improve yourself. In due season, you will come out of the furnace of affliction and see the glory of God in this generation.

> *Psalm 105:17-18 He sent a man before them, even Joseph, who was sold for a servant, whose feet they hurt with fetters: he was laid in iron.*

Until the time that his word came: the word of the Lord tried him.

This 19th verse has kept me sane over the years as I work out my own call before the Lord. For your encouragement, here are a couple of other translations:

> *Psalm 105:19 (GNV) Until his appointed time came,* and *the counsel of the Lord had tried him*

*Psalm 105:19 (CEV) Joseph remained a slave until his own words had come true, and the Lord had finished testing him*

*Psalm 105:19 (AMP) Until the time that his word [of prophecy regarding his brothers] came true.*

The word of the Lord tested *and* refined him. It is interesting to see how my particular trial reveals the hearts of those around me.

*Luke 2:35 (Yea, a sword shall pierce through thy own soul also,) that the thoughts of many **hearts** may be **revealed**.*

As I walk in my calling, I recognize that the word of the Lord is testing and refining me as I stay in the face of God. Circumstances have been brutal, but I stand before the throne awaiting His timing. No compromise.

May you do the same. Jesus is worthy.

Let's Pray:

*Father, there is an appointed time for my gift in the earth. May I continually stay in the press with You, growing, learning, hardening myself against sin. I am learning to accept responsibility and, where necessary, breaking at Your feet. I know what I have heard, and by Your grace, I will obey You for the sake of Your glory, Lord Jesus. Amen.*

# 45

# Timing

Again, I find myself awake in the night.

*Psalm 17:2 Let my sentence come forth from thy presence; let thine eyes behold the things that are equal. Thou hast proved mine heart; **thou hast visited me in the night;** thou hast tried me, and shalt find nothing; I am purposed that my mouth shall not transgress. Concerning the works of men, by the word of thy lips, I have kept me from the paths of the destroyer.*

*Psalm 17:15 As for me, I will behold thy face in righteousness: I shall be satisfied when I awake, with thy likeness.*

This is an excellent passage of encouragement for those of us who recognize the call of God upon our lives.

We must recognize that certain things will only occur in His timing. No matter how much we long for it, our commission will come only at the sentence issued from His lips. In the meantime, we call forth those things that be not, as though they were, believing we receive the things we have been shown and walking it out by faith. We recognize the struggle along the journey. He walks with us and is protecting, delivering us, and refining us, and qualifying us for His commission.

He is determined to make us into the character and likeness of Jesus.

> *Rom 8:29 For whom he did foreknow, he also did predestine to be conformed to the image of his Son, that he might be the firstborn among many brethren.*

The purity of heart and holiness is His goal for us.  People may see our outward actions and consequences, but God views not only our whats but our whys.

> *The heart is used in Scripture as the most comprehensive term for the authentic person.  It is the part of our being where we desire, deliberate, and decide. It has been described as "the place of conscious and decisive spiritual activity," "the comprehensive term for a person as a whole; his feelings, desires, passions, thought, understanding and will," and "the center of a person. The place to which God turns." J. Stowell, Fan The Flame, Moody, 1986, p. 13*

Let us rest tonight in the faith of the psalmist: *"As for me, I will behold thy face in righteousness. I shall be satisfied when I awake, with thy likeness"* Psalm 17:15.

He can change us in the night; He still speaks.

Let's pray:

> *Father, I thank You for the call You have placed upon my life to bring your change and grace to the earth in my generation. Keep forming the character of Jesus in me. I will not fight You in it. May my faith remain unfeigned, unleashed, and undefeated, as Your unconquerable kingdom comes to me and through me in the earth. In Your name, I pray, Lord Jesus. Amen.*

# 46

# Visions of Glory... Walking out Your Heavenly Vision

*Acts 10:19 While Peter thought on the vision, the Spirit said unto him, Behold, three men seek thee.*

Have you ever had an authentic vision from God that you didn't understand? Or that was clearly beyond your personal ability to accomplish?

I am in the midst of that presently. I have a vision from heaven for my life that involves many nations, peoples, and ministries that is revolutionary and will bring wonderful grace, power, and blessing to the earth, in this, my generation.

Daily, as I seek the Lord and think about this vision. Holy Spirit, speak!

When He speaks, He often speaks very specifically and far outside of my comfort zone, but always in terms of something I can do immediately.

Could you imagine crying out to God for His power to be revealed in your life and that He might use you in His gifts and miracles? And then Him speaking: 'Go, spit on the ground, make some mud, and put it in that blind man's eyes.' Yeah, right. Yet, Jesus operated as a man under the anointing of the Holy Spirit under the direction of the perfect voice of the Father.

*John 9:6 When he had thus spoken, he spat on the ground, and made clay of the spittle, and he anointed the eyes of the blind man with the clay,*

Or how about this one: 'spit in the man's face, and he will be healed!' How would you handle this word from the Holy Spirit?

*Mark 8:23 And he took the blind man by the hand, and led him out of the town; and when he had spit on his eyes and put his hands upon him, he asked him if he saw ought.*

I heard a minister testify of how God had used him to raise over 200 people from the dead.

Some of the things God asked him to do in terms of fasting and prayer were very extreme (Like a nine-month fast where he ate three days/week and fasted four).

A more traditional Christian said to him, 'You are out of your mind!'

His reply makes me smile to this day: 'No, I'm not, I'm just out of yours. I'm over in the mind of Christ."

So, have you ever taken an extended time in prayer and fasting to hear exactly why God created you and His vision and plan for your life?

If you have authentically heard the specific voice of God for your life and have written down what He said, you may have a fresh understanding of the little plaque the Oral Roberts used to have on his desk that read: *'Make no little plans here!'*

God usually speaks something so above and beyond what we can ask or think that sets us upon a path that will require daily, specific faith-filled instructions that lead us from faith to faith, strength to strength, and glory to glory.

* * *

It started like so many evenings. Mom and Dad are at home, and Jimmy played after dinner. Mom and Dad were absorbed with jobs and did not notice the time.

It was a full moon, and some of the light seeped through the windows. Then Mom glanced at the clock.

*"Jimmy, it's time to go to bed. Go up now, and I'll come and settle you later."*

Unlike usual, Jimmy went straight upstairs to his room. An hour or so later, his mother came up to check if all was well and, to her astonishment, found that her son was staring quietly out of his window at the moonlit scenery.

*"What are you doing, Jimmy?"*

*"I'm looking at the moon, Mommy."*

*"Well, it's time to go to bed now."*

As one reluctant boy settled down, he said, *"Mommy, you know one day I'm going to walk on the moon."*

Who could have known that the boy in whom the dream was planted that night would survive a near-fatal motorbike crash which broke almost every bone in his body, and would bring to fruition this dream 32 years later when James Irwin stepped on the moon's surface, just one of the twelve representatives of the human race to have done so?" (Bill Hybels, *Who You Are When No One's Looking*, IVP, 1987, p. 35)

* * *

Let's Pray:

199

*Father, show me again Your glory and the purpose for which You created me. I believe that You order my steps and that You will speak to me specifically regarding the particular acts of obedience You require for me to get there.  I seek You, Lord Jesus, and believe I receive the hearing of Your voice for you have promised You will speak to me today. Amen.*

# 47

# Providing Supernatural Oversight

Well, here is a simple teaching on spiritual oversight of the people of God. Much can be said and has been said about pastoral and spiritual leadership. But today, I want to bring a little nugget that the Lord brought to my remembrance for your edification. Over means above; sight is to see. Therefore, oversight means the **view from above**.

> *Ac 20:28 Take heed therefore unto yourselves, and to all the flock, over the which the Holy Ghost hath made you **overseers**, to feed the church of God, which he hath purchased with his own blood.*

Oversight might be better said, as 'implementing the visionary directives of God, into our organizations and ministries.'

> *Eph 2:6 And hath raised us up together, and made us sit together in heavenly places in Christ Jesus:*

We see Paul being led by the vision of the man from Macedonia, and Joseph being led by heavenly dreams and interpretation of dreams.

So, God can lead you through dreams and visions, divine pictures that show you what to do, or what is going on in the realm of the Spirit.

I want to touch on a thought from the ministry of the prophet. That is the spirit of seeing and knowing.

In the following passage, we see the prophet Elisha operating in the spirit of seeing and knowing, where he saw, by the Spirit of God, events that were geographically far away. There is no way he could have heard or seen them naturally. It seems God allowed his human spirit to travel through space to be present at the event where Gehazi lied to Naaman to take an offering that he had expressly forbidden.

> *2 Kings 5:26 And he said unto him,* **Went not mine heart with thee**, *when the man turned again from his chariot to meet thee? Is it a time to receive money, and to receive garments, and olive yards, and vineyards, and sheep, and oxen, and menservants, and maidservants?*

He saw supernaturally and judged, and Gehazi got the very leprosy that Naaman had been cleansed of. God was merciful to him, though, for lepers were banned from the camp of the Israelites; yet Gehazi repented and did right in his latter years. God must have healed him.

> *2 Kings 7:9 Then they said one to another, We do not well: this day is a day of good tidings, and we hold our peace: if we tarry till the morning light, some mischief will come upon us: now, therefore, come, that we may go and tell the king's household.*

Gehazi must have been healed of leprosy because we read about him again, speaking to the king. If he still had the disease, he could not appear before the king, for he would be forbidden to enter the city.

> *Lev 13:45-46 And the leper in whom the plague is, his clothes shall be rent, and his head bare, and he shall put a covering upon his upper lip and shall cry, Unclean, unclean. All the days wherein the plague shall be in him he shall be defiled; he is unclean: he shall dwell alone; without the camp shall his habitation be*

Yet, he must have been cleansed, because here we see him before the king:

*2 Kings 8:4 And the king talked with Gehazi, the servant of the man of God, saying, Tell me, I pray thee, all the great things that Elisha hath done.*

*2 Kings 8:5 And it came to pass, as he was telling the king how he had restored a dead body to life, that, behold, the woman, whose son he had restored to life, cried to the king for her house and for her land. And Gehazi said, My lord, O king, this is the woman, and this is her son, whom Elisha restored to life.*

Supernatural oversight, prophetically by the Spirit of God, is our topic. Jesus did it, operating in the spirit of seeing and knowing.

*John 1:45-49 Philip findeth Nathanael, and saith unto him, We have found him, of whom Moses in the law, and the prophets, did write, Jesus of Nazareth, the son of Joseph. And Nathanael said unto him, Can there any good thing come out of Nazareth? Philip saith unto him, Come and see. Jesus saw Nathanael coming to him, and saith of him, Behold an Israelite indeed, in whom is no guile! Nathanael saith unto him, Whence knowest thou me? Jesus answered and said unto him, Before that Philip called thee, **when thou wast under the fig tree, I saw thee.** Nathanael answered and saith unto him, Rabbi, thou art the Son of God; thou art the King of Israel.*

Jesus saw Nathanial in the Spirit as one called to become one of His disciples when there was no natural way He could have seen him otherwise.

Let's look at the apostle Paul as to how he supplied oversight by the Spirit of God by the spirit of seeing and knowing.

*Colossians 2:5 For though I be absent in the flesh, yet am I with you in*

> *the spirit, joying and beholding your order, and the steadfastness of*
> *your faith in Christ.*

Paul ministered back in the day before the internet and cell phones. And yet he was given supernatural revelation into the spiritual condition of one of the churches he fathered and provided oversight to. Geographically, Paul was not in Colossae any longer. He was absent in the flesh, yet he was with them in spirit. And he could see what was going on in the church because he could 'behold their order.' Behold means 'to look upon,' and this verse literally says that Paul was able to see through time and space and participate in the worship services of one of the churches he provided leadership to.

I wonder how much better we could lead if we were more attuned to what the Holy Spirit is showing us about the ministries He has given us authority and oversight in. Leadership can do this instead of trying to lead by merely sense knowledge.

In this next account, we see God, through Paul, rendering judgment upon an individual involved in incest:

> *1 Corinthians 5:3–5 For I verily, as absent in body, but present in spirit,*
> *have judged already, as though I were present, concerning him that*
> *hath so done this deed, in the name of our Lord Jesus Christ, when ye*
> *are gathered together, and my spirit, with the power of our Lord Jesus*
> *Christ, to deliver such a one unto Satan for the destruction of the flesh,*
> *that the spirit may be saved in the day of the Lord Jesus.*

I am only reviewing to stir up your pure minds in the things of God.

The Spirit of seeing and knowing can see across time and space, to discern spiritual or natural events by the Spirit of God and know what to do about them.

Leaders can walk in this not only in churches but also in communities where we are called to minister. I remembered several years ago how we had pioneered a children's outreach that we called a Big Brothers Club where we took children out of a rough government housing project for swimming, bicycling, hiking, and fishing trips. We would aggressively pray for God to save these children and their parents. Yet, we would do this on Friday nights, and Friday night was check night in the hood, we called it 'King for a Day' where people, either on welfare or working, would take every bit of their money and spend it on Friday and Saturday nights on alcohol, crack cocaine, and marijuana. Sometimes when we would bring these children home after a Friday night swim, the whole neighborhood would be one big party.

Picture if you will: Loud music, clouds of dope smoke, people dancing, fighting, cars squealing rubber, electric atmosphere.

I got tired of it and decided to pray and fast and weep before the Lord, because my heart broke for these poor children having to go home to these drug dens of iniquity.

I remember one Friday after dropping off the children and leaving the community, that the Lord opened my eyes, and I saw a demon hovering over the neighborhood. The Lord caused me to know that this demon was responsible for all drug use and drug trade.

I saw him, and he saw me. I commanded him to leave my community, and instead of leaving, he turned and cried out for help. I saw another demon on some chariot or something fly up beside him. The Lord caused me to know that this other spirit was a party spirit, and he was stirring up the people and causing them to party.

The first spirit pointed to me and said: *"We need to join forces because of him!"* They both looked at me. I commanded them both to go and get out in the name of Jesus. Suddenly, I couldn't see into the spirit anymore.

That community calmed down after that. The police arrested many drug dealers there, and over the next year, we led many children and parents to the Lord from there. I was able to govern the community in the Spirit in prayer, even when I wasn't there. God gave me spiritual oversight there for several years until He moved me out of the country.

Perry Stone tells the story of a minister that saw a demon in the back of a church that the Lord caused him to know had been there for over twenty years preventing the Holy Spirit from moving and growing the church. The minister rebuked it, and the church immediately grew by 1000 members!

Many ministers have been alerted and shown sin in their leaders or congregations that they are able to confront in prayer and the public preaching of the Word, thus protecting the dignity of the person who needed to repent and the integrity of the ministry.

The problem with this type of ministry has always been deception. It's the only weapon Satan has left, for he has been stripped of all power and authority when Jesus rose from the dead.

> *2 Cor 11:14 And no marvel; for Satan himself is transformed into an angel of light.*

> *Gal 1:8 But though we, or an angel from heaven, preach any other gospel unto you than that which we have preached unto you, let him be accursed.*

Satan may be a liar and the father of all lies. Deception is the main weapon that he uses very well on earth, even today. Just as there is authentic prophetic ministry and oversight, there are demonic spirits that emulate the gifts of God with the sole intent of causing ministries and people of God to go astray.

> *Deut 18:10-13 There shall not be found among you any one that maketh his son or his daughter to pass through the fire, or that useth divination, or an observer of times, or an enchanter, or a witch, or a charmer, or a consulter with familiar spirits, or a wizard, or a necromancer. For all that do these things are an abomination unto the LORD: and because of these abominations, the LORD thy God doth drive them out from before thee. Thou shalt be perfect with the LORD thy God.*

From the time in the garden, Satan knew that if he could get the people of God to disobey God, he would have them in his power, for how well he knows the holiness of God.

I wonder what the kingdom of darkness is doing during this Presidential election to seek demonic influence and rule?

*Jer 14:14 Then the LORD said unto me, The prophets prophesy lies in my name: I sent them not, neither have I commanded them, neither spake unto them: they prophesy unto you a false vision and divination, and a thing of nought, and the deceit of their heart.*

Therefore thus saith the LORD concerning the prophets that prophesy in my name, and I sent them not, yet they say, Sword and famine shall not be in this land; By sword and famine shall those prophets be consumed.

And the people to whom they prophesy shall be cast out in the streets of Jerusalem because of the famine and the sword; and they shall have none to bury them, them, their wives, nor their sons, nor their daughters: for I will pour their wickedness upon them.

In this verse, we have prophets that should have been speaking by the Holy Spirit the revelations of God; yet they were hearing and seeing by another spirit, a spirit of divination. And they became deceived in their hearts.

This sends chills down my spine. In the fear of the Lord, I seek holiness. I seek the fear of the Lord and truth above every other thing. None of us is immune to error.

As we study church history in the lives of some of the most powerful servants of God, we see some that went off.

William Branham came to deny the Trinity and perhaps moved in a mix of true prophetic and divination or familiar spirits.

John Alexander Dowie claimed to be a *'reincarnation of John the Baptist'* in his latter years, and on it goes.

What about many today who *'prophesy'* money out of people's pockets in the name of the Lord?

Surely there are true prophets that move in the financial realm, but how many times have we heard an offering taken up that just doesn't sit right in our heart?

*Act 16:16 And it came to pass, as we went to prayer, a certain damsel possessed with a spirit of divination met us, which brought her masters much gain by soothsaying: The same followed Paul and us and cried, saying, These men are the servants of the Most High God, which shew unto us the way of salvation. And this did she many days. But Paul, **being grieved**, turned and said to the spirit, I command thee in the name of Jesus Christ to come out of her. And he came out the same hour.*

We must listen to our hearts and test the spirits. If something doesn't seem right, it probably isn't right.

*John 4:1–4 Beloved, believe not every spirit, but try the spirits whether they are of God because many false prophets are gone out into the world. Hereby know ye the Spirit of God: Every spirit that confesseth that Jesus Christ is come in the flesh is of God. And every spirit that confesseth not that Jesus Christ is come in the flesh is not of God and this is that spirit of antichrist, whereof ye have heard that it should come; and even now already is it in the world. Ye are of God, little children, and have overcome them: because greater is he that is in you than he that is in the world.*

I read a great little book, given to us by Billye Brim, called *The Authority of the Believer*, by John A. Macmillan. It is a great book on spiritual authority and warfare, but the last couple of chapters talk about many cases of demonic interaction with people. One chapter talks about the rise of modern-day spiritism that stems from actual communication with spirits claiming to be the souls of loved ones who had died some years previously. As these spirits communicated through tapping and other methods, the group of adherents to this mess went from two teenage girls to over 10 million. Just because an experience is supernatural, does not mean it is of God.

Please stay grounded in truth as you move in the revelatory gifts of the

Holy Spirit. I have to believe that as I stay rooted and grounded in the Word of God, that God Himself will send both laborers and teaching materials about demonic errors to keep us clean spiritually.

Like any Bible doctrine, there is a ditch on either side of this teaching. One ditch is demonic deception resulting in supernatural revelation coming from demons instead of God. The other ditch is strict legalism, resulting in no tolerance or allowance of prophetic ministry and guidance to the church of the living God. There is a straight and narrow way through these perils!

The cure for misuse of a gift is not no-use, but rather, correct use.

*1 Cor 14:1 Follow after charity, and desire spiritual gifts, but rather that ye may prophesy.*

*1 Cor 14:39 Wherefore, brethren, covet to prophesy and forbid not to speak with tongues.*

Let's pray:

*Father, I take my place in Your kingdom. I am determined to feed, lead, and take oversight over the people You have called me to. Open my eyes to the true state of the ministries You have me leading and give me wisdom on how best to pray, preach, feed, and lead Your people. Deliver me and protect me any false prophetic dreams, visions, or manifestations. Keep me in truth at all costs and prevent me from going astray. In any case that I have heard or seen things in the spirit that are not from You, but are demonic deception, please show me, cleanse me, and keep me pure and holy in Your sight and submitted to Your Word. In Your name, I pray, Lord Jesus. Amen.*

## 48

# What Happened To Sin?

Let's name a few things forbidden in the Word of God so that I do not single out anyone because we have all sinned and fallen short of the glory of God. Jesus died because He loved sinners. He paid the ultimate price for sin and it killed Him. He died upon the cross to bear the full weight of sin for all humanity.

*Gal 5:16-24 So I say, let the Holy Spirit guide your lives. Then you won't be doing what your sinful nature craves. The sinful nature wants to do evil, which is just the opposite of what the Spirit wants. And the Spirit gives us desires that are the opposite of what sinful nature desires. These two forces are constantly fighting each other, so you are not free to carry out your good intentions. But when you are directed by the Spirit, you are not under obligation to the law of Moses. When you follow the desires of your sinful nature, the results are very clear: sexual immorality, impurity, lustful pleasures, idolatry, sorcery, hostility, quarreling, jealousy, outbursts of anger, selfish ambition, dissension, division, envy, drunkenness, wild parties, and other sins like these. Let me tell you again, as I have before, that anyone living that sort of life will not inherit the Kingdom of God. But the Holy Spirit produces this kind of fruit in our lives: love, joy, peace, patience, kindness, goodness, faithfulness, gentleness, and self-control. There is no law against these things! Those who belong to Christ Jesus have nailed the passions and desires of their sinful nature to his cross and crucified them there.*

As I read these verses, written to Christians, I see clearly that we are called to live a life of honor, humility, love, purity, gratefulness, patience, gentleness, holiness, and love in Jesus.

Yet, we see, as the native proverb goes, the battle we all fight within ourselves. If you have read much of my material, you discover the overwhelming thread of what I post is on the love, grace, goodness, and righteousness of God, who we are before His throne, royal children of the Most High God.

If I am a servant of Jesus, I do humanity a disservice if I do not do as Jesus did, commanding men everywhere to repent?

If I call lying wrong, am I a hater?

If I declare homosexuality to be wrong, am I a gay basher?

If I declare that pornography, prostitution, and child sex trafficking are wrong, am I judgmental, critical, non-loving?

How about envy, jealousy, pride? If I call these sins, am I no longer a 'good news preacher'?

You can see where I am taking this line of thought.

The overwhelming tragedy of the human experience is not the depth of degradation people allow themselves to wallow in, but instead, in light of eternity and the power of God available to any human being through the grace given us in Jesus. How far short of His glory, honor, holiness, purity, and love we still choose to live.

When Jesus came to live inside of us, old things passed away, all things became new. I see so many fellow Christians, like dogs returning to their own vomit, living so far below their rights and privileges as believers.

**The Temple of the Living God**

*1 Cor 6:14-16 Don't team up with those who are unbelievers. How can righteousness be a partner with wickedness? How can light live with darkness? What harmony can there be between Christ and the devil? How can a believer be a partner with an unbeliever?* [16] *And what union can there be between God's temple and idols? For we are the temple of the living God. As God said: "I will live in them and walk among them. I will be their God, and they will be my people.*

*Therefore, come out from among unbelievers, and separate yourselves from them, says the Lord. Don't touch their filthy things, and I will welcome you.*

*And I will be your Father, and you will be my sons and daughters, says the Lord Almighty."*

We are called children of the Most High God; we are people who bear His name.

Yet, just like we need to change a few diapers as parents, as our children dirty themselves, even so, we are expected to grow out of the diaper stage into honor and holiness.

Yes, I love people.

Yes, like Jesus, I hate sin, for I see what it does to people, families, communities, and nations.

*Titus 2:11 (AMP)* **For the grace of God** *(His unmerited favor and blessing) has come forward (appeared) for the deliverance from sin and the eternal salvation for all mankind.*

*Titus 2:12 (KJV)* **Teaching us that,** *denying ungodliness and worldly lusts, we should live soberly, righteously, and godly in this present world.*

Yes, we are adopted into the kingdom of God, but we are to become HOLY. Notice here that it is only God's grace that allows us to do this, but that that very grace teaches us.

*2 Timothy 3:16 All Scripture is given by inspiration of God, and is profitable for doctrine, for reproof, for correction, for **instruction** in righteousness,*

God loves us, yet as a good parent, He instructs us on the rules in His family, His kingdom, the ways of righteousness.

Sin kills, and if I am to love you honestly, I must exhort you to holiness.

Let's pray:

*Father, may we see sin and hate it the way You do. In Your love for us, convict us of our sin, and in Your grace, teach us how to leave sinless and live in purity, honor, and love toward You and our neighbor. I ask this, knowing I am heard, for I ask in Your name, Lord Jesus. Amen.*

# 49

# Running Before the Gale

**The Storm at Sea**

*Acts 27:13–15 When a light wind began blowing from the south, the sailors thought they could make it.  So, they pulled up anchor and sailed close to the shore of Crete. But the weather changed abruptly, and a wind of typhoon strength (called a "northeaster") burst across the island and blew us out to sea. The sailors couldn't turn the ship into the wind, so they gave up and **let it run before the gale.***

When I was young and full of fire and adventure, I spent nine months becoming trained as an underwater welder.  I decided to join a company out of Key West named Treasure Salvors headed up by a flamboyant man named Mel Fisher. We hunted Spanish treasure ships off the Florida Keys. It was a great adventure.

Then, as God would have it, I had the opportunity to jump ship and join *The Illusion* expedition, headed up by a man from Brazil. Tony had worked in the oil fields as a diver and had built a 65-foot schooner, fully equipped as a dive vessel. He had been searching archives for many years to unearth the plight of the many treasure ships that had sunk crossing the Atlantic. He had his eyes on a Dutch Schooner said to be sunk in the Madeira Island group off Portugal. We also scoured several other wrecks along the journey.

So, not yet 21, I hired aboard this wild expedition with two Swiss, a German, and a French man from Gabon, Africa. Our captain was a man from Brazil who also brought with him his wife and two-year-old daughter along with two Doberman pinchers.

We had many adventures and some once in a lifetime experience. We found wrecks and went spearfishing while crossing the Atlantic under sail.

We got caught in a force 9 storm, with 50-70mph winds. All we could see are blowing foam and seas mounted to 40-50' waves with the tops being torn off of them by the high winds. We had to keep the boat running before the wind, carefully slicing the waves, or we would breach, overturn, and I might not be writing this story.

For three days and nights, we could do nothing but hang-on. No food, no sleep as the waves were too violent and would throw you out of your bunk. Dark, starless nights, blowing rain, foam, mist, with one thought on all of our minds, survive.

On the third day, the winds let up, and I ate a dry cracker, crawled into my bunk, and slept for a couple of hours. The sound of the baby laughing woke me up. The sun was streaming through my porthole!

I stumbled out of my bunk, being flung side to side, the entire boat creaking and groaning, crashing through the waves. I came above decks to behold a sight.

The wind had stopped in the night, but because it was no longer tearing the tops off of the waves, seas were now 65-80' tall. Our little schooner would surf up one side of a mountain of water, and launch into the air, to come crashing down the other side of these monstrous waves. We would hit the bottom of the trough, and the bow would turn submarine, plunging the front third of the ship underwater, with hatches groaning, like a cork we would bob up again and head for the sky again.

The baby was in her safety strap, hugging one of the dogs, laughing hysterically. One of the Swiss had a camcorder, and he filmed that day. How I wish I had a copy of that video.

We all began to laugh. It was a celebration of life. We were alive to face another day. The sun was shining, and it was going to be alright.

* * *

You know the story, Paul, the mighty apostle with a burning zeal and a passionate fire to see his people saved and right with God. He has met Jesus, and he is going to Jerusalem, the capital of the world, to tell them the good news of who Yeshua really is.

**FAITH is Fantastic Adventures In Trusting Him.**

*Acts 20:22 And now, behold, I go **bound in the spirit** unto **Jerusalem**, not knowing the things that shall befall me there:*

### Bound In The Spirit

There were questions as to whether Paul heard the voice of God to make this particular trip to Jerusalem.

*Romans 8:14 For as many as are led by the Spirit of God, they are the sons of God.*

Surely Paul is a son of God, and He heard God say to go to Jerusalem. Yet we see an interesting interplay here between the office of the apostle and the office of the prophet.

*Acts 21:11-13 And when he was come unto us, he took Paul's girdle, and bound his own hands and feet, and said, Thus saith the Holy Ghost, So shall the Jews at **Jerusalem** bind the man that owneth this girdle, and shall deliver him into the hands of the Gentiles. And when we heard these things, both we, and they of that place, besought him not to go up to **Jerusalem**. Then Paul answered, What mean ye to weep and to break mine heart? For I am ready not to be bound only, but also to die at **Jerusalem** for the name of the Lord Jesus.*

The prophetic word delivered to Paul was accurate, and those around him that loved him interpreted that Paul should refrain from going up to Jerusalem. Yet, to Paul, the apostle, it meant that he was ready to endure any hardship for the sake of the gospel. **The Word strengthened him.**

He hardened himself, recognizing imprisonment and a beating were in his future, but he did not flinch in the face of danger.

> *Isaiah 50:7 For the Lord God will help me; therefore shall I not be confounded: therefore have I set my **face like** a **flint**, and I know that I shall not be ashamed.*

He made it to Jerusalem, underwent imprisonment, and the foretold beating. Yet, though his path was hard, there was an audience of One that he sought to obey and please.

In His prison cell, that One, King Jesus, showed up to personally comfort His servant:

> *Acts 23:11 And the night following the Lord stood by him, and said, Be of good cheer, Paul: for as thou hast testified of me in **Jerusalem**, so must thou bear witness also at Rome*

How is that for an encouraging word?

You obeyed me. Now I am sending you to Rome – (in the belly of a slave ship)—running before the gale.

So, Leader, the storms of life will come. You are either in one, finishing one, or headed into another one. It is the cost of the call, the price tag of leadership, the race run, before our audience of One.

The lonely times leave a mark upon your soul. Perhaps it was this time in Jerusalem that caused Paul to pen these words:

> *2 Timothy 4:16 At my first answer, **no man stood with me**, but all **men** forsook **me**: I pray God that it may **not** be laid to their charge.*

When we enter into the perfect, sovereign assignment of heaven for our lives, all hell may well break loose to prevent us from getting to our goal.

Jesus faced the storm on the sea of Galilee; Paul, the Mediterranean; Joseph, the pit; Moses, the desert.

Jesus suffered alone upon the cross. We who represent Him will find ourselves alone with Him too.

While no earthly help may seem to appear, there is a friend that sticks closer than a brother — One who knows, who cares, and who will never leave nor forsake you.

We did make it to Portugal and discovered the 1611 Dutch trader with 54 silver bars on its manifest, another story, for another day.

You will make it too if you are willing to abandon all for the sake of the call.

Like Mary told her servants so many years ago, at the wedding feast:

> John 2: (KJV) **His mother saith unto the servants, Whatsoever he saith unto you, do it.** *In your hour of trial,* **HE WILL APPEAR, AND HE WILL SPEAK!**

Do not settle for the mere words of men, obey Him, and walk upon the water of His Word. Make headlines in heaven so that this question in the heart of Jesus be answered.

> *Luke 18:8 Nevertheless, when the Son of man cometh, shall he* **find faith** *on the earth?*

Let your answer to this question be a resounding YES! You won't have to look any further, Lord Jesus, for I believe!

Let's pray:

> *Father, let me not shrink back for Your clear mandate for me. While the storms may rage, may I navigate them and run before the wind of Your Holy Spirit, running before the gale. In Your name and for Your*

*glory I pray, Lord Jesus, Amen.*

# 50

# Leadership Development and Timing

*Luke 12:42 The Lord answered, "Who then is the faithful and wise manager, whom the master puts in charge of his servants to give them their food allowance **at the proper time**?*

If we recognize that all authority, whether political or spiritual, comes from God. We, as growing leaders, determine to perform the perfect will of God for our lives and the lives of those we lead. We find ourselves constantly humbly in prayer, seeking His face for wisdom, and studying to learn how to do things better.

*John 13:3-17 NIV Jesus knew that the Father had put all things under his power and that he had come from God and was returning to God; so he got up from the meal, took off his outer clothing, and wrapped a towel around his waist. After that, he poured water into a basin and began to wash his disciples' feet, drying them with the towel that was wrapped around him. He came to Simon Peter, who said to him, "Lord, are you going to wash my feet?"*

*Jesus replied, "You do not realize now what I am doing, but later you will understand."*

*"No," said Peter, "you shall never wash my feet."*

*Jesus answered, "Unless I wash you, you have no part with me."*

*"Then, Lord," Simon Peter replied, "not just my feet but my hands and my head as well!"*

*Jesus answered, "Those who have had a bath need only to wash their feet; their whole body is clean. And you are clean, though not every one of you." 11 For he knew who was going to betray him, and that was why he said not everyone was clean.*

*When he had finished washing their feet, he put on his clothes and returned to his place. "Do you understand what I have done for you?" he asked them. "You call me 'Teacher' and 'Lord,' and rightly so, for that is what I am. Now that I, your Lord and Teacher, have washed your feet, you also should wash one another's feet. I have set you an example that you should do as I have done for you. Very truly I tell you, no servant is greater than his master, nor is a messenger greater than the one who sent him. Now that you know these things, you will be blessed if you do them.*

### Down is Up in God's Kingdom.

The heart of authentic leadership is the call to love and serve people honestly. As we grow in grace and humility, Godly leaders seek to empower, equip, prosper, educate, disciple, heal and love the people God has called us to lead.

It is only natural for the disciples to wonder which of them will be His right-hand man. Even the three disciples who have just seen Jesus's glory revealed in the transfiguration cannot resist the attraction of honor. After all, who has a better claim than they do to being the greatest of Jesus' disciples?

Fortunately, Jesus overhears what is said and is quick to respond in mercy to correct their mistake. Greatness in His eyes doesn't consist of seeing wonders or performing miracles or even fasting and praying. Instead, greatness is about humility and service. These are the heart of the kingdom of heaven.

*Mark 9:35 The Voice (VOICE) He sat down with the twelve to teach them. Whoever wants to be first must be last, and whoever wants to be the greatest must be the servant of all.*

As I am reading yet another book on leadership, allowing my weaknesses of character and understanding to be exposed, I am seeking to be rebuilt upon the firm foundation of the Word of God. I read this quote that prompted the writing of this article.

*"A new moral principle is emerging which holds that only authority deserving one's allegiance is that which is freely and knowingly granted by the led to the leader in response to, and in proportion to, the clearly evident servant stature of the leader. Those who choose to follow this principle will not casually accept the authority of existing institutions. Rather, they will freely respond only to individuals who are chosen as leaders because they are proven and trusted as servants." (Servant Leadership, A Journey into the Nature of Legitimate Power and Greatness, Robert K Greenleaf)*

Perhaps humility and servanthood are new concepts in the business world, but they are not new to the kingdom of God. It seems that down is up in the kingdom, for God gives grace, which is power, authority, wisdom, and influence to the humble.

*2 Corinthians 8:9 You know the grace that has come to us through our Lord Jesus the Anointed. He set aside His infinite riches and was born into the lowest circumstance so that you may gain great riches through His humble poverty.*

The riches of heaven come to us because God, the Creator of Heaven and earth, not only humbled Himself to become a man, Christ Jesus, but then emptied Himself of every earthly rank, position, and privilege and accepted a beggars death upon the cross that the wrath, the judgment, the punishment each of us deserve, might be poured upon Himself. God within God doing the infinite, that we, the finite, might be reconciled, to Him.

As leaders, we become shepherds, called of God to lead, feed, and protect God's people as they grow in their particular gifts and callings.

> *1 Peter 5:2 When you shepherd the flock God has given you, watch over them not because you have to but because you want to. For this is how God would want it not because you'Rev being compensated somehow but because you are eager to watch over them. Don't lead them as if you were a dictator, but lead your flock by example; and when the Chief Shepherd appears, you will be crowned with honor that will shine brightly forever. You who are younger in the faith: do as your elders and leaders ask. All of you should treat each other with humility, for as it says in Proverbs, God opposes the proud but offers grace to the humble. So bow down under God's strong hand; then when the time comes, God will lift you up. Since God cares for you, let Him carry all your burdens and worries.*

Humility is rarely a virtue that our culture values. We're trained from an early age to show our strengths and hide our weaknesses. This type of thinking also spills over into our models of leadership as we learn to dictate to others how they should perform.

Peter, however, says that we should be humble in our relationships with one another and not lead as dictators. In fact, this humility before one another and God is actually the position of the greatest strength. Our enemy desires to consume us, but we find the power to resist him when we are dependent upon God for His strength.

These verses bring me great comfort as I daily prepare for the calling and task before me:

> *James 4:6 But he giveth more grace. Wherefore he saith, God resisteth*

*the proud, but **giveth grace unto the humble***.

*James 4:10 Humble yourselves in the sight of the Lord, and he shall lift you up.*

* * *

When I saw Sadhu Sundar Singh in Europe, he had completed a tour around the world. People asked him, *"Doesn't it harm your getting so much honor?"*

Sadhu's answer was: *"No. The donkey went into Jerusalem, and they put garments on the ground before him. He was not proud. He knew it was not done to honor him, but for Jesus, who was sitting on his back. When people honor me, I know it is not me, but the Lord, who does the job."* Corrie Ten Boom, Each New Day.

In the quote that prompted this article, I am reminded of this verse:

*Psalm 110:3 Thy people shall be willing in the day of thy power, in the beauties of holiness from the womb of the morning: thou hast the dew of thy youth.*

There is, I believe, a day of God's power, an unveiling of a masterpiece, whereby God Himself sets in the public eye a leader that He may have been preparing secretly for many decades. For those of us in that divine development process, this verse should again bring comfort:

*1 Peter 5:6 Humble yourselves therefore under the mighty hand of God that he may exalt you in due time:*

*"To be a leader, a man must have followers. And to have followers,*

*a man must have their confidence. Hence the supreme quality of a leader is unquestionably integrity. Without integrity, no real success is possible no matter whether it is on a section gang, on a football field, in an army, or in an office. If a man's associates find him guilty of phoniness, if they find that he lacks forthright integrity, he will fail. His teachings and actions must square with each other. The first great need, therefore, is integrity and high purpose." (Dwight D. Eisenhower,* Bits & Pieces, *September 15, 1994, p. 4)*

There is a set time and appointed time for the release of our gift into the earth. Perhaps, like me, you clearly see that the time is close, and appears to be, NOW. Yet, despite the incredible vision God has given you and the personal promises He has spoken to you, the time is yet for the appointed time.

*Habakkuk 2:1–3 (KJV) I will stand upon my watch and set me upon the tower and will watch to see what he will say unto me, and what I shall answer when I am reproved. And the LORD answered me, and said, Write the vision, and make it plain upon tables, that he may run that readeth it.*

*For the **vision is yet for an appointed time**, but at the end it shall speak, and not lie: though it tarry, wait for it; because it will surely come, it will not tarry.*

Behold, his soul which is lifted up is not upright in him: but the just shall live by his faith.

Daily, we seek Him, set upon our watch, listening carefully for what He might speak to us, documenting and writing the vision, yet though we press for it in faith. It is for an appointed time, and there is nothing we can do to make it happen any quicker. So, if we are wise, we diligently prepare.

*Psalm 105:16–19 Moreover, he called for a famine upon the land: he brake the whole staff of bread. He sent a man before them, even Joseph,* *who was sold for a servant. Whose feet they hurt with fetters: he was laid in iron. Until the time that his word came: **the word of the LORD tried him.***

The very promises of God, spoken to your heart, are testing and trying you.

You are not testing the word of God – it is testing you!

Notice this verse, though. Before Joseph was brought from the prison to the palace, the Sovereign judgments of God were on the earth. Joseph was tried, trained, and prepared in the brutal circumstances of an Egyptian prison. Yet the hardness worked in Joseph caused him to become a strong leader in what, for Egypt, were some brutal times.

Brutal times are again coming to the earth in many nations as I think of my years as a missionary, working underground in a mine, on boats, in the competitive field of triathlon, and in construction.

There have been tough times, brutal people, and hard circumstances.

Yet, over the decades, in places often far from the comforts of the familiar, I have met Jesus, and walked with Him, daily now, for many, many years.

As much as I love my family, my church, my country, and now this country I am called to, I love Jesus more and know Him. He has been entirely faithful. No matter what people or circumstances have done to you, God is devoted to you, too!

Let's pray:

*Father, keep me focused upon my purpose and Your personal promises to my family and me. May I not become distracted, discouraged, or dismayed as I stay in the press towards the high calling of God in Christ Jesus. May I lead and develop as a servant leader daily, determining to grow and walk in holiness, flying straight and true to the calling You have placed upon my life. In Your name, I pray, Lord Jesus. Amen!*

# 51

# Teach Us To Number Our Days

*Romans 10:9 That if thou shalt confess with thy mouth the Lord Jesus, and shalt believe in thine heart that God hath raised him from the dead, thou shalt be saved.*

We are going to talk about the Lordship of Jesus in our personal lives.

We see here that making Him Lord is a condition for salvation. If Jesus is the Lord, He must be our Lord. If He is our Lord, we must do what He says.

Previously, I have talked about the Lordship of Jesus in our personal lives. We saw how the first commandment, commanding us to love God, precedes service. We talked about seeking first the kingdom of God before doing anything else. We ended with ACTS as a simple method of placing Him first. What does ACTS stand for?

**ACTS:**

- **Adoration**: Praise and Worship
- **Confession** – Confess God's Word back to Him, expecting Him to perform it in your life.
- **Thanksgiving** – Thank Him for your life, your family, His Word, for answered prayer, for this church.

- **Supplication** – Ask Him for those things you need that day. Wisdom, strength, courage to make changes in your life, to talk to others about Him. For your daily needs.

Again, this is not a legalistic formula. The question is simply one of the heart: Are we seeking first Jesus and His will for our lives today?

We are going to look at another aspect of His Lordship. We are going to see from the Word of God if Jesus is Lord of our time.

*Romans 13:11 And that, knowing the time, that now it is high time to awake out of sleep: for now is our salvation nearer than when we believed.*

*2 Corinthians 6:2 (For he saith, I have heard thee in a time accepted, and in the day of salvation have I succored thee: behold, now is the accepted time; behold, now is the day of salvation.)*

Do you realize that this age, the church age, is the greatest season any person serving God has ever seen upon the earth?

God is not just for us but lives in us. Our bodies have become His temple. When He decides to act in the earth, He has obligated Himself to work through one of us!

*Daniel 11:32 (AMP) And such as violate the covenant, he shall pervert and seduce with flatteries, but the people who know their God shall prove themselves strong and shall stand firm **and do exploits [for God]**.*

That would be you and I!

*Ephesians 5:16 Redeeming the time, because the days are evil.*

Jesus has redeemed us, is redeeming us and will redeem us. At the cross, He said, "It is finished."

> *Philippians 1:6 Being confident of this very thing, that he which hath begun a good work in you will perform it until the day of Jesus Christ.*

He is redeeming us. Changing us, molding, and making us into His image and likeness.

Soon, whether by way of the grave or with the triumphant shout of an archangel, we will see Him face to face. He will redeem us. Yet, in this verse, it clearly states that we are to redeem our time.

It has been said that the average Canadian spends 2-1/2 hours each day watching television. Here in the United States, it is likely greater because of the internet and the availability of programming.

- Four out of five of Hollywood executives think there is a link between TV violence and real-life violence.
- 91% of children say they feel upset or scared by violence on television.
- Twelve medical studies since 1985 link excessive television-watching to increasing rates of obesity.
- Two hundred two junk food ads are generally aired during four hours of Saturday morning programming.
- 200,000 – the number of violent acts the average American child season TV by age 18;
- 16,000 – the number of murders witnessed by children on television by age 18.
- 10% of youth violence is directly attributable to TV viewing.
- 73% of Americans believe TV and movies are responsible for juvenile crime.

> *Proverbs 23:7 For as he thinks in his heart, so is he.*

The average Canadian spends 912.5 hours, or 38 days every year, lying there in front of the TV! There are only twelve months in a year. That means that

Canadians spend over one month of every year feeding their flesh.

Sure, it gets cold outside, but there are tons of winter activities that are fun, good fitness, and free!

This message was preached initially while we pastored five years in Canada, where temperatures often hit -30C with two feet of snow on the ground. Yet, here, in Tulsa, people still spend hours in front of the screen, and this time could surely be spent more profitably for the kingdom of God.

Now, if every Canadian were watching two and a half hours a day of excellent anointed television ministry, what a difference we would see.

> *Philippians 4:8 Finally, brethren, whatsoever things are true, whatso-ever things are honest, whatsoever things are just, whatsoever things are pure, whatsoever things are lovely, whatsoever things are of good report; if there be any virtue, and if there be any praise, think on these things.*

We had this verse framed on our wall for many years. It is still true 25 years later.

If what you are watching is not true, honest, just, pure, lovely, of a good report (the news is not generally a good report), full of virtue (not lies), does not cause you to praise God, **do not watch it**.

It is not bringing life to you but is taking life from you.

Even one of our favorite family activities, Facebook, can quickly become an electronic tabloid, broadcasting what satan is doing in the earth instead of glorifying God. Yes, our Social Media needs to bow to the Lordship of Jesus!

> *Psalm 101:3(KJV) I will set no wicked thing before mine eyes: I hate the work of them that turn aside; it shall not cleave to me*

It is sucking the anointing, joy, fruitfulness, presence, and prosperity of God out of you like a giant leech. It is killing your dreams and vitality and polluting your mind. Kill it before it kills you.

I asked my congregation at one point for all of us to take a television fast to spend our daily TV time in the Word, job hunting, volunteering, taking a course, reading our Bible (what a concept), or telling someone about Jesus.

If you seek Him first, He will exalt you.

> *1 Peter 5:6 Humble yourselves therefore under the mighty hand of God, that he may exalt you in due time.*

So, you have made Jesus your Lord. You are praying every morning, seeking Him, craving Him, diligently reading His Word, and trying to do what it says. Your due time is coming. He will exalt you.

Now, we need to do something. You must act now.

Faith is an act!

> *Eccl 11:4 (NLT) If you wait for perfect conditions, you will never get anything done.*
> *Proverbs 14:23 In all labor, there is profit, but the talk of the lips tendeth only to penury.*

NOW faith is, and His name is I AM! Our ever-present help in times of need!

Confession alone will not bring godly success; we must do what we confess.

We need to begin the dos of the gospel.

The most important thing we can do is share the gospel. Only the gospel has the power to turn men from darkness to light, to separate them from hell to turn towards heaven.

In Reinhard Bonnke's book *Time is running out*, he makes this statement:

"If 10,000 people live near your church, according to statistics, four of them die every week. Is it satisfactory then, if only one of the 10,000 is saved every month or even every week? I find it is impossible to exaggerate the urgency of sharing the gospel! The greatest work on earth is to preach the good news, and the greatest need in the world is the need of the gospel."

We believe in healing around here, but Jesus taught, preached and healed.

If you want some simple ways to share the gospel and you are reading this online, here are some articles I wrote. You may simply cut and paste these links to share eternal life, the power of God in speaking in other tongues, or the message of divine healing. You must know someone online. You can share one of these with NOW!

First of all, he went.

Perhaps all God would have you do today is cut and paste one of these articles or one of the links above to one of your friends that you know needs eternal life.

Honestly, are you comfortable with them going to hell?

This can affect your finances. As you get involved in God's work, He gets involved in your business.

*Deuteronomy 8: (KJV) But thou shalt remember the Lord thy God: for it is he that giveth thee power to get wealth, that he may establish his covenant which he sware unto thy fathers, as it is this day*

*Acts 1:(KJV) But ye shall receive power, after that the Holy Ghost is come upon you: and ye shall be witnesses unto me both in Jerusalem, and in all Judaea, and in Samaria, and unto the uttermost part of the earth.*

We believe in financial prosperity around here, yet the power to get wealth is **'to be my witnesses' on the earth.**

We must use our time to win souls for eternity. This life is but a dressing room for eternity.

People we know are going to die. We could have shown them the love of Jesus, fed and clothed them, served them, given them money, even healed them. Yet, if they are not born-again, they will go to hell. Hell is not a theological concept but a very real place.

*Acts 4:12 Neither is there salvation in any other: for there is none other name under heaven given among men, whereby we **must be saved**.*

We are called with a purpose. We are redeemed. Yet, there is a time to grow up and recognize our responsibility to the family business. Our Father in heaven is in the redemption business. Everything we are or hope to be must revolve around that.

I heard a minister state that the secret of successful people is in their daily routine. Stephen Covey, a leadership expert, talks about the book, *7 Habits of Successful People*. The secret of your success is in your daily routine, the daily disciplines that create incredible realities over time.

> *Teach us to number our days aright, that we may gain a heart of wisdom. Psalm 90:12.*

> *Matthew 25:15 And unto one, he gave five talents, to another two, and to another one; to every man according to his several ability; and straightway took his journey.*

God uses people according to their ability.

> *1 Peter 4:11 If any man speak, let him speak as the oracles of God; if any man minister, let him do it as of the ability which God giveth: that God in all things may be glorified through Jesus Christ, to whom be praise and dominion forever and ever. Amen.*

Yet abilities can change. You take a night course to improve your expertise. Take a college course, or take a course online through one of the great Bible schools in the earth: http://www.vbctulsa.com/ http://www.rbtc.org/ http://www.elim.edu/

You deliberately find someone gifted in a particular area and ask them to teach you what you need in that area. When I ran our construction companies, I carefully cultivated relationships with skilled mentors.

Do like me; endeavor to read a new book every week. All that college taught me is how to learn, to research, to grow...face the truth: we are all students for life!

What is your daily schedule? Do you get up and let things happen? Or do you deliberately decide that this week is going to be different, that you are going to make changes for the better?

Are you seeking First Jesus and His Kingdom? Nothing else works unless He is our personal Lord!

There are several great books written on the power of daily discipline. May I recommend just two? *The Slight Edge* by Jeff Olsen and *The Compound Effect* by Darren Hardy encouraged me. I do not know if these guys know Jesus, but they have sure figured out the secrets of daily disciplines that produce success!

In summation:

Win souls!

Get involved with something that presents the gospel to an unsaved person.

> *Proverbs 11:30 The fruit of the righteous is a tree of life, and he that* **winneth souls** *is wise*

**Think Harvest thoughts!** I have learned that everything in the kingdom of God revolves around the harvest. If you are spending your life reaching people with the love of God and the gospel, you will see the presence and power of God daily, and your life will be blessed of heaven.

**Improve yourself.** Apply for a better job. Take a night course. Improve your ability. If you want a change, you need to make a change. The second commandment is to love your neighbor as yourself. If you don't take time to develop yourself, your neighbor is in trouble!

Don't know how to start? PRAY!

> *John 16:13 Howbeit when he, the Spirit of truth, is* **come***, he will guide you into all truth: for he shall not speak of himself; but whatsoever he shall hear, that shall he speak: and he will shew you* **things to come***.*

God will show us things to come! You have specific, unique fingerprints –
and a distinct unique destiny and calling upon your life. As you seek Jesus, He
will lead and guide you to maximize your impact in this life and for eternity–
yet, always remember that He walks with you in the journey. His joy is a
relationship – He is drawing you to Himself in the incredible pilgrimage of
life and life more abundantly – you were never designed to be alone nor to
do life alone.

> John 3:27 John answered and said, **A man can receive nothing**, except
> it be given him from heaven.

Question: What are you going to do with your time tomorrow? How are you
going to use it to affect eternal results and rewards?

Let's pray:

'Father, teach me to number my days right. Make my life count for
eternity! Use me today to make a difference in someone's life. Deliver
me from timewasters! I ask, knowing I am heard, for I ask in Your name,
Lord Jesus. Amen!'

# 52

# Attentive to Serve

*Isaiah 40:31 but they that wait upon the Lord shall renew their strength; they shall mount up with wings as eagles; they shall run, and not be weary; and they shall walk, and not faint.*

*Psalm 123:2 We keep looking to the Lord our God for his mercy, just as servants keep their eyes on their master as a slave girl watches her mistress for the slightest signal.*

Some years ago, I heard a minister say that waiting upon the Lord was not sitting still doing anything but as a waiter in a restaurant, serving attentively with excellence, continually looking to their client's very eye and hand motions, and being ready for their next course or slightest need.

Can we not serve Jesus and His people this way? Attentively, aggressively seeking Holy Spirit for the next need of our Master ready to jump, help, listen, and move as He leads?

*Waiting for God is not laziness. Waiting for God is not going to sleep. Waiting for God is not the abandonment of effort. Waiting for God means, first, activity under command; second, readiness for any new command that may come; third, the ability to do nothing until the command is given.* G. Campbell Morgan

Let's Pray:

Father, grant us attentive, sensitive hearts to hear, obey, and anticipate what Your heart says is needed next. We love You, Lord Jesus, and would serve You today. Amen!

# 53

# Test the Spirits - Love Truth!

*John 4:1 Beloved, believe not every spirit, but try the spirits whether they are of God: because many false prophets are gone out into the world.*

*Hereby know ye the Spirit of God: Every spirit that confesseth that Jesus Christ is come in the flesh is of God: And every spirit that confesseth not that Jesus Christ is come in the flesh is not of God: and this is that spirit of antichrist, whereof ye have heard that it should come; and even now already is it in the world.*

*Ye are of God, little children, and have overcome them: because greater is he that is in you than he that is in the world.*

The problem with authentic prophetic ministry has always been deception. It's the only weapon satan has left, for he has been stripped of all power and authority when Jesus rose from the dead.

*2 Cor 11:14 And no marvel; for Satan himself is transformed into an angel of light.*

*Gal 1:8 But though we, or an angel from heaven, preach any other gospel unto you than that which we have preached unto you, let him be accursed.*

Satan is a liar and the father of all lies, and deception is his weapon, but he uses this weapon very well on the earth even today. Just as there are an authentic prophetic ministry and spiritual oversight, there are demonic spirits that emulate the gifts of God, with the sole intent, of causing ministries and the people of God to go astray.

*Deut 18:10 There shall not be found among you any one that maketh his son or his daughter to pass through the fire, or that useth divination, or an observer of times, or an enchanter, or a witch,*

Or a charmer, or a consulter with familiar spirits, or a wizard, or a necromancer.

For all that do these things are an abomination unto the LORD: and because of these abominations the LORD thy God doth drive them out from before thee.

Thou shalt be perfect with the LORD thy God.

Jesus warned us about false prophets: Matthew 7:15 Beware of false prophets, which come to you in sheep's clothing, but inwardly they are ravening wolves.

*Matthew 24:24*

*For there shall arise false Christs, and false prophets, and shall shew great signs and wonders; insomuch that, if it were possible, they shall deceive the very elect*

*2 Corinthians 11:13-14*

*For such are false apostles, deceitful workers, transforming them-selves into the apostles of Christ. And no marvel; for Satan himself is transformed into an angel of light. 15 Therefore it is no great thing if his ministers also are transformed as the ministers of righteousness; whose end shall be according to their works. John 10:12*

*But he that is a hireling, and not the shepherd, whose own the sheep are not, seeth the wolf coming, and leaveth the sheep, and fleeth: and the wolf catcheth them, and scattereth the sheep. 2 Peter 2 [Full Chapter]*

But there were false prophets also among the people, even as there shall be false teachers among you, who privily shall bring in damnable heresies, even denying the Lord that bought them and bring upon themselves swift destruction. And many shall follow their pernicious ways, because of whom the way of truth shall be evil spoken of. And through covetousness shall they with feigned words make merchandise of you: whose judgment now of a long time lingereth not, and their damnation slumbereth not.

From the time in the garden, satan knew that if he could just get the people of God to disobey God, he would have them in his power, for how well he knows the holiness and raw power of God!

*James 2:19 Thou believest that there is one God; thou doest well: the devils also believe and tremble.*

He knows he has no power against God and that we do have power with God and authority from Him. He hasn't changed; he still whispers, 'Has God really said?' to attempt to get us off of the Word of God, to deviate from the authority of the Scriptures. In a broad sense, he has been successful.

Mohammad went up into a cave to seek God. An angel claiming to Gabriel appeared to him and put him in a spiritual stupor. After clasping him, the angel imparted to him 'the oracle of God' which Mohammad then had written down. That writing is now known as the Quran. Islam now claims to have a billion followers in the earth that are far from Jesus, living a life of fear, violence, hatred, and strife, all because one man listened to another voice, heard another spirit that pretended to be of God.

Remember, demons lie, then deceive. Jesus said, 'by their fruits, you will know them.' And the fruit of Islam has been a blood bath for centuries.

So, it is with Mormonism. A strong leader named Joseph Smith, attempting to lead his people into the promised land honestly, had a vision where Jesus and Mary supposedly appeared to him and gave him 'a complete revelation of the Bible,' and the Book of Mormon was written. Though Mormonism is not as bloody as Islam, Walter Martin in his book, *The Kingdom of the cults*, cites 84 critical differences between Mormon doctrine and the Bible. And so you end up with a moral people, devoid of spiritual power, anointing, and living truth brought alive from the presence and power of Holy Spirit.

*2 Tim 3:5 Having a form of godliness but denying the power thereof: from such turn away.*

Since these two deceptions were the crux of the 2012 US Presidential election, I mentioned them as examples. But I much encourage you to get a copy of Walter Martin's book, *Kingdom of the Cults*, to protect yourself from error.

Dig deep into the Word of God to discover what you believe, based upon the Bible: John 8:31-32 (AKJV)

*Jer 14: 14 Then the LORD said unto me, The prophets prophesy lies in my name: I sent them not, neither have I commanded them, neither spake unto them: they prophesy unto you a false vision and divination, and a thing of nought, and the deceit of their heart.*

Therefore thus saith the LORD concerning the prophets that prophesy in my name, and I sent them not, yet they say, Sword and famine shall not be in this land; By sword and famine shall those prophets be consumed.

And the people to whom they prophesy shall be cast out in the streets of Jerusalem because of the famine and the sword; and they shall have none to bury them, them, their wives, nor their sons, nor their daughters: for I will pour their wickedness upon them.

In this verse, we have prophets that should have been speaking by the Holy

Spirit the revelations of God, yet they were hearing and seeing by another spirit, a spirit of divination. They became deceived in their hearts.

> *Act 16:16 ¶ And it came to pass, as we went to prayer, a certain damsel possessed with a spirit of divination met us, which brought her masters much gain by soothsaying:*
>
> *The same followed Paul and us and cried, saying, These men are the servants of the most high God, which shew unto us the way of salvation. 18 And this did she many days. But Paul, being grieved, turned and said to the spirit, I command thee in the name of Jesus Christ to come out of her. And he came out the same hour.*

We must listen to our hearts and test the spirits. If something doesn't seem right, it probably isn't right.

I just finished a great little book, given to us called *The Authority of the Believer* by John A. Macmillan. It is a great book on spiritual authority and warfare, but the last couple of chapters talk about

many cases of demonic interaction with people. One chapter talks about that the rise of modern-day spiritualism stems from actual communication with spirits claiming to be the souls of loved ones who had died some years previously. As these spirits communicated through tapping and other methods, the group of adherents to this mess went from two teenaged girls to over 10 million.

**Just because an experience is supernatural, does not mean it is of God!**

Remember Moses, when he appeared before Pharaoh and God turned his staff into a serpent? The Egyptian priests did the same thing by demonic power.

Please stay grounded in truth as you move in the revelatory gifts of the Holy Spirit. I have to believe that as I stay rooted and grounded in the Word of God, that God Himself will send both laborers and teaching materials about demonic errors to keep us clean spiritually.

Like any Bible doctrine, there is a ditch on either side.

With this teaching, the two ditches are demonic deception resulting in supernatural revelation coming from demons instead of God. On the other side, strict legalism, resulting in no tolerance or allowance of prophetic ministry and guidance to the church of the living God. There is a straight and narrow way through these perils!

The cure for misuse of a gift is not "no use," but rather, "correct use."

> *1 Cor 14:1 Follow after charity, and desire spiritual gifts, but rather that ye may prophesy.*
>
> *1 Cor 14:39 Wherefore, brethren, covet to prophesy and forbid not to speak with tongues.*
>
> *These are the last days, the season when the anti-Christ spirit will manifest in a man.*

He is described in 2 Thess 2:9 *This man will come to do the work of Satan with counterfeit power and signs and miracles. He will use every kind of evil deception to fool those on their way to destruction,* **because they refuse to love and accept the truth that would save them.**

If we determine to love the truth and embrace it, we will be protected from sinister ministers and snakes in pulpits, wolves in sheep's clothing.

Let's pray:

'Father, I take my place in Your kingdom, determined to walk in truth. Open my eyes to the true state of the ministries You have called me to and give me wisdom on how best to pray, preach, feed, and lead Your people, to best grow them up in You, and Your perfect plan for us. Deliver me and protect me any others from all false prophetic, dreams, visions, or manifestation. Keep me in truth, at all costs, and prevent me from going astray. In any case that I have heard or seen things in the spirit that are not from You, but are demonic deception, please show me, cleanse me, and keep me pure and holy in Your sight and submitted to Your Word. In your name, I pray, Lord Jesus. Amen.'

<h1 style="text-align:center">54</h1>

# Successful

Success has eternal consequence. Luke 8:13 And those upon the rock [are the people] who, when they hear [the Word], receive and welcome it with joy; but these have no root. They believe for a while, and in time of trial and temptation fall away **(withdraw and stand aloof).**

John Maxwell calls it 'The Law of Buy-In,' in his book *The 21 irrefutable laws of leadership.*

I see it in the successful.

We preach the Word to them of God's kingdom, but it is contrary to the way they do things, and **'they withdraw and stand aloof.'**

Question is always: Will we do it God's way and reap eternal rewards, or fall back to the compromised, negotiated, slippery roads we have grown so accustomed to?

We must step up and step out in Jesus and endure the humility that comes from the trial. We do it His way.

"The trouble with being in the rat race is that even if you win, you'Rev still a rat." Lily Tomlin

One leader says to another: "You got to do it this way, now, if you want to survive in the rat race!" Quietly, the elderly man said: 'I'm not a rat; I'm running a completely different race."

It might look like you are losing in the rat race for a while, but hey, you are not a rat; you are a child of the King. Run your race for Him, for He is worthy!

Let's Pray:

'Father, bring truth into my life and reveal Your way to me, no matter how contrary it may appear to the way I was raised or instructed. As You do, please grant me the courage and boldness to do what You show me, no compromise, no fanfare, for Your glory. I ask this, Sir, knowing I am heard and answered, for I ask in Your name, Lord Jesus. Amen!'

55

# Righteousness Exalts a Nation

This message has not changed over the years because Jesus is the same, yesterday, today, and forever. He is the Prince of Peace. If we want peace in our land, we must submit to His Lordship, for His kingdom is righteousness, peace, and joy in the Holy Ghost!

*Proverbs 14:34 Righteousness exalteth a nation: but sin is a reproach to any people.*

*Proverbs 11:10 When it goeth well with the righteous, the city rejoiceth: and when the wicked perish, there is shouting.*

*Proverbs 29:2 When the righteous are in authority, the people rejoice: but when the wicked beareth rule, the people mourn.*

*Psalms 9:8 And he shall judge the world in righteousness; he shall minister judgment to the people in uprightness.*

*Psalms 11:7 For the righteous LORD loveth righteousness; his countenance doth behold the upright.*

*Psalms 23:3 He restoreth my soul:  he leadeth me in the paths of righteousness for his name's sake.*

*Psalms 96:13 Before the LORD: for he cometh, for he cometh to judge the earth: he shall judge the world with righteousness, and the people with his truth.*

*Proverbs 2:9 Then shalt thou understand righteousness, and judgment, and equity; yea, every good path.*

I want to speak about the righteousness of God. Righteousness meaning 'right standing with God.'

First, as a New Testament believer, we need to understand the difference between positional righteousness and practical righteousness.

Positional righteousness is the righteousness that every Christian has before the throne of God. We believe in Jesus, that He is God in the flesh, that He lived a sinless and victorious life here in the earth, performing miracles throughout His earthly ministry. We believe that He died upon the cross as the only acceptable substitute for our sins, that He rose from the grave on the third day and ascended bodily into heaven where He now reigns as King of King and Lord of Lords.

Positionally, we were all lost, but because we placed our faith in Him, He adopted us into the family of God and gave us a new identity.

Ephesians 1:20 Which he wrought in Christ when he raised him from the dead and set him at his own right hand in the heavenly places,

Ephesians 2:6 And hath raised us up together, and made us sit together in heavenly places in Christ Jesus:

You are a child of promise and heir of God. Your life has purpose and destiny upon it. You are no longer a bastard, a slave, or an orphan. You are not a mistake but are a child of the king, training for ruling and reigning in Him throughout eternity. You are the church, a member of the Body of Christ, a warrior in God's army, called to occupy this earth until He comes again. You have been given authority over death, demons, and disease and are no longer your own but have been bought with a price and live under His command. He has commanded us to go into all the world in His strength and authority and to bring it under His Lordship and authority. Today we are going to do some of that.

> *Revelation 1:5 And from Jesus Christ, who is the faithful witness, and the first begotten of the dead, and the prince of the kings of the earth. Unto him that loved us, and washed us from our sins in his own blood,*

> *Revelation 1:6 And hath made us kings and priests unto God and his Father; to him be glory and dominion forever and ever. Amen.*

> *Revelation 5:10 And hast made us unto our God kings and priests: and we shall reign on the earth.*

Practically, many of us are in one of two camps; we either don't fully know what God has for us to do for Him and so are growing in Him, becoming rooted and grounded in His love, seeking His will and Word in all things. Yet, some have flat out gone AWOL. We have long ago forgotten that 'Seek ye first the kingdom of God, and His righteousness' is the primary commandment in the Bible. Loving God first takes precedence over serving Him. There are no morning watch and prayer vigil in our homes. The family altar has long ago fallen away, destroyed and decrepit from disuse, and then the long weary walk of works has begun, living life in a dry and weary land where there is no water. We raise our children. We busy ourselves in our churches. We work hard to provide for our families, but we have lost our first love, the Lord of glory. I know, even as a pastor, my ministerial responsibilities have often crept into my life for long seasons, where I have dried up spiritually and delivered sermons devoid of passion and power. I have fed God's people stale bread from years of Bible study that ministers only to the intellect of man and not his spirit. I had to fall back upon the Rock and be broken. I had to put aside every earthly distraction to again seek the face of God, that I might deliver to His people living waters from His throne, words of Spirit and truth, again a voice for the Lord and not merely an echo.

Today, we will have good old-fashioned altar time to come back to. The Lord will meet you there, for He has sent me.

Yet I must speak today of practical righteousness. Practical righteousness for a Christian is walking in love. You have been made to sit together with Christ in heavenly places. You have been given a high position in the Spirit of God.

We used to attend a men's breakfast monthly up in Canada that was hosted by a group of Christian businessmen who understood the honor of God. They rented a Penthouse ballroom each month in one of the best hotels in town; and they did it right.

The Penthouse is on top of the building. It's a high place. Practical righteousness means to repent. That is, come back to your high place in God. Leave behind the filthy things of your flesh and this world, and come back, you royal child, to your position of honor and holiness before Him.

The Pentagon is also a high place. Every person working in the government of this great nation is called of God to live and do righteousness, for God is holy!

If we love and serve Jesus, we truly do have friends in high places, higher than any earthly relationship. He must become our best friend so that we serve and obey Him, seeking His counsel on the complexities of life more than all the counsel of man. The US Congress used to begin their sessions with the first three hours devoted to prayer.

Quickly, I'll give you a couple of thoughts on sin and will give the Holy Spirit something to work with in this message because I'm a man on a mission. These are critical days, and I'm fixing to change a nation and ultimately the nations of the earth, based upon what happens to you as you hear this word.

Forgive — no time to play with this one. God says if you don't forgive people that have done you wrong, He won't forgive you. Do it now. You will never feel like it, for the pain and offenses are real. Do it because the Word says so as an act of your will. You are commanded to forgive and love people, but you do not have to trust everyone. If someone did you wrong, you must forgive them. Until they exhibit fruits in keeping with repentance, you are not required to reconcile with them. Sin separates, but love covers a multitude of sins. You must forgive and love.

Now let's look at a few more sins.

> *Gal 5:19 Now the works of the flesh are manifest, which are these; Adultery, fornication, uncleanness, lasciviousness, idolatry, witchcraft, hatred, variance, emulations, wrath, strife, seditions, heresies, envyings, murders, drunkenness, revellings, and such like: of the which I tell you before, as I have also told you in time past, that they which do such things shall not inherit the kingdom of God. But the fruit of the Spirit is love, joy, peace, longsuffering, gentleness, goodness, faith, meekness, temperance: against such there is no law. And they that are Christ's have crucified the flesh with the affections and lusts. If we live in the Spirit, let us also walk in the Spirit.*

I had to do a little house cleaning before I could take you into where God wants us to go in this book.

You see, there is power in sacrifice. God is Almighty, and there is no higher power in heaven and earth than the power of the blood of Jesus.

> *Rev 2:18 And unto the angel of the church in Thyatira write; These things saith the Son of God, who hath his eyes like unto a flame of fire, and his feet are like fine brass;*

I know thy works, and charity, and service, and faith, and thy patience, and thy works; and the last to be more than the first.

Notwithstanding, I have a few things against thee, because thou sufferest that woman Jezebel, which calleth herself a prophetess, to teach and to seduce my servants to commit fornication, and to eat things sacrificed unto idols.

And I gave her space to repent of her fornication, and she repented not.

Behold, I will cast her into a bed and them that commit adultery with her into great tribulation, except they repent of their deeds.

And I will kill her children with death, and all the churches shall know that I am he which searcheth the reins and hearts: and I will give unto every one of you according to your works.

But unto you I say, and unto the rest in Thyatira, as many as have not this doctrine, and which have not known the **depths of Satan,** as they speak; I will put upon you none other burden.

But that which ye have already hold fast till I come.  **And he that overcometh,** and keepeth my works unto the end, to him will I give power over the nations:

God wants to give His church power over the nations, but we need to grow into it by overcoming the obstacles satan has arrayed against us. Overcoming takes raw courage, good old-fashioned guts, because many people do not love truth, nor are they willing to walk in honesty and the fear of the Lord. They will oppose you.

*1 Peter 2:2 As newborn babes, desire the sincere milk of the word, that ye may grow thereby:*

*Galatians 3:29 And if ye be Christ's, then are ye Abraham's seed, and heirs according to the promise.*

*Galatians 4:1 Now I say, That the heir, as long as he is a child, differeth nothing from a servant, though he be lord of all;*

But is under tutors and governors until the time appointed of the father.

You don't give a child an atomic bomb. We are the bride of Christ, and look at this:

*Isaiah 9:6 For unto us a child is born, unto us a son is given: and the government shall be upon his shoulder: and his name shall be called Wonderful, Counsellor, The mighty God, The everlasting Father, The*

*Prince of Peace.*

*Isaiah 9:7 Of the increase of his government and peace, there shall be no end, upon the throne of David, and upon his kingdom, to order it, and to establish it with judgment and with justice from henceforth even forever.*

The zeal of the LORD of hosts will perform this.

If you want to see your life influence the nations of the earth, or this nation used of God in the nations of the earth, we must keep growing in Jesus and in the Word of God. As we do, His rule and righteous reign, the absolute highest good of all humankind, will flow through this nation and us.

*Matthew 10:27 What I tell you in darkness, that speak ye in light: and what ye hear in the ear, that preach ye upon the housetops.*

We are the bride of Christ. When we approach God in intimacy, and symbolically place our head upon Jesus's shoulder, He whispers secrets into our spirit. He tells us that these things are to be proclaimed from the rooftops.

Why? Because Jesus has all authority in heaven and earth, and He grants that authority to His church. He will back up His Word with signs following, and even angels wait for the hearing of God's Word in the earth.

*Psalms 103:20 Bless the LORD, ye his angels, that excel in strength, that do his commandments, hearkening unto the voice of his word.*

*Psalms 104:4 Who maketh his angels spirits; his ministers a flaming fire: The government of God must flow through you! You are the ones supposed to be uttering this decree, as you abide in Him. Thou shalt make thy prayer unto him, and he shall hear thee, and thou shalt pay thy vows.*

*Job 22:28 Thou shalt also decree a thing, and it shall be established unto thee: and the light shall shine upon thy ways.*

*Acts 2:17-18 And it shall come to pass in the last days, saith God, I will pour out of my Spirit upon all flesh: and your sons and your daughters shall prophesy, and your young men shall see visions, and your old men shall dream dreams: And on my servants and on my handmaidens I will pour out in those days of my Spirit; and they shall prophesy: And I will shew wonders in heaven above, and signs in the earth beneath; blood, and fire, and vapor of smoke:*

*Isaiah 8:18 Behold, I and the children whom the LORD hath given me are for signs and for wonders in Israel from the LORD of hosts, which dwelleth in mount Zion.*

We seek Him. God pours out His Spirit. The Holy Spirit tells us things God wants to do in the earth. We proclaim these things and declare the decrees of God. God backs up His Word with power, and signs and wonders occur in the earth.

So, when God wants to prune an earthly government, He reveals His will to five-fold ministry gifts in the earth. They declare His decrees. God moves upon His Word, and stuff happens.

*Amos 3:7 Surely the Lord GOD will do nothing, but he revealeth his secret unto his servants the prophets.*

*Isaiah 55:11 So shall my word be that goeth forth out of my mouth: it shall not return unto me void, but it shall accomplish that which I please, and it shall prosper in the thing whereto I sent it.*

*Jeremiah 1:10 See, I have this day set thee over the nations and over the kingdoms, to root out, and to pull down, and to destroy, and to throw down, to build, and to plant.*

*Matthew 4:8 Again, the devil taketh him up into an exceeding high mountain, and sheweth him all the kingdoms of the world, and the glory of them;*

What did Satan show Jesus? I believe he showed him his rulership over nations in the realm of the spirit. Territorial principalities of darkness ruling under his domain. Demons rule the minds of men, for satan is a mind–blinding spirit.

*Hebrews 11:3 Through faith we understand that the worlds were framed by the word of God, so that things which are seen were not made of things which do appear.*

We are to take the Word of God and subdue this world through prayer and the preaching of God's Word until:

*Revelation 11:15 And the seventh angel sounded; and there were great voices in heaven, saying, The kingdoms of this world are become the kingdoms of our Lord, and of his Christ, and he shall reign forever and ever.*

We do this through what we believe and speak.

Hebrews 11:33 Who through faith subdued kingdoms, wrought righteousness, obtained promises, stopped the mouths of lions,

Today, God is going to use us for signs and wonders in the earth. We are going to move in things of eternal consequence for His glory.

There is power in sacrifice. Satan knows this. When you study out pagan religions, part of the worship of Baal and Ashtoreth and Molech in the Old Testament involved human sacrifice. Demon worshippers literally offered their children upon altars of demonic sacrifice, a practice God expressly forbids.

*Leviticus 18:21 And thou shalt not let any of thy seed pass through the fire to Molech, neither shalt thou profane the name of thy God: I am the LORD. Jesus holds the keys to death and hell. Every life in the earth is given by God by divine decree. When blood is shed unrighteously, it cries out to the throne of God.*

For those of you who have read or heard my teaching on 'Redeeming the Land' or have had me come to your property and pray to redeem it, you have learned that this is not merely great preaching but a practical reality.

*Gal 4:9 And the LORD said unto Cain, Where is Abel thy brother? And he said, I know not: Am I my brother's keeper? And he said, What hast thou done? The voice of thy brother's blood crieth unto me from the ground.*

*Rev 6:9–10 And when he had opened the fifth seal, I saw under the altar the souls of them that were slain for the word of God, and for the testimony which they held:*

*And they cried with a loud voice, saying, How long, O Lord, holy and true, dost thou not judge and avenge our blood on them that dwell on the earth?*

When a person dies, his spirit appears before the throne of God. God sees, and He judges.

*Luke 11:51 From the blood of Abel unto the blood of Zacharias, which perished between the altar and the temple: verily I say unto you, It shall be required of this generation.*

So, Satan understands the power of unjust bloodshed and seeks to destroy nations who shed it to provoke God to wrath. The thief comes to kill. 2 Kings 3:

It gives us an account that I believe has a powerful application today. We see a divided kingdom. Israel was ruled by a wicked king named Jehoram.

Judah ruled by a godly king named Jehoshaphat. Jehoram had been raised by an evil father, Ahab. Ahab had ruled over the Samaritans and taxed them heavily. When he died, they rebelled, and Jehoram found himself without God at war. So, he did what many still do today. He tried to find someone to fight with him.

*2 Kings 3:1-12 Now Jehoram, the son of Ahab, began to reign over Israel in Samaria the eighteenth year of Jehoshaphat king of Judah and reigned twelve years.*

*And he wrought evil in the sight of the LORD; but not like his father, and like his mother: for he put away the image of Baal that his father had made. 3 Nevertheless, he cleaved unto the sins of Jeroboam, the son of Nebat, which made Israel to sin; he departed not from there.*

*And Mesha king of Moab was a sheepmaster and rendered unto the king of Israel an hundred thousand lambs, and an hundred thousand rams, with the wool.*

*But it came to pass, when Ahab was dead, that the king of Moab rebelled against the king of Israel.*

*And king Jehoram went out of Samaria the same time, and numbered all Israel.*

*And he went and sent to Jehoshaphat the king of Judah, saying, The king of Moab hath rebelled against me: wilt thou go with me against Moab to battle? And he said, I will go up: I am as thou art, my people as thy people, and my horses as thy horses.*

*And he said, Which way shall we go up? And he answered, The way through the wilderness of Edom.*

*So, the king of Israel went, and the king of Judah, and the king of Edom: and they fetched a compass of seven days' journey: and there was no water for the host, and for the cattle that followed them.*

*And the king of Israel said, Alas! That the LORD hath called these three kings together to deliver them into the hand of Moab!*

*But Jehoshaphat said, Is there not here a prophet of the LORD, that we may enquire of the LORD by him? And one of the kings of Israel's servants answered and said, Here is Elisha, the son of Shaphat, which poured water on the hands of Elijah.*

*Jehoshaphat seeks God and finds a prophet, the mighty man of God Elisha, the successor to Elijah.*

*And Jehoshaphat said, The word of the LORD is with him. So, the king of Israel and Jehoshaphat and the king of Edom went down to him.*

*And Elisha said unto the king of Israel, what have I to do with thee? Get thee to the prophets of thy father and to the prophets of thy mother. And the king of Israel said unto him, Nay: for the LORD hath called these three kings together, to deliver them into the hand of Moab.*

*And Elisha said, As the LORD of hosts liveth, before whom I stand, surely, were it not that I regard the presence of Jehoshaphat the king of Judah, I would not look toward thee, nor see thee.*

*But now bring me a minstrel. And it came to pass, when the minstrel played, that the hand of the LORD came upon him.*

*And he said, thus saith the LORD, Make this valley full of ditches.*

*For thus saith the LORD, Ye shall not see wind, neither shall ye see rain; yet that valley shall be filled with water, that ye may drink, both ye, and your cattle, and your beasts.*

*And this is but a light thing in the sight of the LORD: he will deliver the Moabites also into your hand.*

*And ye shall smite every fenced city, and every choice city, and shall fell every good tree, and stop all wells of water, and mar every good piece of land with stones.*

*And it came to pass in the morning, when the meat offering was offered, that, behold, there came water by the way of Edom, and the country was filled with water.*

*And when all the Moabites heard that the kings were come up to fight against them, they gathered all that were able to put on armor, and upward and stood in the border.*

*And they rose up early in the morning, and the sun shone upon the water, and the Moabites saw the water on the other side as red as blood:*

*And they said, This is blood: the kings are surely slain, and they have smitten one another: now therefore, Moab, to the spoil.*

*And when they came to the camp of Israel, the Israelites rose up and smote the Moabites so that they fled before them: but they went forward smiting the Moabites, even in their country.*

*And they beat down the cities, and on every good piece of land cast every man his stone, and filled it, and they stopped all the wells of water, and felled all the good trees: only in Kirharaseth left they the stones thereof; howbeit the slingers went about it, and smote it.*

*And when the king of Moab saw that the battle was too sore for him, he took with him seven hundred men that drew swords, to break through even unto the king of Edom: but they could not.*

*Then he took his eldest son that should have reigned in his stead and offered him for a burnt offering upon the wall. And there was great indignation against Israel: and they departed from him and returned to their own land.*

*So, he killed his son, a shadow and type of how God offered up His Son as a sacrifice, and the blood of that sacrifice so empowered the demon principality that the Moabites served that the army was empowered to drive back the compromised army of God.*

*We see again and again in the Scripture that when the people of God walked with God in practical righteousness, their enemies rose up. Then God would give a battle plan; and the nation was undefeated. A holy people in the hands of an Almighty God is undefeatable, unstoppable in battle.*

So, abortion, the killing of an unborn child, no matter how it is rationalized in the mind of people, is a literal blood sacrifice being offered up to demon spirits.

Why do world leaders attend meetings at Bohemian Grove for the yearly 'Festival of Fire'? Some think it is merely a political move, but it is not: it is a ceremony where demon spirits are actually worshipped in exchange for political power and authority.

*2 Cor 10:6 And having in a readiness to revenge all disobedience when your obedience is fulfilled.*

Obedience produced God's power and still does today. Ac 5:32 And we are his witnesses of these things; and so is also the Holy Ghost, whom God hath given to them that obey him.

Remember? The Egyptians chased Moses at the Red Sea. God parted the waters, and then God caused the water to drown the Egyptian army. Exodus 17:10 So Joshua did as Moses had said to him and fought with Amalek: and Moses, Aaron, and Hur went up to the top of the hill.

You know the story. Moses lifted his rod, and the armies of heaven marched against the legions of hell in the realm of the spirit, and Israel prevailed in battle. When Moses got tired and let the rod of God fall, the devils empowering the Amalekites surged, and the heavenly host withdrew, and the armies of Israel struggled. With Aaron and Hur's undergirding, Moses was able to keep the rod of God upheld, and Israel won the victory over her enemies.

So, it was during the war in Iraq. As the church interceded and spiritually held up the arms of President Bush and the US and allied armed forces, we saw victory.

I said by the spirit of God, during that war:

"If we let down our guard and become apathetic and prayerless, Al Queda recruits and plots are not revealed to military sources by the Spirit of God. The host of heaven is not empowered to work, and soldiers die, and our borders are not safe."

I can give many stories. When Joshua marched against Jericho under God's authority and commands, the walls fell, and Israel prevailed. When we read the account in Joshua chapter 7, where Achan sinned and stole the cursed things, his sin punched a hole in the dome of God's supernatural protection over Israel. Israel went to battle against Ai and was defeated.

Soldiers died. Joshua prayed. God did not say, "Achan sinned," but rather

He said,

"Israel has sinned." Achan's disobedience in wartime opened the door for demonic penetration of the spiritual covering over the nation of Israel, and Israel was defeated in battle. Achan was discovered, and capital punishment was executed. Israel was undefeated in its next military exploits. There is much I can say about this, but this is enough, for now.

> *2 Sam 5: And the Philistines came up yet again and spread themselves in the valley of Rephaim.*
>
> *And when David enquired of the LORD, he said, Thou shalt not go up; but fetch a compass behind them, and come upon them over against the mulberry trees.*
>
> *And let it be, when thou hearest the sound of a going in the tops of the mulberry trees, that then thou shalt bestir thyself: for then shall the LORD go out before thee, to smite the host of the Philistines.*

What happened here in battle? David sought God for a battle plan. God gave him one that involved the host of heaven. David was to wait until the angels of God marched against the demons that the Philistines served, then go to battle. He did; God did, and again Israel was victorious. Notice again that David was serving God with his whole heart, no compromise.

We see this again, recorded for us from the life of the prophet Elisha:

> *2 Kings 6:15 And when the servant of the man of God was risen early, and gone forth, behold, an host compassed the city both with horses and chariots. And his servant said unto him, Alas, my master! How shall we do?*
>
> *And he answered, Fear not: for they that be with us are more than they that be with them.*
>
> *And Elisha prayed and said, LORD, I pray thee, open his eyes, that he may see. And the LORD opened the eyes of the young man; and he saw: and, behold, the mountain was full of horses and chariots of fire*

*round about Elisha.*

One man with God, in touch with heaven and operating under the authority of heaven, allowed the armies of God to prevail against the host of hell and the people of God were delivered.

My question to you is this: Will you be that man or woman of God?

After we repent of our personal sins and again begin to seek God, there are specific battle plans to be revealed from heaven that will cause the church and the gospel to be victorious in this generation.

Here's what I see at present in the earth. The purposes of God in the earth are at stake again as the destiny of God for the United States hangs in the balance.

So, what are we to pray for this nation?

That the blood of Jesus be applied to the blood of the sacrifice Satan has raised up through abortion.

That God give a revelation to judges and purge the judicial system. May the medical profession and the general public recognized the depth of evil that the abortion industry is.

That the United States of America sell out for Jesus and the kingdom of God and renounce compromise with Islam, abortion, and same-sex marriage and make unholy alliances with agencies within the United States, (ACLU, Islam, the Bohemian grove bunch, and every pro-abortion, or homosexual group) and that God remove from positions of authority those leaders across this land that do.

That the church recognize racism for what it is, an enemy to be destroyed in prayer. It is a spiritual force that must be blasted in prayer, not just social action.

That the church aggressively pray for North American Indian tribes, the host peoples of this land. The broken treaties and innocent bloodshed of these people are screaming before the throne of God, and ONLY the church can fix this through the blood of Jesus.

*Matt 6:24 No man can serve two masters: for either he will hate the one, and love the other; or else he will hold to the one, and despise the other. Ye cannot serve God and mammon.*

*Luke 16:13 No servant can serve two masters: for either he will hate the one, and love the other; or else he will hold to the one and despise the other. Ye cannot serve God and mammon.*

Mammon is simply a term to describe the worldly system, and demonic principalities rule through it. You cannot serve Jesus, claim to know Him, then publicly do exactly the opposite His Word prescribes.

*John 14:15 If ye love me, keep my commandments.*

*John 14:21 He that hath my commandments, and keepeth them, he it is that loveth me: and he that loveth me shall be loved of my Father, and I will love him and will manifest myself to him.*

That the church take her place in this spiritual war and that Islamic infiltration into the US be removed. That terrorist organizations be exposed, dismantled, and removed. That Muslims would be converted, en masse, both here in the US and internationally. The Bible is a book of holiness and love. The Quran is a book of atrocities and hate. There will never be a mix of the two in heaven nor can there be in the earth.

That God protection be restored in this nation. That terrorist plots be exposed and stopped before they are carried out.

That Federal judges or politicians across this land who have been proabortion repent, now, or be removed from office.

The US publicly again stand with Israel.

That prayer and the Bible again return to schools.

That Christians again sell out totally for Jesus and begin to seek your kingdom first, hear your voice, share the gospel, and attend and build healthy local churches across the US.

That the media proclaim the gospel and the truth, not lies.

Those hidden things are brought to light, and those things against the Word of God and the spirit of the US constitution be removed.

That again, this great nation bow its knee to the Lordship of Jesus Christ.

Get in agreement, Church, and declare these things in your authority and agreement and watch God move His hand in revival across the earth again.

Let's Pray:

Father, we ask for mercy, once again, for the horrendous slaughter of our unborn children. Forgive them, Father, for their murder and open their eyes to the carnage they create. Reveal Jesus to them. By faith, in your authority, I plead and apply the blood of Jesus over the blood of abortion and command every evil spirit operating there to leave this nation now. In the name and authority of Jesus.

Father, Thank You for the stand against racism in this nation. Please use all means to provide equity and equal opportunity to all Americans, including blacks and First Nations peoples.

Forgive us, Father, have mercy upon us and open our eyes to see Jesus and to bow to His Lordship. To cut every tie with Islam, abortion, homosexuality, and every treacherous group determined to undermine and destroy the United States. I thank You for the freedom that you have given us and for the liberty to walk in love, honor, and honesty, and justice for all men. I pray for every member of government in the executive, judicial, and legislative branches, every civil authority, and in every state. I pray that they choose Jesus and the Word of God in every area of their leadership, and that they use all of their abilities, authority, and influence to promote the kingdom of God in the earth.

By faith, I stand against Islam in America. I forbid and stop every evil spirit operating through this and command all deception to leave now. I bring the sword of the Spirit to all compromise with Islam and pray for every Muslim that You would reveal to them the love of Jesus and the truth that sets free in the gospel. I bind the fear of death that controls them and set them free to be the people of love, honor, honesty, and truth you have called them to be, in Jesus's name.

Father, Today is the day of salvation, and Your name is I AM. I declare and decree that every politician, judge, or government official that has joined itself to abortion, homosexuality, or Islam, be removed from office and that God-fearing persons be put in their place, today, in Jesus's name. Amen

Father, I ask that The US publicly again stand with Israel in spirit and in truth and would stop supporting her enemies today. That you might again bless this nation.

Father, we ask: "That prayer and the Bible again return to schools." In Jesus's name!

Father, we ask that Christians again sell out totally for Jesus and begin to seek first your kingdom, hear your voice, share the gospel, and build healthy local churches across the US.

Father, by faith, I command the media proclaim the gospel and be cleansed from all perversion, filth, and evil, in Jesus's name.

1. Father, I ask, that hidden things be brought to light, and those things against the Word of God and the spirit of the US constitution be removed from this nation, in Jesus's name. Amen.

- Father, bring this great nation back to You. That again, this great nation bow its knee to the Lordship of Jesus Christ. AMEN!

Praying for America Hidden things to be revealed.

*Isa 45:3 And I will give thee the treasures of darkness, and hidden riches of secret places, that thou mayest know that I, the LORD, which call thee by thy name, am the God of Israel.*

*Isa 48:6 Thou hast heard, see all this; and will not ye declare it? I have shewed thee new things from this time, even hidden things, and thou didst not know them.*

*1 Cor 2:7 But we speak the wisdom of God in a mystery, even the hidden wisdom, which God ordained before the world unto our glory:*

*1 Cor 4:5 Therefore judge nothing before the time, until the Lord come, who both will bring to light the hidden things of darkness, and will make manifest the counsels of the hearts: and then shall every man have praise of God.*

*2 Cor 4:2 But have renounced the hidden things of dishonesty, not walking in craftiness, nor handling the word of God deceitfully; but by manifestation of the truth commending ourselves to every man's conscience in the sight of God.*

That God will reveal to us hidden things:

Hidden keys of knowledge to dismantle and destroy works and roots of darkness.

Hidden keys of wisdom to know what to do, to see the kingdom of God advance and be restored in the United States of America.

That God reveal the very motives of men's hearts, the agendas of godless men, intent on destroying this country. That He, Himself destroy them: Psalm 112:10 The wicked shall see it, and be grieved; he shall gnash with his teeth, and melt away: the desire of the wicked shall perish. That these very desires die, and that God change both the hearts of men and leadership here, or, if necessary, the administration itself, that the government be righteous, holy, and entirely under the Lordship of Jesus.

That the Lord come and reveal the hidden things of dishonesty and iniquity, and that by manifestation of the truth, these be destroyed and cleansed from our land.

That Father God in heaven would have mercy upon this nation, and forgive us, and send His spirit again to reveal Jesus and turn us back to Him.

This is the promise God made to our founding fathers, from which we get our three branches of government:

*Isaiah 33:22 For the Lord is our judge, the Lord is our lawgiver, the Lord is our king;* **he will save us!**

As I reread this verse this week, I am convinced that Jesus will save America! He is going to do it! Continue to stand with me for righteousness and the preservation of this great nation! Amen!

# 56

# What Spirit Do You Serve With Money?

*1 Timothy 6:10 For the **love of money** is the root **of** all evil: which while some coveted after, they have erred from the faith, and pierced themselves through with many sorrows*

*Revelation 13:17 and that no man might **buy or sell**, save he that had the mark, **or** the name*

of the beast, **or** the number of his name.

If we honestly believe that we are living in the last days and that we are in a spiritual battle for the souls of men, then these verses become radically relevant.

Demons work through controlling the minds and thinking of people.

As Jesus moves in great power in this generation, we see multitudes coming into His kingdom, great healing miracles, yet satan still fights the hardest in the financial realm, knowing that generally 'He who owns the gold, makes the rules'.

There are powerful societies that have marshaled great financial empires, and, unless they are fully submitted to the Lordship of Jesus, have become part of this hellish, devilish oppressive system, that keeps the poor, weak and seeks only 'one world order' or power and control of the earth through

267

its resources.

The nature of God is to give, for God so loved the world that He gave... The only way to truly kill selfishness and covetousness is to give.

I do so daily on purpose.

It's the only safe way I know to keep my own pride and selfish nature crucified.

At whatever level of giving we are at, there is always the challenge to use wisdom to give more intelligently.

Can you think of ways to give more today for the purpose of promoting the kingdom of God?

Let's pray:

'Father, You give. Make me more like You. Give me the gift of giving today and show me how to give responsibly.  Increase me in this, and lavishly provide more to give. In Your name, I pray, Lord Jesus. Amen.'

# 57

# Leave a Legacy - Your Leadership Changes the Changes to Come!

*Leadership responsibilities:*

Success without a successor is failure!

**successor**

sksesr/ noun: **successor**; plural noun: **successors**

a person or thing that succeeds another.

"Schoenberg saw himself as a natural **successor to** the German romantic school."

synonyms:

heir (apparent), inheritor,next-in-line

"Mary was the rightful successor to the English throne."

antonyms:

predecessor

If you are a successor to the throne, that means you'Rev next in line when the current royal has to step down. The successor takes over when someone gives up a position or title or when something becomes outdated.

The noun, successor, was first used in the 13th century to mean "one who comes after." It's often used in reference to a royal court where the successor is usually the king's eldest son. If something happens to the U.S. president, the vice president is the designated successor and will assume the position of head of government. ;l It seems like every day there's a new and improved computer, a successor that replaces an earlier model.

*Psalm 102:18 Let this be written for a future generation, that a people not yet created may praise the Lord:*

So, we discover that actions done in this life can affect generations to come:

*2 Kings 10:30 The Lord said to Jehu, "Because you have done well in accomplishing what is right in my eyes and have done to the house of Ahab all I had in mind to do, your descendants will sit on the throne of Israel to the fourth generation."*

Without doing an in-depth study, we see where leaders make decisions that can bless or curse not only their time here in the earth, but also generations to come. Processes can be set in motion that have repercussions, either good or bad, for not only our children but also our grandchildren and people not yet created.

In this passage of Scripture, we see how Hezekiah lived out his leadership, only in the NOW, living only for his lifetime.

*2 Kings 20: 12 At that time, Marduk-Baladan son of Baladan king of Babylon sent Hezekiah letters and a gift, because he had heard of Hezekiah's illness. 13 Hezekiah received the envoys and showed them all that was in his storehouses—the silver, the gold, the spices and the fine olive oil—his armory and everything found among his treasures. There was nothing in his palace or in all his kingdom that Hezekiah did not show them.*

*Then Isaiah, the prophet, went to King Hezekiah and asked, "What did those men say, and where did they come from?"*

*"From a distant land," Hezekiah replied. "They came from Baby-lon."*

*The prophet asked, "What did they see in your palace?"*

> *"They saw everything in my palace," Hezekiah said. "There is nothing among my treasures that I did not show them."*
>
> *Then Isaiah said to Hezekiah, "Hear the word of the LORD: 17 The time will surely come when everything in your palace, and all that your predecessors have stored up until this day, will be carried off to Babylon. Nothing will be left, says the LORD. 18 And some of your descendants, your own flesh and blood who will be born to you, will be taken away, and they will become eunuchs in the palace of the king of Babylon."*
>
> *"The word of the LORD you have spoken is good," Hezekiah replied.*
>
> *For he thought, **"Will there not be peace and security in my life-time?"***

Who knows the pressure and turmoil he had faced, so let's not be too hard on him. But in his unwillingness to cry out to God one last time, he sentenced his descendants to captivity and emasculation! UGH!

I don't know about you, but I love my children and grandchildren more than that, and I love this country that has adopted me as my home, the United States of America. Let it be known that I will not quietly accept the status quo and live only for peace and security in my lifetime. I am aggressively praying, working, and building towards a better future for my children and grandchildren so that the blessing of Almighty God might continue to rest upon not only my family but this great nation.

How many are willing to lift up a cry, once again, of passionate prayer for revival, for righteousness, for virtue, holiness, and truth displayed once again?

I love the words of Joshua, as his life was approaching the twilight of his leadership:

*Joshua 24:14-16 The Message (MSG) "So now: Fear GOD. Worship him in total commitment. Get rid of the gods your ancestors worshiped on the far side of The River (the Euphrates) and in Egypt. You worship GOD.*

*"If you decide that it's a bad thing to worship GOD, then choose a god you'd rather serve—and do it today. Choose one of the gods your ancestors worshiped from the country beyond The River, or one of the gods of the Amorites, on whose land you'Rev now living. As for my family and me, we'll worship GOD."*

Sure, I'm tired; it has been a tough road. I'm sure yours, Child of God, has been no picnic either.

Yet, I am still breathing, and my faith is still alive, active, and making headlines in heaven.  Let's continue to fight our fight of faith standing boldly and passionately for Jesus, until we finally breathe our last here. Or He comes and splits the Eastern sky to come to get us.

Come on, Saints! Let's press for a righteous, honorable America again, an America that's full of humility, truth, justice, love, grace, wisdom, and the resulting favor, prosperity, and manifold blessing righteous living bring!

Let's pray!

'Father, I undergird my friends here with my prayer and my faith and trust in You! Touch us again; reveal Yourself again. Help us to stay not only focused, but led of you, today and every day. In Your name, I pray, Lord Jesus, Amen.'

# 58

# Making the Impossible - POSSIBLE!

All things are possible to them who believe!

The past couple of days, I have been sharing profound, introspective truth, but sometimes, we need to get back to the basics of life. God is Almighty! Jesus is Lord! He will use His power to help us when we believe! Are you facing some impossibilities in your life?

> *Luke 18:27 And he said, The things which are impossible with men are possible with God.*

> *Mark 9:23 Jesus said unto him, If thou canst believe, all things are possible to him that believeth.*

Yes, faith comes by hearing and hearing by the Word of God. Love is the currency of the kingdom by which everything works: Galatians 5:6 but faith which worketh by love.

You must receive the love of God to recognize your worth. John 1:12 But as many as received him, to them gave he power to become the sons of God, even to them that believe on his name:

You are a child of the King, powerful in Him, only because you have received Him. There is no way you can love your neighbor as yourself, unless you receive the love of God for yourself. If you don't know God loves you deeply and intimately, so that your self-worth is established in Him, then your neighbor is in trouble.

We are talking about impossibilities, though, and Jesus said that all things are possible to them that believe. Believe what, you may ask?

Believe that you are precious. Royalty! A child of the King! You are adopted into the most powerful family this earth has ever seen, the family of the Most High God!

You may be in the crosshairs of hell, but heaven's arsenal responds with howitzers in the hands of angels. He has charged His angels to watch over you, the 91st Psalm declares. Heaven has not lost track of you or me; Jesus will never leave you nor forsake you. The host of heaven walks with you. You have guardian angels, and because you serve the Lord of glory, king of heaven, Psalms 34:7 The angel of the LORD encampeth round about them that fear him, and delivereth them.

Do you need encouragement? The God of angel armies is standing by your side!

Though you may feel alone and helpless, Jesus will never leave you nor forsake you. The specific angels assigned to you are delivering you from your current circumstance and trial, even though you might not be able to see, touch, hear, or feel them right now. They are with you, and they fight for you!

You are loved, and because you are loved, your faith will work.

Faith, that is what you believe, moves mountains. Your mouth is what unleashes heavens arsenal against the onslaught of hell against you. That silent belief deep within you has the strength to carry you to untold heights if you would only speak it.

Tears alone do not move God.

Desperation does not intimidate God.

Manipulation does not control God.

Education does not influence God.

Faith is the only voice God respects.

Faith is the only method that impresses God to activate miracles.

Faith has a voice. If you believe something, you are going to say something.

Let the redeemed of the Lord say so!

It's a voice-activated system. Your voice is your address in the realm of the Spirit. Heaven is listening intently for you, Child of God, to cry unto Him to declare into this war-torn, sin-sick earth, His promises, His decrees, and His glory. His answer of power brings glory, honor, and praise, as your testimony creates eternal witness in this generation of His covenant, His faithfulness, His mercy, greatness, and love!

Do you need direction? The word of God declares that it belongs to you. If you are a child of God, you know what to do. Why?

> *1 John 2:20 But ye have an unction from the Holy One, and ye know all things.*

> *John 16:13 New King James Version (NKJV) However, when He, the Spirit of truth, has come, He will guide you into all truth, for He will not speak on His own authority, but whatever He hears **He will speak; and He will tell you things to come.***

After you are heading in the right direction? Do you need to know how to proceed?

> *James 1:5 If any of you lack wisdom, let him ask of God, that giveth to all men liberally, and upbraideth not; and it shall be given him.*

> *Jeremiah 33:3 Call unto me, and I will answer thee, and shew thee great and mighty things, which thou knowest not.*

Faith comes by hearing the voice of God.

He will speak to you!

> *John 10:27 New King James Version (NKJV) My sheep hear My voice, and I know them, and they follow Me. Then after you hear, I'm going to be like Mary.*

*John 2:5 His mother said to the servants, "Whatever He says to you, do it."*

*James 2:26 For as the body without the spirit is dead, so faith without works is dead also.* If you believe something, you are going to do something. Faith can be seen.

*Matthew 9:2 And, behold, they brought to him a man sick of the palsy, lying on a bed: and Jesus seeing their faith said unto the sick of the palsy; Son, be of good cheer; thy sins be forgiven thee.*

Faith can be seen!

*Matthew 16:8 Which when Jesus perceived, he said unto them, O ye of little faith, why reason ye among yourselves, because ye have brought no bread?*

*Luke 5:20 And when he saw their faith, he said unto him, Man, thy sins are forgiven thee.*
    *Not only can faith be seen, but when you exercise it, it will produce sight!*

*Mark 10:52 And Jesus said unto him, Go thy way; thy faith hath made thee whole. And immediately, he received his sight and followed Jesus in the way.*
    *Now some people do 'acts of faith' to impress other people, but this is a waste of time.*

*Jeremiah 17:5 Thus saith the LORD; Cursed be the man that trusteth in man, and maketh flesh his arm, and whose heart departeth from the LORD.*

True faith cares not what people think about what they do but makes headlines in heaven because God sees.

> *Job 28:10 He cutteth out rivers among the rocks, and his eye seeth every precious thing. He bindeth the floods from overflowing; and the thing that is hid bringeth he forth to light. But where shall wisdom be found? And where is the place of understanding? Man knoweth not the price thereof; neither is it found in the land of the living.*

There are times in life when there is no earthly solution to our problems.

All of our work, study, knowledge, and friendships, fail, and we stand face to face with only ourselves looking back in the mirror, alone.

Yet, this is a beautiful place to be in! Why?

Look up, for this verse is clear,

1. But where shall wisdom be found? And where is the place of understanding?
2. Man knoweth not the price thereof; neither is it found in the land of the living.

What we need is not found in the land of the living! It comes from heaven from the throne of God; in His light, we see light!

At the end of our particular stand of faith is One who stands forever faithful, enthroned in the heavens. And though we may appear to have failed in the eyes of all men and even in our own eyes, it is not over yet! There is one move voice to be heard in this situation, the voice of Jesus, and no matter what you are going through, He is well able to deliver you today!

What is more precious to God but to be believed?

His only pleasure is to be trusted.

His greatest pain is to be doubted.

God continually arranges scenarios that require your confidence in Him.

You've looked to books, to men, to the right and the left for deliverance from your dilemma. Look up for your redemption draweth nigh.

Yet, can God see what I'm going through? I thought He was a Spirit.

*Psalms 94:9 He that planted the ear, shall he not hear? He that formed the eye, shall he not see?*

God sees all, knows all, and would guide you if you seek him. Psalms 32:8 I will instruct thee and teach thee in the way which thou shalt go: I will guide thee with mine eye.

*2 Chronicles 16:9 For the eyes of the LORD run to and fro throughout the whole earth, to shew himself strong in the behalf of them whose heart is perfect toward him. Herein thou hast done foolishly: therefore from henceforth, thou shalt have wars.*

God sees alright, and He is looking around the world continuously for one thing. Faith. A heart full of faith will move Him every time. In fact, He will pass over millions, even billions of people, to get to one person who believes.

*Mark 11:22-24 And Jesus answering saith unto them, Have faith in God.  For verily I say unto you, That whosoever shall say unto this mountain, Be thou removed, and be thou cast into the sea; and shall not doubt in his heart, but shall believe that those things which he saith shall come to pass; he shall have whatsoever he saith. Therefore I say unto you, What things soever ye desire when ye pray, believe that ye receive them, and ye shall have them.*

*1 John 3:21 Beloved, if our heart condemn us not, then have we confidence toward God.*

*1 John 5:14 And this is the confidence that we have in him, that, if we ask any thing according to his will, he heareth us: 15 And if we know that he hear us, whatsoever we ask, we know that we have the petitions that we desired of him.*

Do we have confidence toward God?

*Psalms 66:18 If I regard iniquity in my heart, the Lord will not hear me:*

*Are you seeking Him? Is He first place? Repent! Believe! Speak to your mountain! Obey! Move towards your dream, and God will move your dream towards you.*

Faith releases a flow of miracles into your life. Fear releases heartache and misery into your life.

Step back into the miraculous today.

Let's pray!

Father, I choose to believe You today. You said that you would guide me, so I trust You to show me what I need to do. I ask You for wisdom, and, according to Your Word, I receive it right now. I ask You for favor, and I believe You are granting it to me right now. I ask You for provision, and I believe I receive it right now. I ask You for forgiveness and mercy, and I thank You for forgiving me and cleansing me and revealing again to me Your love. Fill me, Lord; heal me, Lord. Grant me boldness and strength to serve You today. In your name, I pray, Lord Jesus. Amen!

# 59

# Obedience: Whatever He says: Do it!

I've read that when Edward VI, the king of England in the 16th century, attended a worship service. He stood while the Word of God was read. He took notes during this time and later studied them with great care. Through the week, he earnestly tried to apply them to his life. That's the kind of serious-minded response to the truth the apostle James calls for in today's Scripture reading. A single revealed fact cherished in the heart and acted upon is more vital to our growth than a head filled with lofty ideas about God.

One step forward in obedience is worth years of study about it.

Chambers, *Our Daily Bread*, March 4, 1993

Jesus is a living Lord, and He speaks to His children!

> **John 10:27 New Living Translation (NLT) My sheep listen to my voice; I know them, and they follow me.**

Some people are so busy trying to make a living; they forget the author of all life.

Like you can have a better plan than Jesus?!?

> *"Christ went more readily ad crucem (to the cross) than we do to the throne of grace." Thomas Watson*

280

It would be good to develop the humility and heart of Jesus earthly mother, Mary, as she says:

**John 2:5 His mother saith unto the servants, Whatsoever he saith unto you, do it.**

Peter T. Forsythe was right when he said, "The first duty of every soul is to find not its freedom but its Master." Warren W. Wiersbe, *The Integrity Crisis*, Thomas Nelson Publishers, 1991, p. 22

It's always a question of Lordship; is Jesus truly in charge of your heart and decisions?

Are we seeking Him first?

**Matthew 6:33 But seek ye first the Kingdom of God and His righteousness, and all these things shall be added unto you.**

It is easy to say Jesus is Lord of our decisions when we are alone with Him in prayer, but challenges will come!

John Kenneth Galbraith, in his autobiography, *A Life in Our Times*, illustrates the devotion of Emily Gloria Wilson, his family's housekeeper:

It had been a wearying day, and I asked Emily to hold all telephone calls while I had a nap. Shortly after that, the phone rang. Lyndon Johnson was calling from the White House.

"Get me Ken Galbraith. This is Lyndon Johnson."

"He is sleeping, Mark. President. He said not to disturb him."

"Well, wake him up. I want to talk to him."

"No, Mark. President. I work for him, not you. When I called the President back, he could scarcely control his pleasure. "Tell that woman I want her here in the White House."

John Kenneth Galbraith, *A Life in Our Times*, Houghton Mifflin, *Reader's Digest*, December 1981

Always obey God, not man!

***Deuteronomy 13:4 Ye shall walk after the Lord your God, and fear Him, and keep His commandments, and obey His voice, and ye shall serve Him and cleave unto Him***

Dr. B.J. Miller once said, *"It is a great deal easier to do that which God gives us to do, no matter how hard it is, than to face the responsibilities of not doing it."* (*Today In The Word*, November 1989, p.11)

***Luke 9:23 And He said to them all, "If any man will come after Me, let him deny himself and take up his cross daily, and follow Me.***

*"It is not the importance of the thing, but the majesty of the Lawgiver, that is to be the standard of obedience...Some, indeed, might reckon such minute and arbitrary rules as these as trifling. But the principle involved in obedience or disobedience was none other than the same principle which was tried in Eden at the foot of the forbidden tree. It is really this: Is the Lord to be obeyed in all things whatsoever He commands? Is He a holy Lawgiver? Are His creatures bound to give implicit assent to His will?"* Andrew Bonar, referring to the laws found in Leviticus, quoted in J. Bridges, *The Pursuit of Holiness*, p. 23.

***Matthew 22:37 Jesus said unto him, "'Thou shalt love the Lord thy God with all thy heart, and with all thy soul, and with all thy mind.'***

***Isaiah 33:22 21st Century King James Version For the Lord is our judge, the Lord is our lawgiver, the Lord is our king; He will save us.***

Imagine, if you will, that you work for a company whose president found it necessary to travel out of the country and spend an extended period of time abroad. So, he says to you and the other trusted employees, "Look, I'm going to leave. And while I'm gone, I want you to pay close attention to the business. You manage things while I'm away. I will write to you regularly. When I do, I will instruct you in what you should do from now until I return from this trip." Everyone agrees.

He leaves and stays gone for a couple of years. During that time, he often writes, communicating his desires and concerns. Finally, he returns. He walks up to the front door of the company and immediately discovers everything is in a mess—weeds flourishing in the flower beds, windows broken across the front of the building. The gal at the front desk was dozing, and loud music was roaring from several offices. Two or three people were engaged in horseplay in the back room. Instead of making a profit, the business has suffered a significant loss. Without hesitation, he calls everyone together and, with a frown, asks, "What happened?

Didn't you get my letters?"

You say, "Oh, yeah, sure. We got all your letters. We've even bound them in a book. And some of us have memorized them. In fact, we have 'letter study' every Sunday. You know, those were really great letters." I think the president would then ask, "But what did you do about my instructions?" And, no doubt, the employees would respond, "Do? Well, nothing. But we read every one!" Charles Swindoll, *Living Above the Level of Mediocrity*, p. 242.

> ***Matthew 7:21 "Not every one that saith unto Me, 'Lord, Lord,' shall enter into the Kingdom of Heaven, but he that doeth the will of My Father who is in Heaven.***
>
> ***James 1:22 But be ye doers of the Word and not hearers only, deceiving your own selves.***

Well, simple preaching, now I need to do what I just preached and get on with the work of my day.

Let's pray:

'Father God in Heaven, Creator of Heaven and earth, You who created me, speak to me, I pray. Lord Jesus, cause me to hear Your voice in every area of my life and grant me the courage to fully obey You above every other voice, **no compromise**. Amen!"

# 60

# The Word of God Shall Talk With THee

The Word of God shall talk with thee!

> *Proverbs 6:22 When thou goest, it shall lead thee; when thou sleepest, it shall keep thee; and* when *thou awakest, it shall talk with thee.*

> *Heb 4:12 For the word of God is quick, and powerful, and sharper than any two-edged sword, piercing even to the dividing asunder of soul and spirit, and of the joints and marrow, and is a discerner of the thoughts and intents of the heart.*

The beautiful thing about the Word of God is that it is alive! The reason it is alive is that the Holy Spirit is the one who breathed upon (pen inspired) them to write exactly what He said. Since God is omniscient and omnipresent, He is literally here every time we open the book. Time, to Him, is simply like a parade. He can see the beginning from the end from His throne in eternity and can enter the parade whenever or wherever He pleases. When He shows up, He is always, 'I Am,' our ever-present help in times of need. One writer stated that the Bible is the only book ever written where the author is always present when we read it.

I have noticed over the years that as I faithfully share the Word of God that is alive and active to me each day, the Holy Spirit makes it alive and active to others too. I realize again that I am simply an instrument in the hand of our ever-living God. He takes my simple offering of preaching, teaching, blogging, or publishing the Word of God, and this very Word is a living organism! It comes in seed form, but when I plant it into the earth in this generation, by faith, and water it with my prayer:

> *Acts 19:20 Thus the **Word of** the Lord [concerning the attainment through Christ **of** eternal salvation in the kingdom **of God**] **grew** and spread and intensified, prevailing mightily*

> Acts 19:20 (DARBY) *Thus with might the word of the Lord increased and prevailed*

Do you see it! The Word of God is alive! It has a life of its own! It grows, and with might, shows forth the glory of God wherever it lands!

> *Psalm 119:130 The **entrance** and unfolding **of** Your **word**s give light; **the**ir unfolding gives understanding (discernment and comprehension) to **the** simple.*

Wherever His Word enters, the light and life of God comes in power!

I cannot count the times this very word has gone into nations I have not yet been to. The Holy Spirit has used my devotionals to heal, deliver, touch, and bless people. It would be unlikely I could ever meet naturally. Things can look fine according to outward appearances, but He looks much deeper within, into not only what we are doing but rather why. When our whys don't agree with His whys, He can gently instruct, correct, counsel, and refine us so that we become more like Him in our thinking and very motives!

> **2 Peter 1:1 (AKJV)** *Simon Peter, a servant and an apostle of Jesus Christ, to them that have obtained like precious faith with us through the righteousness of God and our Savior Jesus Christ: ² Grace and peace*

*be multiplied unto you through the knowledge of God, and of Jesus our Lord, ³ according as his divine power hath given unto us all things that pertain unto life and godliness, through the knowledge of him that hath called us to glory and virtue: ⁴ whereby are given unto us exceeding great and precious promises: that by these ye might be partakers of the divine nature, having escaped the corruption that is in the world through lust.*

Every day, I take time to meditate upon the Word of God. There are different ways I do this, but my favorite, by far, is to simply lay down with the audio Bible playing, simply asking the Holy Spirit to speak to me each time. Faithfully, for years, He has and does!

Let the Word of God talk with thee today!

Each day, I encourage people to seek Jesus first thing each morning and to read through their Bible in some yearly Bible-reading plan. Each night, we have been playing the audio Bible in our house for over twenty years, falling asleep with the prayer: "Jesus, tell me a bedtime story." And He has continually opened His Word to our understanding, making His promises alive to us as He directs us day by day.

Let's Pray:

'Father, I am ever looking towards heaven and your will for my life. Speak to me about the specifics that You have for me today. Not only what I need to be doing, but my reasons for doing it. In Your name, I pray, Lord Jesus. Amen.'

# 61

## Let Your Spirit Free! Create!

In the book, *The E-Myth Revisited*, the author recounts a fictitious account with a business owner named Sarah and the importance of developing systems to produce excellence in her world without her having to do all of it herself. In the dialogue, he accidentally stumbles upon a spiritual law, the law of creating your world with your faith-filled words!

> *Hebrews 11:3 Through faith we understand that the **worlds** were **framed** by the word of*
> *God, so that things which are seen were not made of things which do appear*

> *Romans 10:6 But the righteousness which is of **faith speaketh***

> *2 Corinthians 4:13 We having the same **spirit of faith**, according as it is written, I believed, and therefore have I spoken; we also believe, and therefore speak;*

In dreaming of what her business could be, Sarah decided to unlock her spirit and create a slogan for her business. As she thought on it, I quote:

"There will be no stuffing of the spirit here, my business will say. Maybe I should put it up above the door to remind everyone who comes in what our

288

purpose is. She grinned. "Or maybe better yet, 'Let thy spirit run free!' Yes, that's better; it even feels better" She laughed out loud at the joy of it!

As she continued, it became so clear to me, what a miraculous gift speaking can be.

I saw that Sarah wasn't so much talking to me, but to herself, discovering as she spoke the miracles that lived within her and her experience, within her relationship with her aunt, within her extraordinary imagination. She discovered truths never she never considered before. Discovering all the wealth that was waiting there inside of her to be unearthed, to be explored, to be treasured as the words came tumbling forth.'

As though the words, once freed by the speaking of them combined with the air to become something else again: A vision, Understanding, Expansion.

Do you see the principal?

God placed a dream within her that she had not yet articulated yet. She believed in her heart the dream but had never yet spoken it into existence. When she began to speak, miracles began to happen! God, the Creator, and author of all creativity, breathed upon her dream, just as he breathed upon His own dream way back in the days of creation. When He would speak, His breath, the Person of the Holy Spirit, would create and bring into existence what He spoke, and it was good!

LET YOUR SPIRIT FREE! CREATE!

What is your dream?

We all have one, for we are created in the image and likeness of God.

It needs to be spoken, articulated, and if it is worthwhile, written down, and quantified into some action plan.

Don't die taking to the grave your dream unspoken, unrealized, unfulfilled.

Speak it! If only to a close friend, or into your microphone on your computer, speak it.

Like Sarah, the princess of God, miracles will unlock from deep inside of you, because when you received Jesus into your heart, your heart has become the fertile soil of His beauty, His dreams, His creativity – your lips become His voice in this generation, and your world, your work, becomes an expression of His creativity and love in the earth.

Speak the dream!

Let's Pray:

'Father, I come before You, and I see some of these deep, beautiful things on the inside of me are Your things, that like Mary, I have pondered in my heart for years.  Flow through me, Holy Spirit, with Your words erupting from the depths of my heart, writing Your eternal dreams on the canvas of time, my life being the beautiful expression of Jesus, alive in my generation. Amen.'

# 62

# Leadership Loneliness

*Ex 34:3 No one else may come with you. In fact, no one is to appear anywhere on the mountain.*

Here we see Moses called to come apart unto God to receive the 10 Commandments.  It is very similar to a CEO, business owner, senior pastor, or president set apart to lead their people and organizations.  Corporate guidelines, principals, policies, and governments are always needed that will effectively, fairly empower and prosper the people we are called to lead. These come from God.

For those of us called to leadership, there are seasons where, though surrounded by people, God speaks to us alone.

In this account of Moses, God called him up the mountain without even man's best friend. If he had a dog, it stayed home.

Ex 34: Do not even let the flocks or herds graze near the mountain." *These are places and spaces where only His voice and obedience to His voice will do. I understand those who are in that place, and I'm praying for you.*

There is a straight and narrow way that brings great glory to God. It brings both eternal and temporal impact only as you obey. God still governs human experience

> *1 Corinthians 10:13 (PHILLIPS) No temptation has come your way that is too hard for flesh and blood to bear. But God can be trusted not to allow you to suffer any temptation beyond your powers of endurance. He will see to it that every temptation has a way out so that it will never be impossible for you to bear it.*

Let's pray:

"Father, show me what to do and give me the courage to do it, to obey You, and not to become pulled by the temptations and counsels of people. I need You, Lord Jesus, to strengthen me, now. Amen.'

# 63

# God Goes To Work With Us

There are trendy words these days, like 'Marketplace Ministry,' yet let's read:

> *Acts 18:1 After these things Paul departed from Athens, and came to Corinth; And found a certain Jew named Aquila, born in Pontus, lately come from Italy, with his wife Priscilla; (because that Claudius had commanded all Jews to depart from Rome:) and came unto them. And because he was of the same craft, he abode with them and wrought: for by their occupation they were tentmakers.*

Paul went to Corinth to go work with Aquila, and they opened their home to him. Eventually, they must have got saved and discipled. They raised up a church there. Aquila and Priscilla discipled Apollos and became a missions-sending church and supporter of Paul right out of their home.

Thought of the day: Simply going to work with someone might have great eternal value, if you are allowed to teach them the word of God. Who knows how much fruit they may bear for the kingdom of God eternally?

Let's go to work with Jesus today, seeking to reach the world through the person working next to us.

Let's Pray:

'Father, I commit to fully obey You in the workplace. Help me to live, work, and minister to the people around me in such a way that I make headlines in heaven today. Bless the work of my hands that I be adequately provided for and am able to send missionaries around the world. In Your name, Lord Jesus, do I pray. Amen.'

# 64

# As Successful As The Cross

Clarence Jordan was a man of unusual abilities and commitment. He had two Ph.D.s, one in agriculture and one in Greek and Hebrew. So gifted was he that he could have chosen to do anything he wanted. He chose to serve the poor. In the 1940s, he founded a farm in Americus, Georgia, and called it Koinonia Farm. It was a community for poor whites and poor blacks. As you might guess, such an idea did not go over well in the Deep South of the '40s. Ironically, much of the resistance came from good church people who followed the laws of segregation as much as others in town. The town people tried everything to stop Clarence. They tried boycotting him and slashing workers' tires when they came to town. Over and over, for fourteen years, they tried to stop him.

Finally, in 1954, the Ku Klux Klan had enough of Clarence Jordan, so they decided to get rid of him once and for all. They came one night with guns and torches and set fire to every building on Koinonia Farm. They riddled Clarence's home with bullets. And they chased off all the families except one black family who refused to leave. Clarence recognized the voices of many of the Klansmen, and, as you might guess, some of them were church people. Another was the local newspaper's reporter. The next day, the reporter came out to see what remained of the farm. The rubble still smoldered, and the land was scorched. But he found Clarence in the field, hoeing, and planting.

"I heard the awful news," he called to Clarence, "and I came out to do a story on the tragedy of your farm closing." Clarence just kept on hoeing and planting. The reporter kept prodding, kept poking, trying to get a rise from this quietly determined man who seemed to be planting instead of packing his bags. So, finally, the reporter said in a haughty voice, "Well, Dr. Jordan, you got two of them Ph.D.s, and you've put fourteen years into this farm. And there's nothing left of it at all. Just how successful do you think you've been?"

Clarence stopped hoeing and turned toward the reporter with his penetrating blue eyes and said quietly but firmly, "About as successful as the cross. Sir, I don't think you understand us. What we are about is not success but faithfulness. We'Rev staying. Good day." Beginning that day, Clarence and his companions rebuilt Koinonia, and the farm is going strong today. *Tim Hansel, Holy Sweat, Word Books Publisher, 1987, pp. 188–189*

Maybe wicked people have done horrible things to you today. Outlive them and outlast them by the grace and power of God.

Let's Pray:

'Father, I need your courage and firm resolve today to do what You have called me to do. NO COMPROMISE! I thank you that I am heard and answered, for I ask in Your name, Lord Jesus. Amen.'

# 65

# Laugh Loud At Life

**Don't Stop!**

*Acts 17:5 But the Jews which believed not, moved with envy, took unto them certain lewd fellows of the baser sort, and gathered a company, and set all the city on an uproar, and assaulted the house of Jason, and sought to bring them out to the people. 6 And when they found them not, they drew Jason and certain brethren unto the rulers of the city, crying, These that have turned the world upside down are come hither also.*

In sports and in business, I have heard the statement: 'Just because YOU can't does not mean that I can't. You are not me'. Remember watching one of the episodes of *The Man from Snowy River*, and the bad guys had stolen Macgregor's horses. No one would go with him at first to retrieve them, and he found himself galloping on top of a ridge, high above the outlaws. The lead outlaw said: 'He is no threat. He cannot get down from there." The other replied: 'Don't forget who that is up there.'

Leadership involves championship thinking and actions. You will be opposed by lesser spirits who do not have the same level of faith, commitment, and zeal as you do, and, because of their unbelief or lack of hearing from God, they cause an uproar trying to stop you and the work of God through you.

Welcome to leadership! What are you going to do when all hell appears arrayed against you, and what you believe God has told you to do? Are you going to overcome evil with good and love your enemies?

You will be exercising violent faith against their traps, obstacles, and tumults so that they label you like these first apostles: 'These that have turned the world upside down are come hither also.' Maybe you have not communicated enough with others, and you have operated outside the chain of command somewhat.

Which is worse: Bold, zealous actions for God or paralysis by analysis, where an idea gets wonderfully discussed but never implemented. If you blew it, fess up where you messed up, and don't take yourself too seriously. Happy is the person who can laugh at himself. He will never cease to be amused. It has been said 'that which doesn't kill you makes you stronger.'

One of my favorite redneck verses, when I am falsely accused, is Psalm 50:9: *I will receive no bull out of your house.*

Laugh in the face of adversity, and make the devil mad! Love people, take ground for the gospel and mobilize strategic airstrikes on behalf of the kingdom of God (a prayer that blasts principalities and powers). And keep on turning the world of darkness upside down, until it is all right side up and under the Lordship of Jesus! Remember that Satan is a liar and the father of all lies.

The ABCs of satan are accusations, blame, and criticism. Death by insinuation, that elusive whispering campaign, is designed to slime you, discredit you, and make you feel hopeless, discouraged, and inferior. It's an attack on the favor of God upon your life! Lift up the shield of faith because written: *Psalm 5:11-12 But let all those that put their trust in thee rejoice: let them ever shout for joy, because thou defendest them: let them also that love thy name be joyful in thee. For thou, LORD, wilt bless the righteous; with favor wilt thou compass him as with a shield.*

You have favor with God and man as you believe it, receive it, and proclaim it by faith in the authority granted to you by Jesus!

*Luke 6:22–23 Blessed are ye, when men shall hate you, and when they shall separate you from their company, and shall reproach you, and cast out your name as evil for the Son of man's sake. Rejoice ye in that day, and leap for joy: for, behold, your reward is great in heaven: for in the like manner did their fathers unto the prophets.*

The joy of the Lord is strength, so work yourself up at least a little gleeful giggle today if you are going through stuff because you are a little too bold to be contained in people's current understanding. Love em, instruct them where you can, and then move on in obedience to Holy Spirit.

*Heb 10:32 But call to remembrance the former days, in which, after ye were illuminated, ye endured a great fight of afflictions; No test, no testimony. No guts, no glory. No testimony for the newsletter story. Take time to laugh today; greater is He in you than all those arrayed against you.*

Let's Pray:

'Father, I thank You for boldness today, making me too blessed to be distressed, too anointed to be disappointed, too powerful for the devil and unbelieving men to contain. Jesus! I love you, and thank You for Your goodness and grace and for speaking to me today! You are the way, and my Waymaker, making a way through this, causing me to emerge victorious over it all. For victory is my DNA, the natural result of my obedience to you. Amen!''

# 66

# Run The Race

Know ye not that **they** which **run** in a **race run** all, but one receiveth **the** prize? So **run**, that ye may obtain.

Most of you know that I serve Jesus, determined to grow in spiritual maturity, academic excellence, and physical fitness.

Each day, the Holy Spirit places His finger on one of these areas and challenges me to step up.

Monday, my young daughter and I knuckled down and disciplined ourselves to complete the publication of our book we have been pecking away upon for several months. We completed the cover design and submitted everything to the publisher. Mission accomplished! Yet, while that went well, my workout at the gym was lackluster and not focused and intense.

For those of you who do not know, I have a yearly fitness goal of being able to run under 25 mins in a 5 Km run while maintaining a bench press of 315lbs. I have not been able to do this yet. While my bench is now at 315; to get there, I had to do much strength training to bulk up, and I let my running schedule go. I had my running time down to 25:22 but still have not broken that 25 min barrier again. No small challenge for a man in his late '50s. I call it 'The Great Balancing Act.'

*Hebrews 12:1 Wherefore seeing we also are compassed about with so great a cloud of*

> *witnesses, let us lay aside every weight, and **the** sin which doth so easily beset us, and let us **run** with patience **the race** that is set before us.*

So last week, we decided to walk two ½ mile laps, of a local pond, before breakfast to burn fat. Instead of lifting weights on leg day, I jogged a couple of miles painfully up Turkey Mountain here in Tulsa, tight, brutal miles in heat through the woods.

Yesterday was legs day again. I prayed and felt impressed to rerun the mountain. Yet, the way the schedule worked out, I had to run at 1 PM, in the hot midday heat here. As I asked Jesus how far to run, clearly, the Holy Spirit said:

**'I want you to run the yellow trail, all the way around, without stopping.'**

In years gone by, we loved that 4.3-mile loop around the mountain, but that was when we ran 3-4 times/week. I have not run over a mile since January. Last week's 2-mile run was painful.

Furthermore, my rational mind kicked in. When we run the mountain, we do it early in the morning before the searing Oklahoma heat kicks in. Even when I was in running shape, running at midday was not wise.

Yet, I felt Holy Spirit tell me I could do it, so humbly and intelligently, I asked him: 'How?'

I was reminded of one hot 105F summer day in years gone by. I was scheduled to run and decided it was too hot! Yet, while picking up some supplies for work at Home Depot, I saw a guy out running! He finished right at Home Depot, so I commented to him: 'A little hot for running?' With fire in his eyes, he said, 'Nope, just got back from my tour of duty in Iraq, and we ran every day in 140F. This is just warm, not hot yet."

So, that day I kept my training schedule and ran a couple of miles. (Thank a serviceman or vet today for freedom!)

Gently, I felt Holy Spirit instruct me to drink a full water bottle before I drove the ½ hour over to the mountain, and that I should listen to Him throughout the run.

So, I drank my water and arrived at the start of the trail. It was hot, and I was intimidated!

So, again I asked Him for instruction. Gently, He told me to set a comfortable pace and not to blast the steep inclines but to simply **'keep on moving without stopping.'** This was to become my battle cry.

As I started into the woods, I thought through the upcoming run, the descents, the ascents, and the long winding sections and planned my attack.

From my study of native worship, I immediately sensed the presence of God when a butterfly circled me several times as I entered the woods. A black 'morning glory' that spoke to me of the immediate presence of God with me; creation was speaking of our Creator. The beauty of the butterfly reminded me of the abiding presence of the Holy Spirit with me.

As I approached the first steep hill, about ½ mile in, Holy Spirit gently instructed me to take the long way around with a steady effort, avoiding the steep hill and to **'keep moving after you hit the top.'**

Never was I so aware of Him as my personal trainer, my coach, leading me to fitness and excellence and to push hard in training without overextending.

In a full sweat now, I crested the top. My mind and lungs screamed for me to stop. While My head was pounding from the heat, I remembered His instruction to 'keep moving forward after hitting the top.' Amazingly to me, I was able to do this, and, as the trail leveled out again, I was able to regain control of my breathing again and settle into a steady pace.

The open sections between the trees were searingly hot in the direct sunlight, and I noticed this, and immediately, my coach said: **'Stay to the shady sides of the trail, and avoid direct heat where you can.'**

And so it went, with Him gently encouraging me over the rougher spots in the trail, and then, as I smelled the stench of the sewage treatment plant near the turn-around, I knew I had to climb the mountain again. My doubts reminded me that this was the very place several years ago where our beautiful golden retriever Rusty had collapsed and died and that I needed to stop, walk, and cool down on the steep incline. It was too hot to run it. So, I asked the Holy Spirit
what to do.

Immediately He reminded me of His original instruction to simply '**keep on moving without stopping,**' so I asked Him for strength to keep jogging up the hill. As I came to the looming hill that exploded into a section of direct scorching sunlight at the top, I was intimidated yet decided to try anyway. As I began my ascent, His voice came to me clearly again, "**No heroics here. Just a steady effort throughout the hill, and keep moving at the top.**'

So, I did what He said. I rounded the turn-around and, with lungs bursting and head pounding, exploded out of the trees into the 100 yards or so of heat at the top.

Yet, I managed to keep moving and eventually regain my rhythm and pace. I reentered shade of the trees to begin the jog back. As I did, again, a beautiful morning glory butterfly circled me, and I immediately breathed out a 'Thank-you' to my intimate, never-failing God. I felt His pleasure as He replied: '**Not many notice when I send my creation to encourage them. I'm glad you noticed...**' I found myself asking His forgiveness for the hardness of my own heart. I thought about the times He had forgiven me before when He spoke, and I was too hard to notice until later.

My body was feeling it now. Over two miles had gone by, and I was hot. He sent a breeze!

Ahead of me was a long open section of the path with no shade!

Yet, the footing was sound and the trail pretty level overall . My legs were hurting, but I had found my stride and got into my rhythm of grace.

Before I knew it, I was at 'Heartbreak Hill.' I'm not sure if this is the actual name of this incline or simply one we have given it over the years. Here is why we call it that. On the yellow trail, you circle the mountain and have descended and ascended it so that the final half (If you run it counterclockwise like we usually do) is along mostly the ridge of the mountain. Yet, after 3 miles, when you think you should begin to descend, there is this rough ascent, with loose rocks that climb about 100 yards with some tricky footing as you go up. I find this stretch the most mentally tough part of this run because you have

just completed a mile or so of smooth, easy trail, and by that point, you want to descend and head back to the parking lot.

Again, I felt His presence remind me: '**Keep moving forward, do not stop, just a solid, steady effort,**' solidifying my resolve actually to complete this training assignment and finish this run without stopping.

Made it to the top! Head pounding, a throbbing headache my reward, lungs screaming: "Stop and walk for a while!"

Yet, suddenly, I was surrounded by a swirl of tiny orange butterflies!

Like a victory celebration, I felt His joy, that I had made the top of the hill without stopping, and had actually sent these beautiful little creatures to remind me of His pleasure in my accomplishment.

My quads were hurting now, but I knew I could not stop now. It was only flat and downhill from here, with a little over a mile left to go.

I rounded the corner to the right for the last stretch before the cut-off to the left that descended to the parking lot trail.

I was tired now and knew it; my shirt was a dripping ball in my hand from wiping the burning sweat out of my eyes, my body running rivers of perspiration, but I was beginning to believe I might make it!

As I saw the trail cut off to the left, the Holy Spirit cautioned me: 'Be careful descending!' Suddenly, I saw the danger: I was slightly dizzy from the heat, and there is some treacherous footing headed downhill there. I had to nimbly choose my footing, with legs that felt like tree trunks that were not wanting to be nimble at all.

Furthermore, descending was excruciating! Why does it hurt muscles so much to descend rather than to ascend? Each step down felt bone-jarring, as I felt the impact throughout my entire body.

Yet, I made it to the concrete block trail divider and picked my way down the steep trail to the final ½ mile jaunt back to the parking lot.

Again, my guardian butterflies were with me, signaling my victory over the mountain!

I did it! By the grace of God, I did it!


*1 Corinthians 15:57 But thanks be to God, which giveth us the **victory** through our Lord Jesus Christ.*

Another training milestone laid in my yearly fitness goal, another mental barrier crushed.

In every area, I am convinced that Jesus would give us victory, if we would trust Him, lean upon Him, and learned to submit to the leadership and comfort, and coaching of the Holy Spirit along the way.

He doesn't call the qualified, but He does qualify the called.

Let's Pray:

'Father, show me Your plan, purpose, and destiny. Reveal to me the academic, fitness, and spiritual goals I need to set and give me Your plan to work on all of these simultaneously. I ask this, knowing You love me, You hear, You care, and answer. For I ask in Your mighty name, Lord Jesus. Amen.'

67

# The Lips of The Righteous Feed Many

Use your mouth and words on purpose.

*Prov 10: 21 The lips of the righteous feed many: but fools die for want of wisdom.*

As most of you know, I owned and operated a carpentry company for many years.  As the company grew, I realized my time was far better spent estimating and bidding work, collecting checks, managing projects, ordering materials, and fixing or getting tools on the right job, on time.

One day at work, as I was blazing along on my cell phone, doing sales calls, setting appointments, ordering materials, and moving at incredible speed, a bitter carpenter said to me: *"Must be nice, you don't even work anymore, all you do is talk on that damn phone all day!"*

Even though I was writing that man's paycheck, I took a deep breath. I asked the Lord, what He thought about the man's comment, because there is some truth, in what the man said: Construction is not for the faint-hearted. You must bust a move to make stuff happen because you only get paid for what you get built, and you are constantly working yourself out of a job. The Scripture is plain:

*2 Thessalonians 3:10 For even when we were with you, this we commanded you, that if any would not work, neither should he eat*

When he said, *"all you do is talk on the damn phone all day,"* I was reminded of the verse:

## THE LIPS OF THE RIGHTEOUS FEED MANY

*Prov 14:23 In all labor there is profit: but the talk of the lips tendeth only to penury.*

Another version reads, *"In all labor there is profit, but idle talk leads only to poverty"* Proverbs 14:23 (AMP).

I asked the Lord if I was wasting time on the phone when bold and loud Holy Spirit spoke to me Prov 10:21, *"The lips of the righteous feed many: but fools die for want of wisdom."*

I wasn't using my phone for idle chit-chat, but it was a weapon of war in my hand, as a seasoned leader.

Besides, I was serving Jesus, and had a covenant with God. When I did a moral inventory of my workweek vs. this man's workweek, I realized I worked far more hours with far more stress and responsibility than that man could presently understand.

How much more, as a minister of the gospel! We have authority, anointing, and the very living word of God upon our lips, opening the door to heaven or hell in a person's life as we preach God's Word. I take this responsibility extremely seriously.

God is not joking when we read: Prov 13:3 *He that keepeth his mouth keepeth his life: but he that openeth wide his lips shall have destruction.*

*Prov 18:21 Death and life are in the power of the tongue: and they that love it shall eat the fruit thereof.*

My words, spoken in authority in prayer over your life, mine, and my families, are destroying devilish plots against us, and producing acts of blessing, healing, miracles, revelation, wisdom, joy, peace, provision, and prosperity in us, and our families!

Though I now serve in full-time ministry and part-time construction, through prayer and the release of my confession of faith each day, my lips still feed many.

So should yours!

Let's Pray:

*Father set a watch on my lips and grant me utterance in the Holy Spirit today, as we speak words of faith, power, deliverance, and blessing into the earth, enforcing your love, power, kingdom, truth, will, and way in this generation. In your name I pray, Lord Jesus. Amen!*

# 68

# Seven Principles of Leadership

This is the way I see it, based upon a word from the Lord I received while pastoring:

**7 Principles of Leadership in Ministry**

1. Always remember to meet human needs by the anointing instead of your own strength. "I am Almighty, you are not. You can burn out; I never grow weary."
2. Develop two groups of leaders around you:  Solid faithful men of integrity within the church; Outside Leaders that are not 'Yes' men who hold the same level of responsibility as you have.
3. Stay in your Word, just listening is not enough.  Must read, study, confess, and memorize it also.
4. Schedule two fasts each year and two vacations.
5. Fight to maintain 8-9 hours of sleep each night and maintain a good exercise and nutrition program.
6. Have others administrate finances. Authorize growth and expenditures but have others handle deposits and payments.
7. Continue to date your wife and schedule play dates with your children. Take one day/week off, no work, no ministry.

This is what God told me to do. It is my general guideline. You'll have to pray and ask Jesus what your principles need to be.

# 69

# Leadership – The Fate of the World Depends Upon It!

On top of my daily disciplines of prayer, confession of God's Word, and Bible study, I have determined to read many great books as the Holy Spirit directs. A man I met, Jim Stovall, has disciplined himself to read a book every single day. This might be remarkable in and of itself, but Jim is legally blind! His mind, however, processes information at such a pace that he had the books narrated, and he is listening to them often at an accelerated pace to maintain this daily discipline in his life! I had the privilege of meeting Jim in the waiting room of the Golden Eagle broadcasting television studio, as we were both preparing to film segments of Tom Leding's television show. In the brief 15-20 mins that Jim and I visited, I quickly realized that I was in the presence of an extremely rare individual, and this has proved true in subsequent encounters with Jim.

I set myself a discipline of reading two good books a week from then on and have possibly exceeded that goal this year, devouring good, edifying books, as a parched man would drink after several days in the desert.

The Bible, the Word of God, is the final authority in my life. As I read any book on any topic, I am always mining it for truth, revelation, and keys of knowledge that will better equip me to become a better man, husband, father, leader, and minister of the gospel, determined to make my mark on

311

this generation with the Word of God.

What began as a reading list from Professor Jane Malcolm of Oral Roberts University, has primed my intellectual and spiritual pump so to speak, and helped me develop a lifestyle of continued personal growth, study, prayer, and pursuit of excellence.

My topics of passionate interest are:

- Leadership, morality, and integrity.
- Christian life and world missions.
- The history, plight, and spirituality of the North American Indian.
- Racism, and how to aggressively defeat it.

One of the books on my reading list is *Think and Grow Rich* by Napoleon Hill, first published in 1937. Mark. Hill spent 25 years of his life developing his 13 principles of success by researching and interviewing hundreds of the wealthiest and most successful men in America in his day. Yet, I am no student of mere leadership. Hitler and Stalin were able to move the masses, yet their legacy of evil probably earned them eternal damnation. I wish to lead for Jesus, King of Kings, and Lord of Lords, writing HIS story on the tapestry of time, the brief sliver that is my generation.

I am reminded of Jesus's own words and cautioned by them, whenever I read any other source than the infallible canon of Scripture:

*Matt 16:26 For what is a man profited, if he shall gain the whole world, and lose his own soul? or what shall a man give in exchange for his soul?*

There is a literal Heaven, and a literal Hell and my study, purpose, and actions are governed by a healthy love of the former, and fear of the latter.

*Matt 10:28 And fear not them which kill the body, but are not able to kill the soul: but rather fear him which is able to destroy both soul and body in hell.*

The fear of God is the beginning of wisdom, and the purpose of my study is always the pursuit of wisdom, graciously passed down through the generations, through the written word.

John the Baptist uttered these words during the earthly ministry of Jesus.

*John 3:27 John answered and said, A man can receive nothing, except it be given him from heaven.*

Though they were written to describe the superiority of Christ over the ministry of John the Baptist, yet how much more applicable are they to each of us that would seek to lead, build, and change the world, leaving it a better place for generations to come?

Only in Jesus is there found eternal life; only His gospel has the power to breathe that eternity into any human heart. Only what is done for Him has eternal consequence and reward...

So, as I read the wonderful principles of Mark. Hill, I am interpreting them in light of my understanding of the Scripture to be sure that the principles he expresses are not only applicable in the 1930s in America but rather upon the solid rock of the Word of God, eternally established in the heavens for all ages!

**The Eleven Major Attributes Of Leadership by Napoleon Hill**

*1.) UNWAVERING COURAGE – based upon knowledge of self and one's occupation. No follower wishes to be dominated by a leader who lacks self-confidence and courage. No intelligent follower will be dominated by such a leader very long.*

While I agree that leaders must have unwavering courage, I do not agree as to its source. It is good to study, learn, grow, and understand our particular fields of endeavor, but true courage must come from God and God alone. All true leadership is God-given, and its principles can be mined, understood, and applied through the study of the Word of God.

Here are some verses to develop true courage from, as true faith only comes by hearing, and hearing by the word of God.

*Deuteronomy 31:6 Be strong and courageous.  Do not be afraid or terrified because of them, for the Lord your God goes with you; he will never leave you nor forsake you.*

In this verse, God instructs His people how to act in war in the presence of their enemies – strong and courageous because we recognize we have a covenant with Almighty God, Creator of the Universe. He is with us, and if God be for us, who can stand against us?

We see leadership granted to Joshua after the death of Moses, first by Moses, then by God Himself. In each case, both Moses and God command this leader to do exactly what Mark. Hill would counsel: Be strong, and of good courage!

*Deuteronomy 31:7 Then Moses summoned Joshua and said to him in the presence of all Israel, "Be strong and courageous, for you must go with this people into the land that the Lord swore to their ancestors to give them, and you must divide it among them as their inheritance."*

*Joshua 1:7 "Be strong and very courageous. Be careful to obey all the law my servant Moses gave you; do not turn from it to the right or to the left, that you may be successful wherever you go.*

*Joshua 1:9 Have I not commanded you? Be strong and courageous. Do not be afraid; do not be discouraged, for the Lord your God will be with you wherever you go.*

Obviously, if God, who cannot lie, in His holiness gives a commandment, He must give the power, grace, and strength to fulfill it! God commands us to be strong and of good courage. Therefore, we can and must be!

- **Boldness** – 3954 π´parrhesia par-rhay-see'-ah
  - AV-boldness 8, confidence 6, openly 4, plainly 4, openly + 1722 2, boldly +

- 1722 1, misc. 6; 31
- freedom in speaking, unreservedness in speech
- 1a) openly, frankly, i.e without concealment
- 1b) without ambiguity or circumlocution
- 1c) without the use of figures and comparisons
- free and fearless confidence, cheerful courage, boldness, assurance
- the deportment by which one becomes conspicuous or secures publicity

*Ac 4:13 Now when they saw the boldness of Peter and John, and perceived that they were unlearned and ignorant men, they marveled; and they took knowledge of them, that they had been with Jesus.*

*Ac 4:29 And now, Lord, behold their threatenings: and grant unto thy servants, that with all boldness they may speak thy word,*

*Ac 4:31 And when they had prayed, the place was shaken where they were assembled together; and they were all filled with the Holy Ghost, and they spake the word of God with boldness.*

*2 Cor 7:4 Great is my boldness of speech toward you, great is my glorying of you: I am filled with comfort, I am exceeding joyful in all our tribulation. So, we see here that strength, courage, and boldness are all qualities of leadership granted by God that come by faith. So, let's ask our heavenly Father for these.*

Let's pray:

*Father, I see Your commandments to be strong and of good courage, and how the Holy Spirit granted boldness of speech and action to the early leaders of Your church. So I believe if You did it then, You will do it now in my life and in this generation. I ask You for strength, courage, and boldness of speech and action to lead for You in this generation for the glory and honor of Your name, Lord Jesus. Amen!*

## 2.) Self-Control

*"The man who cannot control himself can never control others. Self-control sets a mighty example for one's followers, which the more intelligent will emulate." Napoleon Hill*

I agree with Mark. Hill here, self-control IS an essential element of leadership, but the question I must ask is, where does self-control come from? Can we read a book on it? Take a course to develop it? Learn it at the feet of a seasoned mentor?

I would state, that true self-control comes from God, the Holy Spirit, operating in the heart of a person fully surrendered to the Lordship of Jesus Christ!

*Proverbs 16:32 Better a patient person than a warrior, one with self-control than one who takes a city.*

*Proverbs 16:32 (AKJV) He that is slow to anger is better than the mighty; and he that ruleth his spirit than he that taketh a city.*

So, we see here, that true self-control is the control of one's heart, or our very spirit.

*1 Timothy 3:2 Now the **overseer** is to be above reproach, faithful to his wife, **temperate, self-controlled**, respectable, hospitable, able to teach.*

The word overseer here translated into modern English and culture, as 'leader.' I have learned this about God: He never gives us a commandment in his Word that He does not give us the grace which is the available power and strength to fulfill His command.

Self-control, is a fruit of the born-again, developed, human spirit, and heart, by the process of the Word and Spirit of God.

*Gal 5: 22-23 But the fruit of the Spirit is love, joy, peace, forbearance, kindness, goodness, faithfulness, gentleness and self-control.*

I have learned that fruit is grown, developed, and produced over time through a walk with God, allowing the cross to meet our selfish passions and desires, and the Word and Holy Spirit to go deep into our souls to root us deeply in the love of God. God's love is patient and kind and does not lash out in anger at people but puts up with their development, graciously, as a parent with a child.

Yes, self-control is an essential part of leadership!

Let us humbly ask Holy Spirit to impart to us, this gift of heart.

*Father God, no matter what is going on, I ask You to grant me the self-control to not act from emotion or situational ethics, but only by the principles of Your Word, and the direct leadership of Holy Spirit. I ask this, knowing I am heard and answered, for I ask in Your name, Lord Jesus. Amen.*

*3.) A Keen Sense Of Justice*

*"Without a sense of fairness and justice, no leader can command and retain the respect of his followers." Napoleon Hill*

*Micah 6:8 He hath shewed thee, O man, what is good; and what doth the Lord require of thee, but to do justly, and to love mercy, and to walk humbly with thy God?*

If we believe we are called of God to lead, we govern ourselves with respect, reverence, and a healthy fear of God, causing us to act responsibly, equitably, and honestly in all of our dealings with people.

> *Matthew 23:23 Woe unto you, scribes and Pharisees, hypocrites! for ye pay tithe of mint and anise and cumin, and have omitted the weightier matters of the law, **judgment**, mercy, and faith: these ought ye to have done, and not to leave the other undone.*

Though I chose the King James Old English version of this verse, I did it on purpose. Jesus, in rebuking religious leaders of the days He walked the earth, spoke of the weightier matters of the Word of God: judgment, mercy, and faith. These are often 'the heart of the matter' in dealing with people. We need to look not only at what they have done but often, why, before we judge.

> *Hebrews 5:14 New International Version (NIV) But solid food is for the mature, who by constant use have trained themselves to distinguish good from evil.*

We must grow in this over years of study of the Word of God, developing our conscience to accurately know good from evil and what is appropriate in each case.

> *Acts 10:34 Then Peter opened his mouth, and said, Of a truth I perceive that God is no respecter of persons.*

God loves each of us equally but does not treat us all the same. He treats us based upon His Word, and our personal development. To whom much is given, much is required.

> *James 3:17 But the wisdom that is from above is first pure, then peaceable, gentle, and easy to be intreated, full of mercy and good*

*fruits, without partiality, and without hypocrisy.*

As leaders, we must daily seek God's wisdom in our daily affairs, and as our responsibility grows, we all find ourselves as Abraham Lincoln did:

Abraham Lincoln met crises on his knees!  During the Civil War, he once said, *"I have been driven many times to my knees by the overwhelming conviction that I had nowhere else to go. My own wisdom and that of all about me seemed insufficient for the day."*

Rather than wait for a crisis, why not prepare for the responsibilities and challenges of the day through prayer.

*Father, grant me a razor-sharp sense of discernment, justice, equity, and fairness in all my dealings with people. Show me clearly when to say and do or when to merely pray and leave the results to You. Lord Jesus, I ask You for Your heavenly wisdom today and each day. Amen*

*4.) DEFINITENESS OF DECISION.*

*"The man who wavers on his decisions, shows that he is not sure of himself. He cannot lead others successfully." Napoleon Hill*

*James 1:8 (KJV) A double minded man is unstable in all his ways.*

This is true.  No matter how much research, counsel, study, and prayer we must perform before we make a decision and after we announce our direction, we must stick to it without compromise.

*James 2:18 Yea, a man may say, Thou hast faith, and I have works: shew me thy faith without thy works, and I will shew thee my faith by my works.*

*James 2:20 But wilt thou know, O vain man, that faith without works is dead?*

*Psalm 15:4 In whose eyes a vile person is contemned; but he honoureth them that fear the Lord.  He that **sweareth to his own hurt**, and changeth not.*

Not much to pray here. When you know clearly what to do, DO IT!

*5. DEFINITENESS OF PLANS.*

*"The successful leader must plan his work and work his plan. A leader who moves by guesswork without practical definite plans is like a ship without a rudder. Sooner or later, he will land upon the rocks."*
*Napoleon Hill*

I remember a quote my dad made as a naval officer with 32 years of service. When I had made a radical life change at one point in my life to get out of a horrible relationship, he succinctly stated, *"Son, course corrections can be brutal in life, but shipwrecks are fatal."*

Our business or ministry plan is like the rudder of our ship. We use our words, work, and deeds to make happen what we believe is God's will for our lives. We must stay with our plan, avoiding distractions or obstacles to our stated purpose.

The classic Scripture quoted in almost every Christian leadership conference I seem to attend is this:

*Habakkuk 2:1-3 (KJV) I will stand upon my watch, and set me upon the tower, and will watch to see what he will say unto me, and what I shall answer when I am reproved. And the Lord answered me, and said, Write the vision, and make it plain upon tables, that he may run that readeth it. For the vision is yet for an appointed time, but at the end it shall speak, and not lie: though it tarry, wait for it; because it will surely come, it will not tarry. Behold, his soul which is lifted up is not upright in him: but the just shall live by his faith.*

In verse two, we see the practical business of getting a ministry, business, or project moving, on-time, on schedule: write the vision.

If it is worth doing, it is worth writing down. Notice the emphasis here is on DOING. I have seen supposed 'think-tanks' that take a God-breathed idea and choke it by paralysis by analysis. Sure, it is good to look at possible scenarios and outcomes and plan for them, but leaders LEAD. Action is their middle name, and the vision, written plainly, should speak loudly with a strong call to action implied in its writing.

*"Make it plain"*—Leave the research, articles, and underlying thoughts in the appendix or footnotes. Make the vision PLAIN, simple to understand, clearly articulated, and blunt if necessary. This is not a research paper, but rather a call to action, a plan to be implemented, with measurable timelines, schedules, and yardsticks for measuring goals accomplished.

*"...That he may run that readeth it"*—Make it so easily understandable, and doable, that when other workers come alongside to make their part of it work, they can do their job quickly with excellence with the minimum of friction to other team members, vendors, or customers.

*Let's pray:*

> *Father, help me to express clearly Your vision that You have ordained me to do or contribute to, adjusting it accordingly, as You add to it in easily understandable terms so that the people called alongside of me to get this great work done can do their part with speed, accuracy, and excellence. In Your name I pray, Lord Jesus. Amen.*

## 6. THE HABIT OF DOING MORE THAN PAID FOR.

> *"One of the penalties of leadership is the necessity of willingness, upon the part of the leader, to do more than he requires of his followers."*
> Napoleon Hill

*Matt 5:41 And whosoever shall compel thee to go a mile, go with him twain.*

'The extra-mile highway is the road less traveled...' business proverb.

One of our company slogans that we borrowed from popular business jargon was "UNDERPROMISE AND OVERDELIVER'.

My previous company was a finish carpentry company. We did this as a company on purpose on every job we performed in general. Here is what we would do.

Our primary market was upper-end homes and nicely paneled offices. When we bid the job, we carefully delineated the scope of work that we would perform for a given price. Yet, our craftsman were so skilled at what we did that we were usually able to run through the fixed scope of work pretty quickly as the design part was already done, and we could simply go by another cute motto: 'If you can see it, we can saw it,' providing quality woodwork quickly on time and on budget. Yet, we, too, know how to design and, as contractors, were often in a lot of more exotic building projects than the average homeowner or even designer or architect. On top of this, we were constantly reading architectural magazines and looking up pictures on the internet. When we found something that would provide a real centerpiece to an office or home (might be a cool ceiling treatment of beams and coffered ceiling, or perhaps a mantle, stair detail, or office paneling treatment), we would offer it to the client at our hard cost, or sometimes, for free, on the condition we could take pictures or show future clients through to showcase our work. In every project, we endeavored to throw in at least one of these exotic 'freebies,' knowing that discerning architects, designers, builders, and the clients' friends would see what we did and would covet our services. It worked well for many years!

*Jesus said, Matt 20:27 And whosoever will be chief among you, let him be your servant:*

*Matt 23:11 But he that is greatest among you shall be your servant.*

*Mark 9:35 And he sat down, and called the twelve, and saith unto them, If any man desire to be first, the same shall be last of all, and servant of all.*

*Mark 10:44 And whosoever of you will be the chiefest, shall be servant of all.*

Let's pray:

*Father, help me to under promise and over deliver with a servant heart, keeping my word and exceeding my commitments by Your grace and power. I ask this, Lord Jesus. In Your mighty name, Amen!*

*7.) A PLEASING PERSONALITY.*

*"No slovenly, careless person can become a successful leader. Leader-ship calls for respect. Followers will not respect a leader who does not grade high on all aspects of a Pleasing Personality." Napoleon Hill*

I personally don't believe in evolution, but I do believe strongly in personal growth. My brutish, callous ways are not acceptable as a leader. They reflect poorly upon Jesus, myself, my family, and the image of the organization I am called to lead.

*Ecc 10:12 The words of a wise man's mouth are gracious; but the lips of a fool will swallow up himself.*

*2 Tim 2:24 And the servant of the Lord must not strive; but be gentle unto all men, apt to teach, patient.*

I believe that leaders should exhibit excellent people skills, and this goes deeper than mere outward actions. People intuitively know when you care for them and hold their best interests at heart. It boils down to love. Mark. Hill calls this a pleasing personality, but I call it the love of God in operation. Sure, we can be movers and shakers, getting things done with stiletto focus, and tough on making goals and deadlines, but we can still exhibit kindness, respect, concern, and gentleness and mercy to those we are called to lead.

I heard that Andrew Carnegie made the statement that the difference between a $50,000 per year manager, and a million-dollar per year executive was only in the way they treated people.

*Prov 16:7 When a man's ways please the LORD, he maketh even his enemies to be at peace with him.*

*Psalm 5:12 For thou, LORD, wilt bless the righteous; with favor wilt thou compass him as with a shield.*

Yes, we are to be strong, courageous, and bold, but not ruthless, brutal, and so direct we crush everyone around us. Empower people, don't break them...
.

Let's pray:

*Father, give me favor and ways pleasing in Your sight that even my enemies might be at peace with me. In Your name I pray, Lord Jesus. Amen.*

*8.) SYMPATHY AND UNDERSTANDING.*

*The successful leader must be in sympathy with his followers. More-over, he must understand them, and their problems." Napoleon Hill*

*Matt 5:7 Blessed are the merciful: for they shall obtain mercy.*

*Luke 6:36 Be ye therefore merciful, as your Father also is merciful.*

I heard of a Japanese leadership style that requires all auto executives to work a full week on the assembly line so that they can better understand not only the process but also the daily grind auto plant workers face each day. They can be more understanding and compassionate (and I'm sure, intimately aware of the production process to ensure, not only better production, but also better working conditions for their staff).

*2 Cor 1:3 Blessed be God, even the Father of our Lord Jesus Christ, the Father of mercies, and the God of all comfort;*

*2 Cor 1:4 Who comforteth us in all our tribulation, that we may be able to comfort them which are in any trouble, by the comfort wherewith we ourselves are comforted of God.*
*Life can be hard. Make it easier on the next guy wherever possible.*

Let's pray:

*Father, Your gentleness, love, mercy and compassion for me are what has caused me to become great. Protect me from pride and the brutality of my own self-will, so that I might be gracious, compassionate, merciful, and understanding with others. I ask this in Your mighty name, Lord Jesus. Amen!*

*9.') MASTERY OF DETAIL.*

*"Successful Leadership calls for mastery of details of the leader's position." Napoleon Hill*

John Maxwell says: *"Those that don't organize, agonize."* There are administrative or organizational gifts that are given to people directly from God. If you don't have one, quickly ask God for one and surround yourself with people who can help you with this. In order for any organization to run smoothly, there must be an administrative process. As leaders, we must implement and oversee these processes and then refine or eliminate them if they become too cumbersome.

> *1 Cor 12:5-6 And there are differences of **administrations,** but the same Lord. Having then gifts differing according to the grace that is given to us, whether prophecy, let us prophesy according to the proportion of faith;*

> *Rom 12:7 Or ministry, let us wait on our ministering: or he that teacheth, on teaching; Or he that exhorteth, on exhortation: he that giveth, let him do it with simplicity; he that ruleth, with diligence; he that showeth mercy, with cheerfulness.*

Let's Pray:

> *Father, help me to fully organize and administrate with excellence that which you have given me to lead. Grant me gifts of administration. I pray in Your name, Lord Jesus. Amen!*

*10.) WILLINGNESS TO ASSUME FULL RESPONSIBILITY: "The successful leader must be willing to assume responsibility for the mistakes and shortcomings of his followers. If he tries to shift the responsibility, he will not remain the leader. If one of the followers made a mistake and shows himself incompetent, the leader must consider that it is he who failed." Napoleon Hill*

**Leadership Equals Responsibility!**

*Joshua 7:1 But the children of Israel committed a trespass in the accursed thing: for Achan, the son of Carmi, the son of Zabdi, the son of Zerah, of the tribe of Judah, took of the accursed thing: and the anger of the LORD was kindled against the children of Israel. And Joshua sent men from Jericho to Ai, which is beside Bethaven, on the east side of Bethel, and spake unto them, saying, Go up and view the country. And the men went up and viewed Ai.*

*And they returned to Joshua, and said unto him, Let not all the people go up; but let about two or three thousand men go up and smite Ai; and make not all the people to labor thither; for they are but few. So there went up thither of the people about three thousand men: and they fled before the men of Ai.*

*And the men of Ai smote of them about thirty and six men: for they chased them from before the gate even unto Shebarim, and smote them in the going down: wherefore the hearts of the people melted, and became as water.*

*And Joshua rent his clothes, and fell to the earth upon his face before the ark of the LORD until the eventide, he and the elders of Israel, and put dust upon their heads.*

*And Joshua said, Alas, O Lord GOD, wherefore hast thou at all brought this people over Jordan, to deliver us into the hand of the Amorites, to destroy us? would to God we had been content, and dwelt on the other side Jordan! 8 O Lord, what shall I say, when Israel turneth their backs before their enemies.*

*For the Canaanites and all the inhabitants of the land shall hear of it, and shall environ us round, and cut off our name from the earth: and what wilt thou do unto thy great name?*

*And the LORD said unto Joshua, Get thee up; wherefore liest thou thus upon thy face?*

*Israel hath sinned, and they have also transgressed my covenant which I commanded them: for they have even taken of the accursed thing, and have also stolen, and dissembled also, and they have put it even among their own stuff.*

*Therefore the children of Israel could not stand before their enemies, but turned their backs before their enemies, because they were accursed: neither will I be with you any more, except ye destroy the accursed from among you.*

*Up, sanctify the people, and say, Sanctify yourselves against tomorrow: for thus saith the LORD God of Israel, There is an accursed thing in the midst of thee, O Israel: thou canst not stand before thine enemies, until ye take away the accursed thing from among you.*

In this account, one man, Achan, had stolen some articles of demonic ritual, but notice God's response: **v11, Israel has sinned!**

Joshua, in crying out to God and taking responsibility to seek Him for understanding, got the entire nation of Israel delivered.

*Daniel 9:3 And I set my face unto the Lord God, to seek by prayer and supplications, with fasting, and sackcloth, and ashes:*

*And I prayed unto the LORD my God, and made my confession, and said, O Lord, the great and dreadful God, keeping the covenant and mercy to them that love him, and to them that keep his commandments;*

*We have sinned, and have committed iniquity, and have done wickedly, and have rebelled, even by departing from thy precepts and from thy judgments: Daniel assumed responsibility for the sin of the entire nation of Israel before God!*

God can hear and answer the prayer of a leader on behalf of their entire organization for deliverance and blessing, and it is clear from these verses that He will hear and answer if the leader is right with Him!

Let's pray:

*Father, make me responsible and strong enough to never blame shift. Give me faith to trust You to show me how to handle any problem I might face in my leadership and courage to take decisive action to rectify it. I ask this, Lord Jesus. Again in Your name I pray. Amen.*


*11.) COOPERATION.*

> *"The successful leader must understand and apply the principles of cooperative effort and be able to induce his followers to do the same. Leadership calls for POWER, and powers calls for COOPERATION."*
> *Napoleon Hill*

All that Mark. Hill has discovered here is the Biblical principle of unity-producing power.

People will help you for much more than a paycheck when you are following God accurately:

> *Psalm 110:3 Thy people shall be willing in the **day of** thy **power**...If you are doing the right things, the right way, in right timings of God, people with you will count it an honor to serve...*

Every leader must bring unity of vision and purpose to his or her team.

> *Eph 4:3 Endeavouring to keep the unity of the Spirit in the bond of peace.*

> *Psalm 133:1–3 Behold, how good and how pleasant it is for brethren to dwell together in unity! It is like the precious ointment upon the head, that ran down upon the beard, even Aaron's beard: that went down to the skirts of his garments; As the dew of Hermon, and as the dew that descended upon the mountains of Zion: for there the LORD commanded the blessing, even life for evermore.*

In this psalm, we see the principle taught that unity produces a commanded blessing from God. The problem in this is the account given to us in:

*Gen 11: 6 And the LORD said, Behold, the people is one, and they have all one language; and this they begin to do: and now nothing will be restrained from them, which they have imagined to do.*

Here we have people unified around an ungodly purpose.  God Himself destroyed their work and purpose.

It is critical then that whatever we intend to build must be according to the will of God. The ends do not justify the means!

This is the end of Napoleon Hill's eleven principles of leadership, and they are good!

Yet, without Jesus, they have no eternal worth or consequence.

*Matt 6:33 But seek ye first the kingdom of God, and his righteousness; and all these things shall be added unto you.*

I believe that putting God first in all of our affairs is the most important thing we must do, no matter what it may appear to cost, personally, at the time.

Jesus had 12 disciples, one was a traitor, so 11 is a good number to choose by Napoleon Hill.

# 70

# Check The Facts Jack!

*"Gossip is the deadliest microbe. It has neither legs nor wings. It is composed entirely of tales, and most of them have stings."* Morris Mandel in Bits & Pieces, June, 1990, p. 22

Recently, we went through a wonderful trial, that occurred when another person accused us of some financial mismanagement that was totally untrue. Gossip is like a serpent's venom. It poisons people against you. It may take years to rebuild trust in relationships.

Just because '**Everyone is saying it,**' does not make it true!

The Bible says we are kings and priests unto God, and we must conduct ourselves as royalty!

*Proverbs 16:10 A divine sentence is in the lips of the **king**: his mouth transgresseth not in judgment.*

As leaders, we hear a lot of stories, and we need to judge not only actions but motives. There was a situation where we wanted to donate building materials to a certain ministry. One of the businesses needed to know exactly where the materials donated were going. So, I sent him an email with the minister's name and location of the construction project we were planning because he grew up in that state and knew the area. It seems another person who 'wanted to get involved' asked for the material list I sent my former client, so I sent it to them. They got involved alright. Instead of helping, they accused me of 'taking up offerings in the name of the other ministry,' and then spread the 'rumor' of this to many, many other ministries. I could not believe they had done this! I attempted to meet with them to discuss it, but they would not return telephone calls nor emails.

As far as I'm concerned, I have forgiven them and am aggressively using my faith to believe the best of them and for them, declaring these two verses over their lives:

> *Philippians 1:6_Being confident of this very thing, that **he** which hath begun a good work in you will perform it until the day of Jesus Christ:*

> *Philippians 2:13 For it is God which **worketh in you** both to will and to do of his good pleasure.*

Faith works by love, and so I am using my faith on purpose for their growth and instruction in the things of God. Check the facts before you judge, leader. It is for your glory and promotion.

> *Proverbs 25:2 It is the glory of God to conceal a thing: but the honor of **kings** is to search out a matter.*

In the midst of my particular trial, I had a good friend of mine who was studying to be a rabbi who lives in Jerusalem call me.

I told him what I was going through, and he said, *"Interesting, Chris. Did you know that I am Israel? We take character assassination of more consequence than even murder?"*

He then reminded me of a story I had heard before that he had heard in the synagogue.

* * *

If you don't say it, they can't repeat it. Yiddish folklore offers a telling tale about gossip-makers. One such man had told so many malicious untruths about the local rabbi that, overcome by remorse, he begged the rabbi to forgive him.

*"And, Rabbi, tell me how I can make amends." The rabbi sighed.*

*"Take two pillows, go to the public square, and there cut the pillows open. Wave them in the air. Then come back."*

The rumormonger quickly went home, got two pillows and a knife, hastened to the square, cut the pillows open, waved them in the air, and hastened back to the rabbi's chambers.

*"I did just what you said, Rabbi!"*

*"Good." The rabbi smiled.*

*"Now, to realize how much harm is done by gossip, go back to the square..."*

*"And?"*

*And collect all your feathers."*

From *Hooray for Yiddish.*

* * *

It looks like the work of this person has blown feathers all over America. I must believe the blood of Jesus can wash away their mess... I need to believe what I preach.

Here are a couple of thoughts before speaking and decision making:

*I once formed a mutual encouragement fellowship at a time of stress in one of my pastorates. The members subscribed to a simple formula applied before speaking of any person or subject that was perhaps controversial.*

*T—Is it true?*
*H—Is it helpful?*
*I—Is it inspiring?*
*N—Is it necessary?*
*K—Is it kind?*

*If what I am about to say does not pass those tests, I will keep my mouth shut! And it worked. (Alan Redpath, A Passion for Preaching)*

God is love, and He will work it all out as only He can.
Let's pray:

*Father, I come before You, determined to walk free from offense and in Your love. Give me grace to see correctly into situations, and before I judge, to investigate to see what is being done and why. May I victoriously obey You, and press forward towards the mark of the high calling in Christ Jesus. Amen.*

# 71

# The Invisible Kingdom

*Act 12:21 And upon a set day Herod, arrayed in royal apparel, sat upon his throne, and made an oration unto them.*

And the people gave a shout, saying, It is the voice of a god, and not of a man.

And immediately the angel of the Lord smote him, because he gave not God the glory: and he was eaten of worms, and gave up the ghost.

But the word of God grew and multiplied.

If we believe that the kingdom of God is simply the rule and authority of God in heaven and in the earth, then we must understand that the most important thing for us, as Christians, is how to fully walk in the kingdom of God - even when the political system of the day may be directly opposed to the righteous and holy reign of Jesus in a particular time and space in the earth.

God only has two authority structures in the earth: The political system (Rom 13:1-5, 1 Tim 2:1-4) and His Church that rules and reigns with him (Eph 2:6).

In the above passage, we see how an earthly kingdom collided with the kingdom of God.

Here is an example of the thoughts and kingdoms of men colliding with the kingdom of God.  King Herod overstepped his earthly authority in proclaiming himself to be a god, just like the old adage: See the writing on the wall...

Somewhere in that generation was a church on fire for God, praying for God's power and authority to be released. And it was! God sent an angel and struck Herod dead that it might be known there is only one true God in heaven and earth, and that Jesus is Lord to the glory of the Father.

Like the old worship song, we sing: *"Kings, and kingdoms, will all pass away, but there's something about that name."*

Greece, Rome, and the Ottoman empire have all passed away, but the kingdom of God still stands. America will too, as long as she stands with the Word of God and Jesus, but if she would depart, she too would end up in the boneyard of history.

So, we pray that each of us, from the least to the greatest, might meet Jesus personally and serve him fully in holiness and in the unique and high calling each of us were created to fulfill.

This is where I find myself in the kingdom, using every available resource, influence, and moment of my life to promote, build, establish, and enforce the kingdom of God in the earth, for it is the answer for every situation, every problem because its nature is love.

*"Yes, Jesus loves me, for the Bible tells me so."*

He loves you too and really does have an incredible plan for your life.

*"If we only had eyes to see and ears to hear and wits to understand, we would know that the Kingdom of God in the sense of holiness, goodness, beauty as close as breathing. His Kingdom is crying out to be born both within ourselves and within the world. We would know that the Kingdom of God is what we all of us hunger for above all other things even when we don't know its name or realize that it's what we'Rev starving to death for. The Kingdom of God is where our best dreams come from and our truest prayers. We get a glimpse of it at*

*those moments when we find ourselves being better than we are and wiser than we know. We catch sight of it when at some moment of crisis, a strength seems to come to us that is greater than our own strength. The Kingdom of God is where we belong. It is home, and whether we realize it or not, all of us homesick for it."* Frederick Buechner

Let's pray:

*Father, You have said that I am to be in this world, but not of it. Bring me to my place in Your kingdom, and teach me Your way of walking through this life. May I not waste time on other things, but may I settle for nothing less than the high calling You have placed upon my life through you, Lord Jesus. Reveal Your Kingdom to our lives, our nation, our families... Amen.*

# 72

# Reigning Through Humility

Jesus has given us all things, as kings and priests, now, wash feet...

> *John 13:3 Jesus knowing that the Father had given all things into his hands, and that he was come from God, and went to God. Here we read of Jesus about to go to the cross, and, like Abraham, God has established His covenant with Him as a man. He has now been given all things. And so God, our Father, has done for you and for me.*

> *Romans 8:32 He that spared not his own Son, but delivered him up for us all, how shall he not with him also freely give us all things?*

We who were lost, directionless, purposeless sinners have been redeemed, forgiven, and into His royal family and granted position, power, prominence in heaven, in the kingdom.

> *1 Pet 2:9 But ye are a chosen generation, a royal priesthood, an holy nation, a peculiar people; that ye should shew forth the praises of him who hath called you out of darkness into his marvelous light:*

Now, we have been given authority over the earth, and its works of darkness...

*Rev 1:5 And from Jesus Christ, who is the faithful witness, and the first begotten of the dead, and **the prince of the kings of the earth.** Unto him that loved us, and washed us from our sins in his own blood, 6 And hath **made us kings and priests unto God and his Father**; to him be glory and dominion for ever and ever. Amen.*

Priests pray and offer sacrifice; kings rule and reign.  Now, we are the sacrifice. Our lives laid down in love are a sweet aroma before the throne of God.

*1 Pet 2:9 But ye are a chosen generation, a royal priesthood, an holy nation, a peculiar people; that ye should shew forth the praises of him who hath called you out of darkness into his marvelous light:*

Yet all of this comes only by faith, and this is a gift from God.

*Eph 2:8 For by grace are ye saved through faith; and that not of yourselves: it is the gift of God:*

So, we realize that faith is the currency of heaven. We begin to allow the word to become flesh in us and develop our faith. Suddenly, Abraham's life becomes very interesting to us. We discover that what God did and promised Abraham, He, by covenant, is willing to do for us...

*Gal 3:6 Even as Abraham believed God, and it was accounted to him for righteousness. 7 Know ye therefore that they which are of faith, the same are the children of Abraham. 9 So then they which be of faith are blessed with faithful Abraham. That the blessing of Abraham might come on the Gentiles through Jesus Christ; that we might receive the promise of the Spirit through faith. And if ye be Christ's, then are ye Abraham's seed, and heirs according to the promise. And, after all this wonderful study, we find ourselves back in the life of Abraham, studying what promises God made to Him.*

*Gen 14:18 And Melchizedek king of Salem brought forth bread and wine: and he was the priest of the most high God. 19 And he blessed him, and said, **Blessed be Abram of the most high God, possessor of heaven and earth:***

Do you see this? In this verse, we see the covenant of God operating through Abraham where everything he had, he had pledged to God. Yet, in this verse, we see the total commitment of God to His part of the covenant.

Here we see that God had given Abraham all of Himself, **making Abraham God's covenant man, possessor of heaven and earth!**

*John 13:35 Jesus knowing that the Father had given all things into his hands, Suddenly we see it.*

We are covenant people, **and all things in heaven and in the earth, have been given to us!**

*Gen 14:20 And blessed be the most high God, which hath delivered thine enemies into thy hand. And he gave him tithes of all. Yet, as great as these truths are, there is one far greater: Jesus is Lord!*

**Apart from Him, we can do nothing.** And so, we go... into all the world, our families, our neighborhoods, our workplaces, and to the nations of the world, bringing His love, truth, power, miracles—GOOD NEWS!

*Matt 28:18 And Jesus came and spake unto them, saying, All power is given unto me in heaven and in earth. 19 Go ye therefore, and teach all nations, baptizing them in the name of the Father, and of the Son, and of the Holy Ghost: 20 Teaching them to observe all things whatsoever I have commanded you: and, lo, I am with you alway, even unto the end of the world. Amen.*

Kings and priests, yes, we are so, John 13:14: *If I then, your Lord and Master, have washed your feet; ye also ought to wash one another's feet. For I have given you an example, that ye should do as I have done to you.*

OBEY HIM! Jesus only did the will of our heavenly Father, and even as He was in His generation, so are we called to do in ours. His strength is made perfect in our weakness, and His power, that is His grace, is only given to the humble.

*1 Peter 5:5 Likewise, ye younger, submit yourselves unto **the** elder. Yea, all of you be subject one **to** another, and be clothed with humility: for God resisteth **the** proud, and giveth **grace to the humble**.*

As my pastor once said: *"If you consistently **humble yourself** before God, then God will never have to humble you before men."*

Let's Pray:

*Father, we are Your children, sons and daughters of the Most High! Thank You for redeeming us, restoring us, disciplining us, and sending us out into this world as kings and priests unto You in Your power and authority. As we go, may we walk in complete obedience to You, Holy Spirit, in humility, gentleness and wisdom before all men, seeking to serve, bless, love, and understand, even when we are mistreated. May Your Kingdom come and Your will be done in our lives and in the earth. May Jesus receive the reward of His suffering. For the sake of His glory, we go! Amen.*

# 73

# Don't Whitewash – Build Upon Truth!

*Whitewash (Merriam Webster) –to make (something) whiter by paint-
ing it with whitewash*

- to prevent people from learning the truth about (something bad, such
  as a dishonest, immoral, or illegal act or situation)
- to defeat (an opponent) easily by winning every game, point, etc.

**Ezekiel 13:10 (CEV)** *Those prophets refuse to be honest.  They tell
my people there will be peace, even though there's no peace to be
found. **They are like workers who think they can fix a shaky wall by
covering it with paint.***

There was a saying in carpentry: 'Putty and paint are what a carpenter ain't.'
    The implication is that no amount of fine finish is a substitute for good
workmanship.
    In life, there is no substitute for building our life upon the truth of the
Word of God.

*Matthew 7:24 "Therefore, whosoever heareth these sayings of Mine* *and doeth them, I will liken him unto a **wise man**, who **built** his house upon a rock. And the rain descended and the floods came, and the winds blew and beat upon that house; and it fell not, for it was founded upon a rock. And every one that heareth these sayings of Mine and doeth them not, shall be likened unto a foolish man, who built his house upon the sand; and the rain descended, and the floods came, and the winds blew, and beat upon that house; and it fell, and great was the fall of it."*

The Storms of life come to us all. Yet, those who have carefully built their lives upon Jesus and His Words will stand through the storms strong! Whatever you do, do it well, so that it will last.

Let's Pray:

*Father, I bring Your word before You, and like Paul prayed Phil 1:9–11: And this I pray, that your love may abound still more and more in real knowledge and all discernment, so that you may approve the things that are excellent, in order to be sincere and blameless until the day of Christ having been filled with the fruit of righteousness which comes through Jesus Christ, to the glory and praise of God.*

# 74

# Timing in the Call of God!

Timing... He is preparing your place.

*John 14:2 In my Father's house are many mansions: if it were not so, I would have told you. I go to **prepare a place for you.***

*John 14:3 And if I go and **prepare a place for you**, I will come again, and receive you unto myself; that where I am, there ye may be also.*

*Deut 31:8 And the LORD, **he it is that doth go before thee**; he will be with thee, he will not fail thee, neither forsake thee: fear not, neither be dismayed.*

*Isa 45:2 **I will go before thee**, and make the crooked places straight: I will break in pieces the gates of brass, and cut in sunder the bars of iron:*

*Luke 1:17 And he shall go before him in the spirit and power of Elias, to turn the hearts of the fathers to the children, and the disobedient to the wisdom of the just; **to make ready a people prepared for the Lord.***

*Eph 4:11-16 And he gave some, apostles; and some, prophets; and some, evangelists; and some, pastors and teachers; For the perfecting of the saints, for the work of the ministry, for the edifying of the body of Christ till we all come in the unity of the faith, and of the knowledge of the Son of God, unto a perfect man, unto the measure of the stature of the fulness of Christ that we henceforth be no more children, tossed to and fro, and carried about with every wind of doctrine, by the sleight of men, and cunning craftiness, whereby they lie in wait to deceive; But speaking the truth in love may grow up into him in all things, which is the head, even Christ: From whom the whole body fitly joined together and compacted by that which every joint supplieth, according to the effectual working in the measure of every part, maketh increase of the body unto the edifying of itself in love.*

**So, you have a call to kingdom leadership, and it burns like a fire shut up in your bones!**

You know you have an offering to contribute, a gift to bring, but it seems every door is closed at present.

Your frustration mounts as the days turn into months, into years, as you faithfully stay before the Lord in prayer, worship, and diligent study of His Word.

Yet, know this. The kingdom of God is no longer a new entity on the earth. The church has been here for 2000 years! For your gift to effectively operate, it must work alongside and in conjunction with many other gifts in the Body of Christ. For you to step into your place, others, perhaps elder than you, need to recognize, test, and respond to your gift.

At present, they may not even like you, for your particular gift is designed to impact this generation, not theirs. Your fire and zeal may be uncomfortable to them because God has led you far outside their mental box.

*Luke 1:17 And he shall go before him in the spirit and power of Elias, to turn the hearts of the fathers to the children, and the disobedient to the wisdom of the just; to make ready a people prepared for the Lord.*

Your gift must operate cross-generationally, and there are at least four generations of believers surrounding you now. And somehow, you must build generational bridges and create pathways for people to flow supernaturally, gracefully through each season of their life and calling.

*Isa 58: 10 And if thou draw out thy soul to the hungry, and satisfy the afflicted soul; then shall thy light rise in obscurity, and thy darkness be as the noonday.*

There are particular needs and ministry needs in each season of life.

It will take much wisdom from God to seek to meet these.

There is nothing new under the sun. You are not the first nor the last to experience this frustration. If you like, you can throw off the fetters of the established order and explode into the earth as the new entity God has called you to be. Many have done this, and sometimes it is the passion of the Holy Spirit for the harvest that authentically compels them.

Others, like me, are learning to temper their fire with wisdom. In the making of a true Samurai sword, the layers of leavened steel are heated up at least seven times and quenched in various processes to instill the right temper and spring into the steel. US soldiers discovered that these swords could slice through their gun barrels in WW2!

*Isa 41:2 Who raised up the righteous man from the east, called him to his foot, gave the nations before him, and made him rule over kings? He gave them as the dust to his sword and as driven stubble to his bow.*

*Isa 49:2 And he hath made my mouth like a sharp sword; in the shadow of his hand hath he hid me, and made me a polished shaft; in his quiver hath he hid me;*

True leaders entering an existing organization recognize they must become a lover and historian of the people, places, and things that God has built in previous years, even if they see precisely what must happen to experience the explosive kingdom growth that will occur when they are given a platform to lead!

Understand the heart of Jesus! He is still a great, gentle shepherd, and He is dealing with seasoned hearts in tenderness and wisdom to prepare them for you, even as He has spent years in your development.

Perhaps, you are honestly ready to step into your office, call, and appointment, but they are not. Let love prevail!

King David, a man after God's own heart, refused to touch God's anointed, even though his daily circumstances were brutal.

Let's say, my past couple of years have been no picnic either.

God clearly anointed David. The prophet Samuel himself came to his house to pour oil upon his head and set him apart as king of Israel.

*1 Sam 16:13 Then Samuel took the horn of oil and anointed him in the midst of his brethren: and the Spirit of the LORD came upon David from that day forward. So Samuel rose up, and went to Ramah.*

By the anointing, he slew the lion, the bear, and Goliath. Yet, he was not king...YET!

*1 Sam 18:10 And it came to pass on the morrow, that the evil spirit from God came upon Saul, and he prophesied in the midst of the house: and David played with his hand, as at other times: and there was a javelin in Saul's hand. 11 And Saul cast the javelin; for he said, I will smite David even to the wall with it. And David avoided out of his presence twice.*

*And Saul was afraid of David because the LORD was with him and was departed from Saul.*

God anointed David but not yet appointed him king. He had to dodge spears from Saul's throne to the deserts and rocks for years, but he fully trusted in God and His timing. And though there were several times God delivered

Saul into David's hands, David refused to hurt him.

Notice the exclamation point, folks, because I have urgently wanted to blast godly authority sometimes when they are obviously wrong.  BUT I WILL NOT TOUCH GODS ANOINTED, NOR WILL I SOW DISCORD AMONG THE BRETHREN.

> *1 Sam 24:6 And he said unto his men, The LORD forbid that I should do this thing unto my master, the LORD'S anointed, to stretch forth mine hand against him, seeing he is the anointed of the LORD.*

### God HATES

> *Prov 6:19 A false witness that speaketh lies, and he that soweth discord among brethren.*

Eventually, David was appointed king.  Notice there were many years between the **anointing** of God and the **Appointing** of God!

> *2 Sam 2:4 And the men of Judah came, and there they anointed David king over the house of Judah. And they told David, saying, That the men of Jabesh and Gilead were they that buried Saul.*

I could study it out, but I'm not sure how long David ran from Saul in battle or hiding amongst his enemies, yet refusing to take matters into His own hands.

I asked Holy Spirit why David had to stay in the wilderness, and I felt Him say: **'David had to learn to accurately hear my voice in life and death circumstances before he was fully qualified to lead my people.'**

> *Isa 42:8 I am the LORD: that is my name: and my glory will I not give to another,*

Yes, the gifts and callings of God are without repentance, but many are called and few are chosen. Therefore there is difference between the **CALL** of God and the **COMMISSION** of God.

As you cry out to God, as I do daily, one of two things will happen, either those around you currently in positions of authority will eventually respond to the direction and wooing of the Holy Spirit, or He will move them out of your way. As for me, I fear God, and we reap what we sow. I am walking in love towards all men, even my persecutors and opposers.

He will move you out of the way! Currently, I find myself, like David, Paul, and other Biblical characters, completely removed from my church home, as I radically obey Holy Spirit into some wilderness areas. His voice is clear here, and there is great intimacy in the desert with Him!

Why? I would rather have the grace and resulting power with God that comes to the humble than that which the strength of my own arm, or even the violence that my own faith can produce. Obedience and intimacy with Him are my first priority, and I will pay any price to fully obey Him without compromise.

There is a set time, and I will walk in it, even if, like my First Nations brothers, I create my own personal 'trail of tears' towards my destiny.

> *Psalm 75:6 For promotion cometh neither from the east, nor from the west, nor from the south. But God is the judge: he putteth down one, and setteth up another.*

We are called to be like Jesus:

> *Heb 5:7 Who in the days of his flesh, when he had offered up prayers and supplications with strong crying and tears unto him that was able to save him from death, and was heard in that he feared;*

Sure, it is hard. Brutal at times, but remember that He makes everything beautiful in His time.

Let's Pray:

*Father, what I do affects eternity and generations to come, should Jesus tarry. You lead with gentleness those with young, how much more organizations and kingdom constructs You have raised up to minister to them. Give me patience, grace, and strength to endure, as my fire and passion find release in praise, prayer, and violent faith. In your precious name, I pray, Lord Jesus. Amen.*

# 75

# The Sin of Sodom

*Ezekiel 16:49 Now this was the sin of your sister Sodom: She and her daughters were arrogant, overfed and unconcerned; they did not help the poor and needy.*

I'm sure I could create a long devotion to the sin of Sodom and its wickedness. Many have used the destruction of Sodom as a text for preaching against homosexuality. I understand how the gay predators tried to rape the angelic strangers that visited Lot's house as the traditional interpretation of the destruction of Sodom and Gomorrah.

Homosexuality is wrong as is any sex outside of a marriage covenant in the eyes of God but look at this verse, tucked away in the book of Ezekiel.

The real sins of Sodom mentioned here are (1) Pride and arrogance, (2) Gluttony, and being overfed. (3) Unconcern for the help of the poor and the needy.

I have a very simple one: Pride is simply having a better idea than God in any area of life.

*2 Corinthians 10:5 casting down imaginations, and every **high thing** that exalteth itself against the knowledge of God, and bringing into captivity every thought to the obedience of Christ.*

Anytime, anywhere any person has thoughts opposed to the word of God, they are in pride. They may be sincere, yet in God's eyes, they are sincerely wrong. Someone might not have their chest puffed up or be walking in the arrogance of way, yet be proud nonetheless, in that they are doing their own thing, not God's.

This past couple of years has been interesting for me and my family as we went from a comfortable income, able to go and eat whatever we wanted, to no income, having to eat at food banks, to finally turning my truck back into the bank. Then our house went through foreclosure. There has been a wonderful walk of discovery from what is truly a need or merely a want. Things that I had taken for granted when removed, become prayer points, where I discover where my heart has really been at.

Learning to survive for weeks without a dime in our pocket, no vehicle, eating at food banks, has quite honestly changed me and made me a far better human being, far more accepting and willing to help, non-judgmental, and grateful for the little things in life. Now, I am able to simply see and listen to the poor of this nation and learn many things that I could never have heard before.

I remember hearing the story of Heidi Baker. After receiving her Ph.D. from seminary, she asked Jesus what He would have her do. The Lord instructed her to go to Mozambique with her husband with nothing but faith in God and to 'sit with the poor and learn of my kingdom'

I reach out internationally to Christian brothers and sisters serving the Lord who honestly have to trust the Lord not only for their next meal but in many cases, the meals of those orphans that have come under their care. They live a sacrificial life at a level that we here in America cannot comprehend. As I cry out to God for our daily needs, I am acutely aware that the God I am praying to loves them exactly as much as He loves me and my children. The nature of my prayers has radically changed.

The old cliché' is true: *"You never truly discover that Jesus is all you need until He is all that you have."*

He can create a humble pathway of provision, that requires radical, strict obedience. I am convinced that He is doing exactly that in my life. I am a prosperity preacher! I honestly believe that one of the benefits of serving Jesus is financial prosperity:

> *3 John 1:2(KJV) Beloved, I wish above all things that thou mayest prosper and be in health, even as thy soul prospereth.*

Yet, as I have walked this pathway of radical obedience, I have discovered that many, many things in my life were simply wants, soulish desires, that were often born in the world and this culture, not birthed in the fire of the Holy Spirit and the Word of God.

Let's talk about a couple of these:

Fitness: I love to stay in shape. My body is a temple of the Holy Spirit, and I like to be strong in the Lord and the power of His might.  To do this, I used to live P90X. For those of you who know what that is, this involved 6-10 workouts/week, a structured diet, many protein and bodybuilding supplements, and of course high dollar multivitamins. These all cost money, usually around an extra $200-300/month, plus a gym membership fee. Money has been non-existent, and in many cases, so has food, any food, so workouts have been in my makeshift gym in my backyard, 3-4 times/week, and then, and only then, when we actually have enough food in the house to justify it, because I have children to feed.

Coffee: I love me some good coffee. Yet, the days of exotic coffees have long gone, and I drink regular Folgers when we have been able. I can live with it, or without it.

Desserts: When we have ice-cream or some sweets for dessert or at a church function, I am simply grateful. I'm fighting for healthy meals for the family, simply putting decent calories on the table with nutrition in them. Sweets are low on the priority.

Pets: We have two dogs, a cat, a rabbit, and an aquarium.  They eat well, but as I see orphans around the world starving, can I justify the expense of feeding pets, when I should be feeding people, starving children that honestly need food?

Entertainment: I used to hit the movies, and watch the latest and greatest flicks at the theater. Netflix, internet access, and movie nights have not been possible which have led to family time together where we actually talk to each other, read the Bible, have tickle fights, and love one another. A walk by the river and building sandcastles is free, yet builds memories for a lifetime. We still hit movies at the dollar theater as we are able, but my appetites have changed. We enjoy the things of God far more now because Jesus draws close to us there as we have drawn close to Him.

Vehicle: For many years, we have had two vehicles. For over a year, we had none. We walked each day to the library for internet and home school and accomplish a fitness activity. We often skip and sing our way here, laughing as we go. I have believed God for another reliable vehicle, and He has surely heard and answered that prayer. But know this: I will be far more grateful to Him and far more sensitive to driving others around, for I know intimately what it is like to walk by faith. (He has answered, providing for us a 1998 jeep Cherokee, for which I am very grateful)

Utilities: I have never been without them before. For over a year and a half, we went without water, gas, and electricity for several extended periods of time. There is nothing like dark nights, cold showers, or hauling water to simply flush the toilet to make you appreciate services that up until now, we have simply taken for granted. After we moved from our home, we have lived with friends, learning that there are radically different ways to do family life than we knew. We have learned much from each family home we have stayed with. As we traveled to Indian reservations and spent time with natives, we discovered many have no heat, nor running water, in often extreme climates, yet they are a resilient people, with deep joy and peace, that has been a great example to us.

The sin of Sodom was in my face, for I now see how I have not only committed all of these three sins but have lived in them for many years.

*1 Timothy 6:17 Charge them that are rich in this world, that they be not **high**-minded, nor trust in uncertain riches, but in the living God, who giveth us richly all **things** to enjoy;*

We cry out for revival, that we are willing to pay any price, yet the price God requires is a heart change. There IS financial prosperity in the kingdom of God.

*2 Corinthians 8:9 For ye know the grace of our Lord Jesus Christ, that, though he was rich, yet for your sakes he became poor, that ye through his poverty might be rich.*

Jesus died upon the cross for our poverty, our sin, and our sickness. Yet, during this season of my financial poverty, I am changing, where human eyes cannot see. Deep in my soul, I am prospering, and in my due season, wealth and riches shall again be my portion in life. Gratefully, humbly, in wisdom, will I again walk in the wealth of this world.

Why? Because I believe, no longer blindly, but because Jesus has spoken to me personally about my finances. One morning, in fervent prayer, He reminded me of who He is, King of the Universe, and He said: '**Son, you cannot seek me the way you have these past years, and come away diminished!**' True faith always has a good report!

*James 2:5 Hearken, my beloved brethren, Hath not God chosen the poor of this world **rich in faith**, and heirs of the kingdom which he hath promised to them that love him? This season too, shall pass, and Jesus, my faithful Lord, shall again honor His Word in my life and cause me to prosper, increase, and walk in wealth, for I have believed.*

*Ecclesiastes 3 To every thing there is a season, and a time to every purpose under the heaven: A time to get, and a time to lose; a time to keep, and a time to cast away; He hath made everything beautiful in his time: also he hath set the world in their heart, so that no man can find out the work that God maketh from the beginning to the end.*

I know that there is no good in them, but for a man to rejoice, and to do good in his life.

And also that every man should eat and drink, and enjoy the good of all his labor, it is the gift of God. How about you?

I think in my testimonies I have discussed how gluttony has died its horrible death in my life, but let me talk about concern for the poor.

I have honestly not been able to give anything to the poor; despite the thousands of requests we receive for financial aid from those who read my blog. Not one goes by unnoticed anymore. I honestly fervently pray with compassion for every need, trusting Jesus to do what I personally cannot.

I have faced many days of trouble, and I need the Lord to deliver me as the days have come. Jesus said the poor you will always have with you. Consider them, love them, do not oppress them, and help wherever you can to alleviate human suffering.

Let's pray:

*Father, in every season of life, there are lessons to be learned. Help us to recognize the season You have us in, and to be content and faithful in it. May we be quick to learn the lessons we must learn, now, deep within our soul, that in the season of our promotion and favor, we remain humble, grateful, and fully dependent upon You, Lord Jesus, Amen.*

# 76

# Balaam – Prophet for Hire!

Okay, let's look at this Bible character named Balaam, who is probably in hell today, to see if we can learn what not to do as leaders.

The Word of God is wonderful in that it tells the truth, and we can learn from even bad examples what not to do.

> *Psalm 19: 8 The statutes of the LORD are right, rejoicing the heart: the commandment of the LORD is pure, enlightening the eyes... Moreover by them is thy servant warned: and in keeping of them there is great reward.*

Here we see the end of the story, Balaam the prophet, being killed by the people of God:

> *Numbers 31:8 And they slew the kings of Midian, beside the rest of them that were slain; namely, Evi, and Rekem, and Zur, and Hur, and Reba, five kings of Midian: Balaam also the son of Beor they slew with the sword.*

> *Joshua 13:22 Balaam also the son of Beor, the soothsayer, did the children of Israel slay with the sword among them that were slain by them.*

**Question is, why did God have Balaam killed?**

*Num 13:15-17 And Moses said unto them, Have ye saved all the women alive? Behold, **these caused the children of Israel, through the counsel of Balaam, to commit trespass against the LORD** in the matter of Peor, and there was a plague among the congregation of the LORD. Now therefore kill every male among the little ones, and kill every woman that hath known man by lying with him.*

*Numbers 31:16 Behold, these caused the children of Israel, through the counsel of Balaam, to commit trespass against the LORD in the matter of Peor, and there was a plague among the congregation of the LORD. **What was the counsel of Balaam?***

*Jude 1:11 Woe unto them! for they have gone in the way of Cain, **and ran greedily after the error of Balaam for reward,** and perished in the gainsaying of Core.*

Here we see the error of Balaam and his motive. He was greedy and sold out the gift of God for a reward.

*Revelation 2:14 But I have a few things against thee, because thou hast there them that hold the doctrine of Balaam, who taught Balac to cast a stumbling block before the children of Israel, to eat things sacrificed unto idols, and to commit fornication.*

Yet, here, we see what he did. He counseled the enemy of God to tempt the people of God to eat food sacrificed to idols and to have sexual relationships out of marriage.

*Numbers 25:1 And Israel abode in Shittim, and the people began to commit whoredom with the daughters of Moab. And they called the people unto the sacrifices of their gods: and the people did eat, and* *bowed down to their gods. **And Israel joined himself unto Baalpeor:** and the anger of the LORD was kindled against Israel.*

*Deuteronomy 23:4 Because they met you not with bread and with water in the way, when ye came forth out of Egypt; and because **they hired against thee Balaam** the son of Beor of Pethor of Mesopotamia, to curse thee.*

*Deuteronomy 23:5 Nevertheless the LORD thy God would not hearken unto Balaam; but the LORD thy God turned the curse into a blessing unto thee, because the LORD thy God loved thee.*

*Joshua 24:9 Then Balak the son of Zippor, king of Moab, arose and warred against Israel, and sent and called Balaam the son of Beor to curse you:*

*Joshua 24:10 But I would not hearken unto Balaam; therefore he blessed you still: so I delivered you out of his hand.*

*Nehemiah 13:2 Because they met not the children of Israel with bread and with water, **but hired Balaam against them,** that he should curse them: howbeit our God turned the curse into a blessing.*

*Micah 6:5 O my people, remember now what Balak king of Moab consulted, and what Balaam the son of Beor answered him from Shittim unto Gilgal; that ye may know the righteousness of the LORD.*

*2 Peter 2:15-22 Which have forsaken the right way, and are gone astray, following the way of Balaam the son of Bosor, who loved the wages of unrighteousness; But was rebuked for his iniquity: the dumb ass speaking with man's voice forbad the madness of the prophet. These are wells without water, clouds that are carried with a tempest; to whom the mist of darkness is reserved for ever.*

*For when they speak great swelling words of vanity, they allure through the lusts of the flesh, through much wantonness, those that were clean escaped from them who live in error. While they promise them liberty, they themselves are the servants of corruption: for of whom a man is overcome, of the same is he brought in bondage.*

*For if after they have escaped the pollutions of the world through the knowledge of the Lord and Savior Jesus Christ, they are again entangled therein, and overcome, the latter end is worse with them than the beginning. For it had been better for them not to have known the way of righteousness, than, after they have known it, to turn from the holy commandment delivered unto them. But it is happened unto them according to the true proverb, The dog is turned to his own vomit again; and the sow that was washed to her wallowing in the mire.*

*Jude 1:11 Woe unto them! for they have gone in the way of Cain, and ran greedily after the error of Balaam for reward, and perished in the gainsaying of Core.*

*Revelation 2:14 But I have a few things against thee, because thou hast there them that hold the doctrine of Balaam, who taught Balac to cast a stumbling block before the children of Israel, to eat things sacrificed unto idols, and to commit fornication.*

So, we see it. Balaam, the prophet who heard and knew the voice of God, sold out his gift for money and position. It cost him his life, and he is eternally in hell today.

What he did is amazingly wicked!

Three times Balak hired him to curse the children of Israel; three times God flowed through him pronouncing a blessing instead of his intended curse. Had he been smart and righteous, he should have left Balak and joined the people of God. He could have won every battle and lived for God.

Yet, he got greedy. Obviously, the Midianites and Moabites had material wealth, and he wanted him some of it.

He was once a broke prophet living peacefully in his hut, and now he has kings knocking at his door. So, what does he do?

He knows that God is holy and cannot lie. In fact, he had even prophesied it:

> *Num 23:19–22 God is not a man, that he should lie; neither the son of man, that he should repent: hath he said, and shall he not do it? or hath he spoken, and shall he not make it good? Behold, I have received commandment to bless: and he hath blessed; and I cannot reverse it. He hath not beheld iniquity in Jacob, neither hath he seen perverseness in Israel: the LORD his God is with him, and the shout of a king is among them. God brought them out of Egypt; he hath as it were the strength of an unicorn. Surely there is no enchantment against Jacob, neither is there any divination against Israel: according to this time it shall be said of Jacob and of Israel, What hath God wrought!*

Do you see it?

God was with Israel! His manifest presence, His glory, His power, His blessing, His anointing, and surely the host of heaven, angel armies were protecting His people.

Yet, in this verse we see why.

The children of Israel are living according to the law of God. They are fully separated unto Him, so that the prophet, by the Spirit of God proclaimed:

'He beheld no iniquity in Jacob, nor has he seen perverseness in Israel.'

**Holiness produced power!**

Fully obedient people were met, blessed, protected, delivered, and prospered by the person and presence of the living God, Creator of heaven and earth!

Here is where amazing wickedness occurred:

Balaam knew God and knew His word. He saw this by the Holy Spirit and knew that the people of God, with God, were unstoppable.

So, what does he do? He counsels Balak to throw a party for the men of Israel. Get your best delicacies and the prime cuts of meat cooking that you have sacrificed to your gods, demon spirits. Then, get your women dressed seductively and have them seduce the men of God to have sex with them.

When you do, God Himself will withdraw from His people and will destroy them Himself.

This he did, and Scripture records:

> *Number 23: 16 Behold, these caused the children of Israel, through the counsel of Balaam, to commit trespass against the LORD in the matter of Peor, and there was a plague among the congregation of the LORD.*

Now, what are we to learn from this today?

We are those that bear the holy offices of God, five-fold ministry gifts, set into the earth to train, equip, and edify the people of God, the Body, the Bride of Christ.

Well, we are to prepare a holy bride for Jesus: one without a spot or wrinkle.

> *James 4:4 Ye adulterers and adulteresses, know ye not that the friendship of the world is enmity with God?  whosoever therefore will be a friend of the world is the enemy of God.*

> *2 Cor 6:17 Wherefore come out from among them, and be ye separate, saith the Lord, and touch not the unclean thing; and I will receive you,*

> *2 Corinthians 10:6 and having in a readiness to **revenge all disobedience**, when your obedience is fulfilled.*

God is still holy, and again I find myself stuck on this theme.

I am convinced that a holy, obedient people, in the hands of our God is unstoppable.

Strong, healthy, wealthy, blessed, joyful, loving, victorious in the trials of life!

Yet, how many of us fail the money test?

We get an extra couple of dollars, and we spend it watching a worldly movie or attending a worldly event.

We say: 'Father, if You give me an extra $50 this week, I will spend it on (missions, orphans, our ministry building program, or whatever the financial need is before us in the kingdom), yet we flunk the prosperity test.

God gives the money, and instead of using it for the work of God, we go out whoring with the world.

Does God give prosperity?

Yes!

> *Deut 8:18 But thou shalt remember the LORD thy God: for it is **he that giveth thee power to get wealth**, that he may establish his covenant which he sware unto thy fathers, as it is this day.*

Give your money a mission. Wealth is given to establish His covenant in the earth or in this dispensation the gospel.

> *Mark 4:19 And the cares of this world, and the deceitfulness of riches, and the lusts of other things entering in, choke the word, and it becometh unfruitful.*

> *Rom 13:14 But put ye on the Lord Jesus Christ, and make not provision for the flesh, to fulfil the lusts thereof.*

> *Gal 5:24 And they that are Christ's have crucified the flesh with the affections and lusts.*

> *1 Tim 6:9 But they that will be rich fall into temptation and a snare, and into many foolish and hurtful lusts, which drown men in destruction and perdition.*

Do I preach prosperity?

Yes!

I cannot see in the word of God anywhere that people of God who were fully serving God, were not prospered.

Yet, beware of the sin of Balaam.

That is compromising the Word of God in any area for financial gain.

To whom much is given, much is required.

In my life, I have withdrawn from many great business opportunities simply because I do not feel strong enough in my office and calling to take the chance of mixing ministry and business. I fear God and seek purity of heart and holiness. I am coming out of the business world, having stepped again into full-time ministry.

My message will always be holiness unto the Lord, to be pure and ALL IN, 100% sold out to Jesus without compromise. I will use all of my position, influence, words, wealth, and teaching to promote only the cause of Christ. I feel that the time is short, and there is no time to do anything else in these last days.

Yet, I have seen the sin of Balaam at work, yea even here in Tulsa, Oklahoma, bless the holy city.

I drove a friend home from Friday night prayer one night, and he lives in an apartment complex, known for weekend partying and gang activity. This man is sold out for Jesus and is doing great things in reaching people with the gospel. As we drove, he shared his vision of raising up a strong ministry in the Northside of Tulsa to reach youth for Christ.

When we pulled into his parking lot, I was full of the Holy Ghost and fire. I rolled down my window as four youths with a case of beer on one guy's shoulder were approaching the truck, obviously on their way to party somewhere. So, I called out to them: 'Hey, my friend and I were talking about getting some sort of ministry going around here that would be relevant to your lives, to reach you for Jesus. What do you think would work?'

Now I wouldn't try this approach in an area other than Tulsa, where there are 1400 or so churches and many Christian television and radio stations.

You would think that everyone here has at least heard the gospel, once.

Well, one of the guys gave me a dirty look and kept walking, but the two girls with them approached the truck. One of them sat cross-legged on the ground beside my driver's window, and we began to talk.

She said, *"Are you serious? Do you really want to know what it would take?"*

I said, *"Yes, tell me, sister!"*

She said, *"I am 19 years old, pregnant with my third child. The first two children are from youth pastors who I slept with. They will not admit we had sex. I'm not saying that what I did was right, but if you want a ministry to reach youth here, in this community, you must solve the zipper problem with most of the ministers."*

Ah, the old-fashioned Billy Graham statement comes alive: *"As a man of God, don't touch the girls, the gold, or the glory!"*

Charisma does not equal character.

Balaam had charisma. Imagine if you will, the great pomp and ceremony, by which he built the altars of God and ceremonially sacrificed before the Lord the animals required. He had anointing. He had the gifts of the spirit.

He had a reputation as a prophet of God. He had a heavenly office.

Yet, he did not develop the character to carry the call.

Here is where I live: fighting daily, to watch over my words to fulfill them. Fighting to avoid any appearance of evil with women, money, or pride. I seek the Holy Spirit to go deep inside my heart, searching my deepest motives and transforming me, so that even my motives are right before the Lord.

I am not content to only do the right thing, but seek to do the right thing for the right reason: that is for the glory and love of Jesus.

I shared my heart for a reason as a man of God.

You are right there with me. The pressure, the subtle flirtatious innuendo's of seductive women (yes, they are real, it's not personal. It's just demons working through carnal women to destroy you and your ministry), the business deals and multi-level 'opportunities' that flood your inbox, the praise of flatterers' testing are common to every leader, and you must not fail.

*Proverbs 27:21 KJV As the refining pot for silver and the furnace for gold, so is a man tried by praise.*

Whether you are called in ministry, business, government, education, or media, or whatever your vocation, holiness is the standard: a clean, pure life, free from sin.

*Isaiah 52:11 Depart **ye**, depart **ye**, go **ye** out from thence, touch no unclean thing; go **ye** out of the midst of her; **be ye clean**, that **bear** the vessels of the Lord.*

I have questioned my motives for publishing this particular book, as there is clearly the potential of great financial benefit to my family in publishing it. Yet, I feel strongly that this initiative is of the Lord as a tool to help US leaders submit their leadership to the Lordship of Jesus Christ, to help turn the USA back to God and righteousness.

Jesus spoke of the differences between hirelings and true shepherds who lovingly lay down their lives to protect God's people:

*John 10:12 But he that is an **hireling**, and not the shepherd, whose own the sheep are not, seeth the wolf coming, and leaveth the sheep, and fleeth: and the wolf catcheth them, and scattereth the sheep. The **hireling** fleeth, because he is an **hireling**, and careth not for the sheep. Be strong, courageous, holy, and fulfill your heavenly office and calling without compromise.*

This is not a job or any mere earthly vocation, but a heavenly office and calling. Be the true shepherd you are created to be.

If you are compromised, let God forgive, purge, prune, and deliver you from your unhealthy relationships and business deals that make merchandise of the flock in your care.

Let's pray:

*Father, I pray for the brother or sister reading this today. May they fully consecrate to holiness, obedience, purity, and excellence of conduct, in whatever You have called them to do. Bring Your power, and truth to extricate them from situations, relationships, business dealings, and distractions that are contrary to Your will for their lives. May they live their lives led by You, in purpose, passion, joy, and victory. I ask this, knowing I am heard. For I ask in Your name, Lord Jesus. Amen.*

77

# YOUR Great Commission – Embracing YOUR Destiny!

### The Call of God

*Matt 10: 1 And when he had called unto him his twelve disciples, he gave them power against unclean spirits, to cast them out, and to heal all manner of sickness and all manner of disease.*

In this passage of Scripture, we see Jesus commissioning His twelve disciples. There is much that we can learn from this, for Jesus is the same, yesterday, today, and forever. And even as He commissioned these people, He has a specific commission for you and your life.

Notice the word 'power' used here.  In English, we have two words we translate as power. One used is 'exousia' which we understand as authority; the other word, *dunamis* means explosive power, like dynamite. In this case, they were granted authority in the kingdom of God, and that authority was over all demons, sickness, and disease. When they commanded these things to leave, it was expected that demonstrated explosive power would result, expelling diseases and healing the sick.

Many think that once we become born-again, and perhaps even filled with the Holy Spirit, that we need to GO into the harvest field He has provided for us. Yet, there is a call of God, then, after sufficient preparation. There is a commission of God. I remember my father in serving in the navy after four years of officer training, was granted his first commission as an officer. Though he had the rank when he enlisted, he did not yet have the authority to command men and equipment, until his commanding officers granted him a commission.

In this case, Jesus had been training, disciplining, growing, and teaching his disciples for a period of years in the Word of God.  They had been handpicked and called by Him. Yet, they were not yet commissioned. Notice that the call does not equal the commission! The qualification for the call is character – a seemingly forgotten message any more in the Body of Christ. (The job description of Christian leaders is 1 Tim 3:1-7)

I have also painfully learned that the call and office of God will come with a corresponding supernatural anointing to perform signs, wonders, and miracles. Anointing does not equal appointing!

Just because I have received supernatural power with my heavenly calling, I need to learn how to walk in that power, so that I use it only to destroy darkness and devils, not people and ministries.  Christ is not Jesus's last name but actually means 'the anointed one,' referring to the oil of anointing upon His life, similar to that used to set one apart unto God in the office of a prophet or a king.  In the case of the kingdom of God, this anointing oil refers to the presence and power of the Holy Spirit upon our lives. We are Christians, anointed ones, endued with supernatural power from God to perform signs, wonders, and miracles. Supernatural acts should be normal in our lives. Although it may take time, study, and discipline to grow into the fullness of our office and calling by the anointing, God has a day of appointing in the timing of the Father. How often I have run ahead of God, excited about His supernatural acts in my life, instead of allowing the deeper work of instruction, sanctification, and purification of my motives to be performed inside of me. When God does this work, I can actually be set apart in the fullness of my leadership capacity.

*Matt 10:1-12 These twelve Jesus sent forth, and commanded them, saying, Go not into the way of the Gentiles, and into any city of the Samaritans enter ye not: But go rather to the lost sheep of the house of Israel. And as ye go, preach, saying, The kingdom of heaven is at hand. Heal the sick, cleanse the lepers, raise the dead, cast out devils: freely ye have received, freely give. Provide neither gold, nor silver, nor brass in your purses, nor scrip for your journey, neither two coats, neither shoes, nor yet staves: for the workman is worthy of his meat. And into whatsoever city or town ye shall enter, enquire who in it is worthy; and there abide till ye go thence. And when ye come into an house, salute it. And if the house be worthy, let your peace come upon it: but if it be not worthy, let your peace return to you.*

Notice here that to have authority, one must be under authority. Jesus is Lord, King, and commander in chief of our lives. We must be submitted and committed to His leadership and be seeking first the kingdom of God and His way of doing things in every area of our lives. To do this, we must constantly study the Word of God and be carefully listening to the voice and promptings of the Holy Spirit.

*Matt 10:5 These twelve Jesus sent forth, and commanded them, saying, Go not into the way of the Gentiles, and into any city of the Samaritans enter ye not. But go rather to the lost sheep of the house of Israel.*

Jesus told them WHERE not to go (to the Gentiles or Samaritans) and WHERE to go (to the lost sheep of the house of Israel).

Jesus has specific places for you to go, also, and places and countries NOT to go. I know of people who have received open visions of countries they are called to go minister to, even as children. Yet, in many cases, they reach middle age before God actually releases and sends them to the nation they have known about all their life.

I know of a woman who at age seven had a vision of serving as a missionary in India as a child, and yet she married a military officer who put her through literal hell on earth with his alcoholism and immorality. Yet, he provided well for their family, and they raised six children together. After their children were grown, at around 60 years of age, her husband retired and attended a Full Gospel

Businessman's meeting. He gave his life to Jesus and was filled with the Holy Spirit. Immediately, God dealt with him to go as a missionary to India and by the time they were 65, off they went, mom and dad Hallas, to go preach. They have now, more than ten years later, won multitudes to Christ and have an organization that oversees 200 churches and ministries across India.

It is never too late to obey God!

One morning in prayer, as I was praying for many nations, Holy Spirit spoke to me:

***'The earth is my playground for obedient children!"***

Hence the name of our ministry, AOM Ministries from Psalm 2:8, *"Ask of me, and I shall give thee the heathen for thine inheritance, and the uttermost parts of the earth for thy possession."* I have asked for nations, and He has given them. When I go, either in word or in person, He has given me authority there **AS I OBEY.**

He will give you spaces and places where you are called. His grace has made a way for you. It remains for you to ask Him for nations and to hear accurately WHERE you are to serve and WHEN.

> *Matt 10:7–8 And as ye go, preach, saying, The kingdom of heaven is at hand. Heal the sick, cleanse the lepers, raise the dead, cast out devils: freely ye have received, freely give.*

Next, we see that He told them WHAT to preach. You can never go wrong in preaching the gospel, the power of God.

Yet, we are to teach the whole counsel of God, not merely salvation. Notice here He told them to preach that 'the kingdom of heaven is at hand'. This is deep and, rather than try and teach the fullness of it here, I would refer you to the kingdom series of books by Dr. Myles Munroe. Let me simply say, that the 'kingdom of God', or the 'kingdom of heaven', is the 'supreme rule and reign of Jesus.' Everything we need for life and godliness has already been provided for us in God's Word by his exceedingly great and precious promises. When His promises are publicly proclaimed, He produces power to perform that which He has decreed, and His kingdom destroys all opposition. God then answers the deepest needs of every human heart.

The gospel, or good news, is the 'manifest love and rule of Jesus,' and where He rules, there is peace for He is the Prince of peace! When the Word of God is embraced and set in place in our lives, our families, communities, states, and nations, there comes peace – Shalom, literally 'nothing missing, nothing broken.' The answer to every problem in life in every area is Jesus. WHAT do we preach? WHATEVER part of the kingdom the greatest need of the people is.

Now, I have learned over the years that Jesus is *"the Word was made flesh"* (John 1:4).

As we study and practice what we have learned, the word becomes flesh in us.

If we understand that the kingdom of God is the supreme rule and reign of God in the earth, then we see something interesting. The kingdom first must come to us, inside of us, as we learn the highest ways of the Word of God. As we live, teach, and preach what we have learned and applied to our own lives, the kingdom of God flows through us to the people in need.

So how do we prepare?

I am convinced that the fastest way to do this is to attend a Bible school. There, a myriad of instructors, seasoned from a multitude of years of walking with the Lord, can teach, train, and equip you for your specific gift and calling to this generation. It was a privilege for me to attend Bible school full time in a new city and country so that I could become immersed in the Word of God for the two-year course of study. I know many Christians cannot do that, but perhaps they could do courses part-time days or nights through correspondence or online. In any case, get it done! No one can qualify you, but you yourself.

It is worth any price on earth to be fully equipped to bear eternal fruit and reap eternal rewards with our lives.

Yes, we learn certain things through our local church, through Christian schools, and through many great teaching ministries. We apprentice through serving in various areas of our church, or on short term missions trips. These are wonderful opportunities to help us raise the right questions in our hearts, as we see the screaming needs of humanity. We can then go to God in prayer, and He answers by opening His Word to our understanding.

So then, while academic learning is essential, there must be corresponding life application, or we become mentally competent, yet practically inept.

Certain things in the kingdom must be done, not merely learned. To say that you can lay hands on the sick, and they will recover is great, but unless the disciple starts actually laying hands upon and praying for the sick, the instruction is only mental. There are things the Lord teaches us over the years in a divine healing ministry that did not come in a day, or in my case, even many years. I am still praying for the sick, still seeing them healed, and often, having to go back to the Lord, asking Him WHY certain people did not get healed...yet Jesus healed them all! As we become more like Him, we, too, will see more and greater healings and miracles! It is a journey of lifetime growth.

When you preach, you will demonstrate. This demonstration is a drug for which I am ever addicted. As the sick are healed, demons destroyed, miracles wrought, and mighty signs, wonders, and miracles accompany the preaching of His Word, I am ever humbled at the majesty, love, mercy, graciousness, and power of God. It never gets old. Every time I see a wheelchair emptied, a blind eye opened, and a deaf ear opened, I stand amazed at His great love and goodness.

> *Job 9:10 Which doeth great things past finding out; yea, and wonders without number.*

WHEN to go, WHERE you are supposed to go, speaking WHAT He gives you to speak will be followed by a demonstration of the kingdom in power, might, glory, and love that humbles us and ignites worship, praise, and passion like nothing else will.

When the 70 were sent out:

*Luke 10:17-21 And the **seventy returned again with joy,** saying, Lord, even the devils are subject unto us through thy name.*

*Yet, Jesus did not end his instruction there. He warned them of **the pride of satan,** And he said unto them, I beheld Satan as lightning fall from heaven.*

*Behold, I give unto you power to tread on serpents and scorpions, and over all the power of the enemy: and nothing shall by any means hurt you. Notwithstanding in this rejoice not, that the spirits are subject unto you; but rather rejoice, because your names are written in heaven. Yet, He was happy they went. In that hour **Jesus rejoiced in spirit,** and said, I thank thee, O Father, Lord of heaven and earth.*

Let's live to continually put a smile on Jesus' face. You got to **GO** to do that. Finally, let's look at HOW we are supposed to go. Godly vision can be spelled **MONEY.**

*Matt 10:8 freely ye have received, freely give.*

We may NEVER charge for the power and gifts of God in us!

*Matt 10:9-13 Provide neither gold, nor silver, nor brass in your purses, Nor scrip for your journey, neither two coats, neither shoes, nor yet staves: for the workman is worthy of his meat. And into whatsoever city or town ye shall enter, enquire who in it is worthy; and there abide till ye go thence. And when ye come into a house, salute it. And if the house be worthy, let your peace come upon it: but if it be not worthy, let your peace return to you."*

Now, in this case, Jesus told these disciples to go, bringing nothing but the Word and power of God, and that people would care for their every need, food, clothes, transportation, and they did not need a weapon. I know people that live just that way: He speaks, and they move. He then supernaturally moves on the hearts of people to open homes, stores, and businesses to them, and around the world, they go.

Yet, I believe it is a fair prayer to ask the Lord when and HOW He would have us go to places He has called us.

At the last supper in Luke:

*Luke 22:35-36 And he said unto them, when I sent you without purse, and scrip, and shoes, lacked ye anything? And they said, Nothing. Then said he unto them, But now, he that hath a purse, let him take it, and likewise his scrip: and he that hath no sword, let him sell his garment, and buy one.*

In the first commissioning, He sent them to Israel, where the people had hospitality laws for strangers, and where they were generally protected, needing no weapon. Now, He sends them to the nations, and He commissions them to get a weapon and to have money.

HOW are you going to go? By faith surely, but faith is not blind.

Faith sees ahead and can provide for upcoming expenditures, and plans for the future.

Yes, surely there are times He may simply say, GO! Yet, there are other times He will specifically direct you on how to raise financial support for something He wants to be done, and He will speak to others to get involved with your vision, and directive.

Your provision is inaccurately hearing and writing your specific vision, so that those called alongside to support you, can run with you in it.

*Hab 2:2 And the LORD answered me, and said, **Write the vision,** and make it plain upon tables, that he may run that readeth it.*

*Hab 2:3 For the vision is yet for an appointed time, but at the end it shall speak, and not lie: though it tarry, wait for it; because it will surely come, it will not tarry.*

This is the topic of the entire teaching, but let me say this: You were created for a purpose, on purpose. There is a reason and season for your life, and God, if you seek Him, will reveal to you your specific vision.

It is progressive. In January 2013, God clearly told me to birth AOM Ministries and to close my companies to go full time in ministry.

Though preached, taught, and prayed often eight hours a day, it was not until April of last year that I was able to have a 15-point yearly mandate that I have been aggressively working on since then.

Hearing accurately, then committing your current life's mandate to words accurately, will take time. As you are doing this, recognize this principle: We often hear God accurately but err in interpretation or application in our attempts to obey what He said.

Here is a perfect example of this:

In 2013 I felt the Lord tell me to pioneer 100 Bible schools through the Victory IVBI program.

So, I interpreted that by trying to do it the way I had heard other ministers succeed. I thought I should immediately travel to many countries, perhaps with evangelists hosting mass crusades, and then introduce the need for Bible schools at leadership meetings. I would then carefully follow up with those leaders interested in hosting Bible schools in their churches.

Being a man of action, I began planning speaking engagements in several foreign countries and sent out a support letter to make the need known, believing that God would speak to people to pay my expenses.

Money did not come. So, I stayed faithful with my daily disciplines of reading my daily Bible reading, completing my faith confessions, journaling, and spending hours each day praying in the Holy Spirit. I began to post the daily Bible reading on my Facebook page to both encourage others to read through their Bible each year and to keep myself accountable to this discipline. I then began to write up a daily Devo for people to read, and the rest is history.

This little devotional now goes out to thousands of people each day. It is growing in popularity daily as people read, share, cut and paste, and email it around the world using Social Media and various internet.

This has resulted in contacts and Skype calls with many leaders that I refer directly to Victory. My records show that as a result of these simple referrals, there have been fifty-three applications for schools in eight countries! Only Heaven will be able to fully record the fullness of this!

I say this to make a point. Did I hear the Holy Spirit accurately?

YES!

Yet, I erred in interpretation and application. Truthfully, my two actual mission trips last year to Canada and Mexico have not yet yielded even one school, while this Social Media outreach is growing, blossoming, and bursting at the seams!

> *Acts 6:7 And the word of God increased; and the number of the disciples multiplied in Jerusalem greatly; and a great company of the priests were obedient to the faith.*

It is this Word of God that is needed in the earth, not me or my great intellect, personality, charisma, or zeal and passion.

Jesus is Lord, not me. It is truly He that commissions and watches over His Word to perform it, not me.

> *Job 33:15 In a dream, in a vision of the night, when deep sleep falleth upon men, in slumberings upon the bed;*

Then he openeth the ears of men, and sealeth their instruction,

That he may withdraw man from his purpose, and hide pride from man. When He performs His Word, He gets the glory, for He can handle it, for He is worthy!

When we perform His Word, we can become guilty or, at least, in danger of pride. Satan himself, chief worship leader of heaven, fell from before the very throne of God through pride.

How much more can we sinful, broken humanity err.

He will provide if we remain humble. You have a call, a commission, a message, and a place and space where you have been provided for your great commission.

Let's Pray:

*Father, we say yes to Your call, Your preparation and instruction. You commission Your wisdom, clarity and direction as we go, and You give specific instructions as to how You have provided for me, my family, and the needs of those I am called to. Move in our lives today and reveal, correct, direct, anoint freshly, and protect and provide for us as we obey. Deliver and protect us from distractions. In Your name I pray, Lord Jesus. Amen!*

# 78

# A Shark Story

When I was young and full of fire, living for adventure, I completed the Underwater Skills program at Seneca College in King City, Ontario, qualifying me as a commercial diver and underwater welder. When I was 16, my dad had been posted to Norfolk, VA, to take the next level of his officer training as a naval officer, and they had a great youth program, that allowed me to take my NAUI scuba certification. I loved diving and the ocean, and so Seneca's training was a great fit for my adventurous personality. After graduation, I went up to Honey Harbour, Ontario, and worked a couple of seasons on a cable laying barge, laying telephone cable that connected telephone lines to what is known as the '10,000 islands' on the East side of Georgian Bay. Roundabout October, or November, when things were starting to freeze up, I would buy myself a ticket and head south to Key West, Florida to go treasure hunting with Mel Fisher. Got to work one winter for Mel's son, captain Kane, aboard the 'Dauntless'.

Now, this treasure hunting is quite an experience. Mel had 8 or nine boats working for him in his fleet, and people signed a contract for a percentage of treasure found. Mel had previously discovered the 'Marguerita', with 22 million dollars of silver and gold recovered, and investors made money, as did crew members that year, for contracts were signed by the year, anticipating the find of the sister ship, 'the Atocha', that historians record as having sunk in the same storm with hundreds of millions of gold and silver bullion aboard.

There were generally two types of boats in the fleet, search boats and dive boats. Search boats tow various metal detecting equipment, and dive boats are equipped with digging equipment, as the area the ships were known to have been lost, is known as 'The Quicksands', with the bottom covered with constantly moving and shifting underwater sand dunes, that are often 30-40' high. The dive boats are equipped with airlifts, and a neat thing called 'mailboxes'. These mailboxes are huge elbow-shaped tubes, that fold down over the propellers of the ship. We had little Boston whaler skiffs with outboard motors, that we would use to fly anchors out on three or four sides of the dive boat so that these mailboxes could be folded down over the propellers of the dive boat, and pinned in place. The boat would them rev up its engines, and blast the prop wash down into the bottom, quickly digging a hole in the bottom 30' or deeper, all the way down to bedrock. Then, the engines are idled back, to direct a stream of clear, surface water down into the hole. We then, as divers, would grab metal detectors and would scoot down to the bottom, to see if any silver, gold, or lead musket balls had been uncovered by the blast.

We were allowed to keep our first silver or gold coin found, I still have my 1622 silver piece of eight to this day.

There was a wonderful side-benefit to all of this digging in the sand. When we dug the first hole in the morning, the props would immediately uncover any clams, worms, crabs, etc, that had been under the sand. Huge schools of fish would begin to congregate around the digging area so that by the end of an 8-10 hour day of digging, there were literally thousands of fish swimming around the hole with us as we continue to work our metal detectors. We would begin to view the menu for the evening's feast throughout the day...

Now, we were not allowed to spearfish during the day, as any blood in the water would attract sharks, but at the end of the day, just as the sun was setting, we would descend with spear guns, and shoot a dozen or so fish, for Hor Deut Orby's (hors d'oeuvres). Probably 8-10 of these fish were grouper or snappers, or some type of delicacy, that we would quickly fillet and hand to the cook, to bread and fry up, as we began the evening chores of washing out dive equipment, greasing 'O' rings, filling tanks, cleaning the deck, etc, as we began the three-hour ride into the harbor, where we would anchor out for the night. These were gratefully served as snacks en route, before our evening feast. Usually, we anchored at Marquesis Key, as its channel enters into the only coral atoll in US waters.

We would take all the fish guts, scales, etc, with any trash fish we had speared, and put this in a 45-gallon garbage container, with about 5 gallons of seawater. Someone, over the years, had welded a shark hook to a 3' length of chain, that we would attach to a clevis on the end of one of our spare anchor lines.

Then after the traditional nightly feast, we play cards on deck, and then hook up a 2-5 lb trash fish to this shark hook, and let the line drift back behind the boat 50-100 yards. Every couple of minutes, we would scoop up some of the blood and guts from the 45-gallon trash can, and we would chum for sharks.

For a couple of weeks, all we caught was one skinny little 5' hammerhead, so I had a hard time believing the stories of the monster sharks the crew had caught in previous years. Sounded like fish stories to me...

Well, one night, there was a 'glow in the dark' plankton bloom that was awesome to see. The water was really clear and calm, and you could look down into the dark, and anywhere something moved, these plankton would light up, leaving a glowing trail when a fish swam. Every crest of every wavelet would light up, and it was really peaceful and picturesque. Looked like those greenish glow sticks that people wave around on July 4th fireworks: Really beautiful.

Around 10-11 pm, Captain Kane told me to pull in that shark hook and go to bed. I was really tired, and nodding off, but I really wanted to catch one of those big sharks everyone talked about. I pleaded with him to leave the shark hook out, and he said I could on one condition: *"If you hook a big tiger shark, and it fouls that line in the props, you are the first diver in with a knife, to cut the props free."*

*"Sure!" I said!*

So, I dumped the whole trash can full of chum over the side and rinsed out the container. Then I thought: 'How will I know if I get a bite in the middle of the night?' So, I pulled in about 40 feet of rope and wrapped it in a figure-eight around a 70 lb spare Danforth anchor that we had stowed around a set of bollards behind the cabin where we slept. I figured that if a shark hooked itself, it would rattle that anchor on the metal deck, and I would wake up and pull him in.

Finally, I went to bed and fell into a deep, exhausted sleep.

In the middle of the night, I was woken by the sound of a loud 'clang', and the boat was shaking, and everyone was up, and men were yelling: *'We got a shark, we got a shark!'* There was the sound of gunshots, as I sleepily ran to the back deck of the Dauntless. They had a spotlight, trying to spot the fin of this huge shark exploding through the surf behind the boat. When the monster had taken the bait, it had flown that 70lb anchor 40' through the air, and the anchor was pinned against the back guard rail so hard that two men, could not pull it off. As the fish exploded from side to side behind the boat, it seemed like the entire ocean lit up from the line, like a 'glow in the dark' football field. A couple of us tried to pull it in, but the rope just tore open our hands, and the entire boat was shaking from the fight!

Each time the fin of this thing would surface, captain Kane would squeeze off a couple of rounds from the .303 rifle we kept on clips for sharks and pirates.

*"Bam, Bam! I think I hit him! Bam! Bam!"*

Finally, someone had an idea to fire up the big 6–71 Jimmy motors and hook up one of the winches we used for pulling anchors. Quickly, a snatch block was run off the side, and the rope ran through it. We then engaged the winch and began hauling this beast in. As it got closer, Kane managed to get a couple of rounds into it's head, and the fight was over. Yet, we couldn't lift it!

So, we placed the rope around a brace, and began winching it in, to discover we had caught a 9 foot, 550 lb lemon shark. Teeth, going somewhere to happen.

Problem was, that even though the fish was dead, it's jaws would still clamp shut involuntarily, and I had to duct tape a fillet knife to the end of a broom handle to cut the hook out. I wanted to gut it, and put it in our walk-in cooler, but Kane wouldn't let me, so as the knife did its work, the body of the beast dropped off, and descended into the deep, clear waters. We followed it with the spotlight into the deep, and I remember the words my father had ingrained in me as a young boy.

*"Son, if you are going to kill something, you better eat it!"*

I thought about what a waste of good meat that was, and how that shark would never have bothered us diving, or probably even come close to us, as lemon sharks are fish eaters, not generally known to attack people.

Well, here's the moral of the story:

Sharks are rather amazing creatures I've found. A shark's primary sense is a keen sense of smell. It can detect one drop of blood in a million drops of water (25 gallons or 100 liters) and can smell blood 0.25 mile (0.4 km) away.

By throwing ladlefuls of blood into the water behind the boat, sharks would hone in on the scent trail, and would readily take the bait placed for them.

So it is in our life. God is love, and we who know Jesus, are His children, designed to walk in love, life, light, strength, power, and authority in the earth. With Him, we are invincible, and satan knows this.

So, he has to do something to get through our impregnable armor.

God forgives us, but commands us to forgive others.

*Colossians 3:13 Be gentle and forbearing with one another and, if one has a difference (a grievance or complaint) against another, readily pardoning each other; even as the Lord has [freely] **forgiven** you, so **must** you also [**forgive**].*

*Luke 6:37 Do not judge, and you will not be judged. Do not condemn, and you will not be condemned.* **Forgive**, *and you will be forgiven.*

**Mark 11:25–26** *And whenever you stand praying, if you have anything against anyone,* **forgive** *him and let it drop (leave it, let it go), in order that your Father Who is in heaven may also* **forgive** *you your [own] failings and shortcomings and let them drop.* But if you do not **forgive**, neither will your Father in heaven **forgive** your failings and shortcomings.

God commands us to forgive people who do us wrong, but in the business of life, people can tick us off, and we can get offended. This is the bait of satan, designed to get us out of the will of God for our lives. John Bevere has a tremendous book called *The Bait of Satan.*

**2 Corinthians 2:11** *To keep Satan from getting the advantage over us; for we are not* **ignorant** *of his wiles and intentions.*

This is one of the wiles of satan, a trap designed to destroy us. Unforgiveness to the devil is like blood is to a shark.

**1 Peter 5:8** *Be well balanced (temperate, sober of mind), be vigilant and cautious at all times; for that enemy of yours, the devil, roams around like a* **lion roaring** *[in fierce hunger], seeking someone to seize upon and devour.*

Satan is a predator, trying to devour our lives. He cannot touch us when we are fully walking with God, in love towards our fellow man, so, he sends people to do us wrong, with the intent purpose to get us in unforgiveness. Why?

Remember the story Jesus told in Matt 18 about the servant who owed a huge debt he could not pay, and how he was brought before the king? He asked for mercy, and the king graciously forgave him, and released him from his debt. This man then went out, saw another guy that owed him a small amount, and had the man thrown in prison. Servants told the king, who then had him arrested and brought back to court. His verdict?

> *Mat 18:33–34 (NIV) Shouldn't you have had mercy on your fellow servant just as I had on you? In anger his master turned him over to the jailers **to be tortured**, until he should pay back all he owed.*

I want you to see this. **Unforgiveness will produce torment in your life.** When you or I choose not to **forgive**, we go into bondage. You get turned over to the tormentors.

> *Mat 18:35 This is how my heavenly Father will treat each of you unless you **forgive** your brother from your heart.*

Unforgiveness brings torment into our lives, and allows the devil to come and do what he does, kill our dreams, steal our joy, blessing, or perhaps our lives, and destroy things that may have taken us years to build.

Grudges only hurt us, not the person we hate or stonewall, for they allow demonic spirits to torture us, and steal our peace. Forgive: It's your life at stake...

**Homework:**

1. Come clean with God. Ask Him to show you all the things you've done that offend him, and ask Him to Forgive you Come clean with others. Ask God to show you all the people who have hurt you, and forgive them. I had to make a 21-page list, forgive them, then burn the list.
2. Come clean with yourself. Ask God to show you all the areas of your life where you are beating yourself up, and forgive yourself.
3. Ask God to show you other people that are caught in this trap, and pray for them. There will be healing in it for you. *(Job 42:10 NIV) After Job had prayed for his friends, the LORD made him prosperous again and gave him twice as much as he had before.*

# 79

# Thoughts, Words, and Deliberate Deeds

### *Thoughts*

*2 Cor 10:5 Casting down imaginations, and every high thing that exalteth itself against the knowledge of God, and bringing into captivity every thought to the obedience of Christ;*

*Rom 12:2 And be not conformed to this world: but be ye transformed by the renewing of your mind, that ye may prove what is that good, and acceptable, and perfect, will of God.*

We work on getting our minds transformed by the Word of God, and we constantly, in this fight of faith, must take our thoughts captive to the Word of God. We resist, rebuke, and stand against thoughts that appear contrary to the Word of God. In a general sense, this we must do in order to live a holy life in thought and in the purity of heart.

Our heart of hearts, our human spirit, the place where Jesus lives when we received Him, only has three gates: Our eye gate, ear gate, and mouth gate.

To walk in holiness and purity, we must guard what we look at, hear, and speak.

Yet, sometimes we move according to the Word of God, assuming we know to do right, and discover troubling Scriptures, ones that allow the living

God, breathing room. Imagine the distress of Joseph when he discovered Mary, the mother of Jesus, was pregnant!

He loves her. However, the law would have her stoned for her unfaithfulness. Yet, he decides to simply break the engagement and to put her away quietly.

Outwardly, I would agree with his decision, yet God speaks to hearts. We know the story:

> *Matt 1:20 But while he thought on these things, behold, the angel of the Lord appeared unto him in a dream, saying, Joseph, thou son of David, fear not to take unto thee Mary thy wife: for that which is conceived in her is of the Holy Ghost.*

His godly principals got rocked by the voice of the Creator of the universe! We think godly thoughts, for this we are commanded to do:

> *Isa 55:7 Let the wicked forsake his way, and the unrighteous man his thoughts: and let him return unto the LORD, and he will have mercy upon him; and to our God, for he will abundantly pardon.*

Yet, while Joseph was fighting his internal battle of decision, he was interrupted by the higher thoughts of God: For my thoughts are not your thoughts, neither are your ways my ways, saith the LORD. For as the heavens are higher than the earth, so are my ways higher than your ways, and my thoughts than your thoughts.

***Moral of the story: It is good to be a man of principle, a godly man, but when God Himself speaks, it is better to be a man of God!***

The same thing goes with **words:**

Jesus taught us in Matthew.

> *Matt 5:48 Be ye therefore perfect, even as your Father which is in heaven is **perfect**.*

*James 3:2 For in many things we offend all.  If any man offend not in word, the same is a **perfect** man, and able also to bridle the whole body.  So, we need to watch our words, to grow in maturity.  Then, there are our **deeds:***

*James 1:22 But be ye doers of the word, and not hearers only, deceiving your own selves.*

*James 1:23 For if any be a hearer of the word, and not a doer, he is like unto a man beholding his natural face in a glass:*

The primary work of faith is words, yet God expects us to do something with what we believe. We need to act upon what we believe. And what these corresponding actions need to be to manifest and demonstrate our faith, boil down to this: **Whatever He says: 'DO IT!'.**

It seems this phrase has become my battle cry these past couple of years, as daily I seek His face and His voice for clear direction in this calling upon my life. You do too.

Quickly, as you sell out to Jesus, you discover, that what Matthew says.

*Matt 4:4 But he answered and said, It is written, Man shall not live by bread alone, but by every word that proceedeth out of the mouth of God.*

It is a spirit-led lifestyle that pleases God, a living relationship with a living God, not merely a religious exercise.

Jesus was our example; He only did the will of our heavenly Father. We can too.In general, we carefully guard our thoughts, our words, and our lifestyle and walk forward in faith in sometimes nothing else than His written Word.

Yet, there are times we face impossibilities, and, if we are honest, we do not know what to do.

We ask Him for wisdom and for His way to be revealed, but if we don't know, we don't know.

Spiritual intelligence in leadership is in this verse:

*1 Cor 4:5 Therefore judge nothing before the time, until the Lord come, who both will bring to light the hidden things of darkness, and will make manifest the counsels of the hearts: and then shall every man have praise of God. We know in part, and prophesy in part.*

Let's pray:

*Lord Jesus, You are my Lord, my Shepherd, my Pastor. May I be faithful to think right, speak right, and act right before You today.  For the brutal or unknown circumstances of my life, may I have the courage to wait, and hear what You would reveal I must do in light of what Your reveal. May I ever hear Your voice, and whatever You say, may I instantly obey. In your name I pray, Lord Jesus. Amen.*

# Resources


- Hagin, Kenneth E, A Commonsense Guide To Fasting, Faith Library Publications (February 2, 2011)
- Johnston, Jon. *Courage.* Wheaton, IL: Victor Books, 1990.
- Davidson, Herbert A. *Moses Maimonides: The Man and His Works.* New York, N.Y.: Oxford University Press, 2005.
- Capps, Charles. *Dynamics of Faith and Confession.* Tulsa, Okla.: Harrison House, 1987.
- James Allen, As a Man Thinketh, Value Classic Reprints (February 24, 2017)
- John Maxwell, 17 Irrefutable Laws of Teamwork, HarperCollins Leadership; Reprint edition (April 1, 2013)
- E.W. Kenyon, The Blood Covenant, Kenyon's Gospel Publishing Society (1999)
- Today In The Word, August, 1989, p. 21.https://www.todayintheword.org/

- James Strong, Strongs Exhaustive Concordance of the Bible, Hendrickson Publishing (January 1, 2009)
- Charles R Swindoll, The Quest for Character, Multnomah Pub (June 16, 1987)
- Today in the Word, Moody Bible Institute, January 1992, p.31. https://www.todayintheword.org/
- Robert Ingersoll, The Best of Robert Ingersoll: Selections from His Writings and Speeches Prometheus (January 1, 1993)
- Cooke, Graham. *Developing Your Prophetic Gifting.* Grand Rapids, MI: Chosen Books, 2003.

- Horatio Alger, Abraham Lincoln, the backwoods boy; or, How a young rail-splitter became president, November 15, 2013
- https://www.jampole.com/blog/trust-but-verify-who-actually-said-it/
- Napolean Hill, Think and Grow Rich, Sound Wisdom; Original Edition edition (December 13, 2016)
- Tim Hansel, Holy Sweat, W Pub Group (July 1, 1987)Sermonillustrations.com #silence
- Merriam-Websters, Websters Dictionary, Merriam-Webster, Inc.; New Edition edition (June 1, 2019)Sermonillustrations.com #justice
- Luis Paleau, Experiencing God's Forgivenes: Being Freed from Sin and Guilt, Multnomah Books (March 1, 1984)
- https://www.brainyquote.com/quotes/abraham_lincoln_388944
- John Bevere, The Bait of Satan, Charisma House; Anniversary edition (January 7, 2014)
- Terry L Wilder with Chad Brand and Eric Mitchel, Holmans Illustrated Bible Dictionary, Holman Reference; Revised, Revised and Expanded edition (November 1, 2015)
- Baker, Heidi. *Compelled by Love.* Lake Mary, Fla.: Charisma House, 2008
- John A. Macmillan, The Authority of the Believer, Jawbone Digital (June 30, 2015)

# About the Author

Chris Walsh is a missionary, the President of AOM Ministries. This blog now reaches over 100,000 people each day! Chris is the author of three books: Parable of the Sower, Worship – Not Just a Song, and now 'Welcome to the Grand Illusion, a prophetic prayer strategy to take America back!' The Walsh family has completed over 20 missions trips since April 2014, and is committed to bringing the Word of God to the nations, by every available media. Over the years, he has been involved in outreaches to native Americans, Africa, and now orphans.

**You can connect with me on:**

- https://www.chrisaomministries.com
- https://twitter.com/ChrisWalsh5
- https://www.facebook.com/chriskaren.walsh